Michael Jones

Michael Jones was awarded a history PhD by Bristol University, and subsequently taught at Glasgow University and Winchester College. He is a Fellow of the Royal Historical Society and works now as a writer, media historical consultant and presented. He has written books on the battles of Bosworth, Agincourt, Stalingrad and, most recently, on the siege of Leningrad, and for the last few years has conducted battlefield tours of the Eastern Front.

Praise for *The Retreat*:

'Michael Jones is already the author of good books on Stalingrad and Leningrad. Now, he addresses the 1941–2 winter battle for Moscow, one of the decisive campaigns of the conflict. His is overwhelmingly a soldiers' story, a vivid exploration of Soviet and German personal narratives' Max Hastings, *Sunday Times*

'As a fresh popular account of the battle, this volume has much value . . . The strength of this work . . . is the view from the trenches, and here will be its attraction to readers. The book consists of eyewitness testimonies by front-line officers and soldiers, constructed into a gripping narrative . . . The battle of Moscow was a hell on earth, a terrible, bloody event for both invaders and defenders. A mass of first-person material has been cleverly assembled here to paint a striking picture' *BBC History Magazine*

Also by Michael Jones

The King's Mother
Bosworth 1485 – Psychology of a Battle
Agincourt 1415 – A Battlefield Guide
Stalingrad: How the Red Army Triumphed
Leningrad: State of Siege

The Retreat

Hitler's First Defeat

MICHAEL JONES

JOHN MURRAY

First published in Great Britain in 2009 by John Murray (Publishers)
An Hachette UK Company

First published in paperback in 2010

1

A CIP catalogue record for this title is available from the British Library

ISBN 978-0-7195-6972-2

Typeset in Monotype Bembo by Servis Filmsetting Ltd, Stockport, Cheshire

Printed and bound by Clays Ltd, St Ives plc

John Murray policy is to use papers that are natural, renewable and recyclable products and made
from wood grown in sustainable forests. The logging and manufacturing processes are expected to
conform to the environmental regulations of the country of origin.

John Murray (Publishers)
338 Euston Road
London NW1 3BH

www.johnmurray.co.uk

Dusk is falling. The crack of artillery fire – and white smoke rises above the forest. The harsh reality of war: gruff cries of command, struggling with ammunition through the snow. And then, a surprising question – 'Did you see the sunset?' Suddenly I thought: how grievously we have broken the peace and tranquility of this land.

Wolfgang Buff, Siniavino, Russia, 10 February 1942

Contents

List of Illustrations

Acknowledgements: The photographs of Leopold Höglinger (1, 4–8, 10–14, 20 and 27) are reproduced by kind permission of Justin Warman; those of Josef Perau (30 and 31) have generously been made available by Eugen Perau. Remaining German soldiers' photographs (2–3, 9, 15–19, 21–26, 28–29, 32–34) are from the Eastern Front collection of Scott Pick.

List of Maps

Preface

On 15 December 1941, German soldier Heinz Otto Fausten fled from a Soviet tank attack on his retreating column. Risking his life, he later returned to one of the baggage carts to retrieve his diary. Fausten was in an elite Wehrmacht unit – the 1st Panzer Division – the troops who had spearheaded Adolf Hitler's assault on Moscow. Now, as the unit collapsed all around him, in a hellish retreat in extreme winter weather, Fausten felt his experience to be so remarkable that he should record and preserve it. He clung on to his diary.

On 6 December Joseph Stalin had launched his great counter-offensive, repulsing the German armies from Moscow. It was the Wehrmacht's first failure of the Second World War. I want to focus on the human story – the experiences of soldiers, prisoners of war and civilians. It tells of a military retreat, but also a retreat from human values, as an already brutal war degenerated into mass killing of the innocent and the unprotected. At its heart is one of the greatest human tragedies of the war in the east – the death of more than two million Red Army POWs in German custody in the winter of 1941–2.

It is often said that we learn most about people in adversity, when things go badly wrong and a response has to be made to a crisis. In the winter of 1941 Hitler's invincible army met a serious rebuff before the gates of Moscow. The German Wehrmacht, which prided itself on technological proficiency, saw that proficiency torn asunder in temperatures below −30 degrees Celsius, as vital equipment malfunctioned or no longer worked at all. Incredibly, this highly professional army had gone unprepared for winter fighting. And it had badly underestimated the desperate courage of Russian fighters determined to defend their capital to the last man. Soviet soldier Georgi Osadchinsky said: 'We resolved to never let the Germans capture Moscow, our dearly beloved city – the symbol of our power, our people's pride and the bearer of our national spirit.'

In the terrible German retreat that followed, both sides were transfixed by the spectre of Napoleon Bonaparte's disintegrating *Grande Armée* of 1812. At a crisis point in mid-December 1941, Hitler decisively intervened, sacking the head of the German Army, Field Marshal Walther von Brauchitsch, and putting himself in Brauchitsch's place. The Führer then issued a draconian 'Stand Fast!' order, intended to prevent another 'Napoleonic disaster'.

The Wehrmacht was pushed to the brink of catastrophe, but was not routed – and Hitler claimed the credit for this. He now resolved to remain as head of the German Army and personally lead the war in the east. The terrible consequences of that decision – which saw brutal fighting all the way from Stalingrad to Berlin – will be told in a companion volume, *Total War*. In *The Retreat* I focus on the critical period from December 1941 to March 1942, when Stalin's armies strove to repeat Russia's triumph of 1812, and to utterly destroy the invaders. They came tantalisingly close to success.

Many veterans on both sides of the conflict have given their unstinting support, and allowed me access to diaries, memoirs and photographs. On the German side – where my principal emphasis lies – I have benefited from the generous help of Heinz Otto Fausten of the 1st Panzer Division and Hans-Erdmann Schönbeck of the 11th Panzer Division. Eugen Perau has kindly allowed me access to the photographs and personal memoir of Josef Perau – a divisional chaplain during the German retreat – which I have used in conjunction with Perau's diary. Justin Warman has made available the diaries and photographs of his father-in-law, Leopold Höglinger, a radio operator with the German 137th Infantry Division. Valuable additional material has been drawn from the

Wehrmacht's many unit histories, and I have benefited greatly from recent research on this period of the war – particularly that of Johannes Hürter.

On the Russian side, I have been kindly assisted by veterans Georgi Osadchinsky, who has made available to me his detailed notes and diary of the counteroffensive, Boris Baromykin and Dmitry Vonlyarsky. I am grateful to Lena Yakovleva for translation and interpretation work, and her help setting up some of the key interviews, and to the Russian Council of War Veterans in Moscow for facilitating additional meetings. Artem Drabkin has pointed me towards material about veterans on his 'I Remember' site, on www.russianbattlefield.com, and a companion site, 'Soldiers of the Great War', on www.pobediteli. ru.

Fellow military historian Richard Hargreaves has been a constant source of help and encouragement, providing me with extracts from rare German unit histories and also a portion of Wolfram von Richthofen's diary from the Bundesarchiv in Freiburg. He has also read and commented on a number of the chapters. Jason Mark, Robert Kershaw and Robert Forczyk have also assisted with some of the German material; David Glantz, Geoffrey Jukes and Yan Mann with the Russian material, and Yan also commented on several chapters in draft. Tony Gillham has provided translations of some of the Russian veterans' accounts, and Ray Smith some of the German accounts. Lena Karsten has translated some of the German testimony and also kindly allowed me access to the letters of her grandfather Dietrich Karsten, who fought and died on the Eastern Front in January 1942. I use the names of soldiers' regiments and divisions – where they exist – as pointers, but have deployed such information selectively, so as not to overburden the dramatic narrative. In general, I have followed sources' transliterations from Cyrillic script, although on occasion I have standardised spellings of forenames and word endings. I have preferred the place names Kalinin and Gzhatsk to their modernised forms of Tver and Gagarin.

The German retreat from Moscow was a major turning point

in the Second World War. It is also a timeless story of cruelty and courage, horror and heroism. I want to bring that story back to life through a mosaic of personal experiences – and show the human cost of Hitler's first defeat.

THE GERMAN ADVANCE ON MOSCOW
2 October to 5 December 1941

KALININ

Klin

Yakhroma

Krasnaya Polyana

Volokolamsk

Istra

MOSCOW

Borodino

Panzer
Group 3
(Reinhardt)

VYAZMA

Mozhaisk

SMOLENSK

Maloyaroslavets

Kaluga

TULA

Panzer Group 4
(Hoepner)

Sukhinici

Bryansk

Mtensk

OREL

5 December

Panzer Group 2
(Guderian)

13 November

[Guderian's advance begins
30 September]

N

- - - - - The front on 2 October
— — — — The front on 13 November
· · · · · · · · · The front on 5 December

Encircled Russian troops

0   25   50   75   100
miles

THE SOVIET COUNTER-OFFENSIVE,
6 December 1941 to 21 April 1942
Showing German Army Groups and Soviet Fronts

FINLAND

Lake Ladoga

Leningrad Front

Baltic Sea

Volkhov Front

Leningrad • • Lyuban

ESTONIA

Northwestern Front

Volga

ARMY GROUP NORTH

Staraya Russa • • Demyansk • Kholm

Kalinin Front

Kalinin

Okhvat

Velikiye Luki • • Andreapol • Klin

LATVIA

Rzhev • MOSCOW

Mozhaisk

LITHUANIA

Dvina

• Vitebsk • Vyazma

Western Front

Smolensk • Yukhnov • Kaluga

EAST PRUSSIA

ARMY GROUP CENTRE

• Orsha

Tula • Bogoroditsk

• Minsk

Roslavl • • Sukhinici

Southwestern Front

Dnieper

• Bryansk

BELORUSSIA

Orel • • Kromy

Gomel •

Livny •

• Kursk

Don

POLAND

UKRAINE

• Kiev

ARMY GROUP SOUTH

Kharkov •

Dniester

Southern Front

HUNGARY

Zaporozhye •

ROMANIA

Odessa •

Sea of Azov

Caucasus Front

Black Sea

CRIMEA

• Sevastopol

▬▬▬ Limit of German
advance, Dec 5 1941

Areas reoccupied by Soviet forces
from Dec 6 1941 to
21 April 1942

0 — miles — 200
0 — kms — 200

xviii

Timeline

22 June 1941: Operation Barbarossa begins.

28 July 1941: Army Group Centre successfully concludes encirclement battle at Smolensk.

21 August: Adolf Hitler orders German forces south, to fight fresh encirclement battle at Kiev.

6 September: The Führer makes Moscow the last German objective before the winter.

30 September: Colonel General Heinz Guderian launches preparatory attack towards Orel.

2 October: Operation Typhoon commences.

6 October: Russian counter-attack at Mtensk; Germans capture Bryansk.

7 October: Germans capture Vyazma, trapping four Soviet armies.

8–9 October: Three Soviet armies encircled at Bryansk.

14 October: Kalinin captured by German 1st Panzer Division.

15–19 October: Battle of Borodino.

16 October: Panic in Moscow – resolved when Stalin decides to stay in the city.

27–29 October: First phase of Operation Typhoon halted by autumn rainy season, logistical problems and increasingly determined Russian resistance.

7 November: Traditional parade, marking the anniversary of the Bolshevik Revolution, held on Red Square.

13 November: German conference at Orsha resolves to continue attack on Moscow.

16–18 November: Colonel General Erich Hoepner's Panzer Group Four advances along Volokolamsk-Moscow motor highway.

23 November: Germans capture Klin.

26 November: Germans capture Istra.

1–2 December: High-water mark of German offensive – some Wehrmacht units within 20 miles of Moscow.

4–5 December: Failure of Guderian's last attempt to surround Tula.

6 December: Soviet counteroffensive launched.

9 December: General Georgi Zhukov orders Red Army units to bypass German strongpoints and break through on flanks.

10 December: Three German divisions surrounded at Livny.

11 December: Soviet forces recapture Istra and Solnechnogorsk.

13 December: *Pravda* headlines 'Defeat of German Army on the approaches to Moscow'.

14–15 December: Germans abandon Klin.

16–18 December: Hitler dismisses Field Marshal Walther von Brauchitsch as head of the German Army and takes command himself. Issues 'Stand Fast!' order forbidding any further retreat.

19 December: Field Marshal Günther von Kluge replaces Field Marshal Fedor von Bock as commander of Army Group Centre.

20 December: Hitler orders 'scorched-earth' policy against Russian towns and villages.

26 December: Guderian dismissed for withdrawing forces without Hitler's authorisation.

1 January 1942: Maloyaroslavets recaptured by Soviet forces.

5–6 January: Soviet high command launches second phase of counteroffensive, seeking complete destruction of German Army Group Centre.

8 January: Hoepner dismissed for retreating without permission.

15 January: Hitler partially rescinds 'Stand Fast!' order, allowing retreat to Rzhev–Yukhnov line.

19 January: General Walther Model takes over command of German Ninth Army.

24 January: German garrison at Sukhinici relieved.

17–18 February: Battle of Rzhev culminates in destruction of Soviet Twenty-Ninth Army

28 February: Secret German report acknowledges that 'the vast majority of the 3.6 million Soviet prisoners of war held by us have already perished through starvation or disease'.

23–24 March: Soviet Lieutenant General Andrei Vlasov's Second Shock Army surrounded at Lyuban.

21 April: Germans relieve Demyansk.

5 May: Germans relieve Kholm.

I

In the Shadow of Napoleon

EARLY ON THE morning of 22 June 1941, Germany invaded the Soviet Union and a torrent of troops, guns and tanks rolled eastwards. Leopold Höglinger, a radio operator with the German 137th Infantry Division, remembered the war's beginning: 'At around 3.15 a.m. our offensive began with a long barrage of artillery fire,' he wrote in his diary, 'and squadrons of our planes flew overhead. There was no resistance from the enemy. A few hours later, as our troops began moving forward, some Russian bombers did appear – but they were immediately shot down. Soon the first prisoners started coming in.'

This was modern warfare at its most lethal in which the destructive power of fighter and bomber aircraft was harnessed to support invading ground troops. At its onset the Germans played a trump card, using the Luftwaffe to obliterate the enemy. In the skies above the advancing Wehrmacht, the Russian air force was literally blown to pieces – with many planes destroyed even before they got off the ground. Soviet pilot Ivan Konovalov remembered the destruction of his airfield: 'All of a sudden there was an incredible roaring sound. Enemy planes were overhead. Someone yelled "Take cover!" and I dived under the wing of my plane. Everything was burning – a terrible, raging fire. At the end of it all, only one plane was left intact.'

Those pilots who survived were stunned by this sudden attack. 'The Russians that managed to get up in the air flew poorly,' commented Luftwaffe commander Wolfram von Richthofen, 'and we were able to bring most of them down.' Red Air Force pilot Stephan Mikoyan said: 'Our superiors had ordered no defensive measures, and at the airfields we had our planes parked next to each other, in neat orderly rows. The Germans hit us hard. More than 800 planes were destroyed on the ground in those first few hours and another 300 were shot down soon after take-off. It was a total disaster. On the first day of the war we lost more than a thousand planes.'

This was a dramatic overture. Hitler, inspired by the awesome power of this new technology, invoked a sense of destiny to accompany his invasion, announcing – as his forces were unleashed upon the Soviet Union – that 'the world would hold its breath'. For another great European onslaught on Russia, Napoleon's nineteenth-century invasion, had been launched at almost exactly the same time of year. On 23 June 1812 the emperor of France had marched into Russia with a huge army. One of his followers recalled its might and grandeur: 'All the finest men, in full dress, all the most beautiful horses, were assembled . . . The sun shone on the bronze of twelve hundred cannon – ready to destroy anything – and on the tempered steel of the weapons of soldiers and officers. Nobody doubted the success of the enterprise.' Hitler's army enjoyed a similar, heady optimism. The early days of the war were a jubilant time for German soldiers. 'Yesterday I knocked off a Red Army tank, as I had done two days earlier,' Karl Fuchs wrote proudly on 25 June. 'The Russians are fleeing everywhere and we follow them. All of us believe in early victory!'

In 1812 the French had marched deep into Russia, fighting a bloody but inconclusive battle at Borodino and then occupying Moscow. Napoleon had hoped that the capture of this city would form a triumphal conclusion to his campaign, but it proved a hollow victory. The Russians set Moscow alight, and the French army was forced to camp out in its smouldering ruins. With supplies running low, Napoleon's forces retreated westwards in terrible winter weather – and, in a ghastly denouement, most lost their lives to cold, starvation and the marauding Cossack cavalry.

Some German generals, inspired by the Wehrmacht's string of successes in the first two years of the Second World War, which had brought most of Europe under the sway of the Nazi regime, began to see – in political terms at least – Adolf Hitler as a Napoleonic figure, and made comparisons between the two leaders. In his quest for European mastery Napoleon had also first struggled to subdue Britain – and then, failing to achieve this, had turned east against Russia. Hitler seemed to be following a similar path. In the summer of 1940, with the war against France successfully concluded, the Führer and many of his generals had visited Napoleon's tomb at Les Invalides in Paris. One of Hitler's commanders, General Gotthard Heinrici, struck by this moment and impressed by his leader's audacity, paid tribute to Hitler's attack on France: 'The Führer's decision is indeed Napoleonic – great and bold.'

Although Hitler had subdued much of Europe, Britain remained defiant. Plans to destroy the Royal Air Force and then launch a seaborne invasion came to nothing. Napoleon had once hoped to launch an invasion of Britain, after destroying the British navy, but his ambitions had been thwarted. Stationed on the French channel coast during the autumn of 1940, waiting for an invasion that never came, Heinrici developed his comparison between the two leaders further: 'The strong statements in *Mein Kampf* about Russia are unlikely to be merely empty words . . . We are inevitably drawn into even greater affairs – ones which at first we did not plan for.' Heinrici was captivated by Germany's role as an arbiter of European affairs, yet he underestimated the depth of Hitler's hatred of the Slavs. He continued: 'Many things today bear similarities with Napoleon. He too marched on Moscow, but not willingly – rather because the struggle against England forced him to do it.'

Napoleon had not regarded the invasion of Russia as a mere consolation prize after failing to conquer Britain. He undertook it at the summit of his power, and as a means to consolidate his sway over Europe. Similarly, for Hitler, a war against a Bolshevik state he both feared and detested was, in his view, always inevitable. But, although he and many Germans admired the might of Napoleon's ambition, the sobering lessons of the French emperor's 1812 campaign provided them with a terrible warning.

Napoleon was the greatest military leader of his age. He had won a succession of stunning victories against other European powers. Veterans of these earlier triumphs formed the backbone of his invading army in 1812; their morale, tactical mastery and professionalism made them seemingly unassailable. Yet, on the retreat from Moscow, this once mighty force lost all cohesion, power and discipline, and in the appalling cold collapsed into a disorderly rabble.

Napoleon left Moscow towards the end of October 1812. The disintegration of his army began when temperatures dropped, following the first November snowfall, to around −10 degrees Celsius. His troops lacked proper clothing to withstand the winter weather. Many of the uniforms were more decorative than practical, the cloth was in any case flimsy. Greatcoats were thin and the quality of material poor. Soldiers began to be found frozen to death at night. The cold finished off thousands of the horses, rendering many cavalry and artillery units useless, and leaving the army vulnerable to the pursuing Cossack cavalry. As supplies ran out, and equipment had to be abandoned, it was impossible to feed the French troops properly. Their shelter was utterly inadequate, for they were retreating along a route already laid waste by the Russians and most of the villages had already been destroyed.

After Napoleon's crossing of the river Berezina, the situation dramatically worsened, as temperatures at the beginning of December plummeted to −30 degrees Celsius. Frostbite was now widespread. French soldiers murdered comrades for their coats, and robbed the wounded of their boots. 'Necessity had turned us into swindlers and thieves,' one wrote, 'and without a trace of shame, we stole from each other whatever we required.' Incidents of cannibalism began to occur. 'One has to have felt the rage of hunger to appreciate our position,' commented Sergeant Adrien de Bourgogne. 'Had there been no human flesh, we would have eaten the devil himself, if someone had cooked him for us.'

On 6 December 1812 the temperature dropped to −37 degrees Celsius. 'We were covered in ice,' one wrote, 'the breath coming out of our mouths was as thick as smoke, and it formed icicles on our hair, eyebrows, moustaches and beards.' The following day was even colder. Men died where they stood; others were reduced to total apathy. Napoleon's great army, which had entered Russia that summer more than 600,000 strong, had now dwindled to an effective fighting strength of little more than 10,000 tottering soldiers. 'I made a mistake in the manner in which I waged this war,' Napoleon said starkly to Armand de Caulaincourt, who later wrote an account of this terrible campaign. 'I stayed too long in Moscow.'

The more one considers this ghastly sequence of events, the more incredible it seems that the German military machine, priding itself on meticulous planning and logistics, and with full knowledge of earlier history, could have allowed that history to repeat itself: unprepared winter war in Russia. It is clear that Hitler and the German Army high command did not believe Napoleon's warning applied to them. What is less clear is why. They were certain they could fight and win a summer campaign, and there was no alternative strategy in place if the first one failed. In 1812 Russia had known of Napoleon's intentions in advance. In 1941, by contrast, the Soviet Union was not expecting Hitler's attack and was caught unprepared for war. It therefore appeared that the Führer could indeed succeed where the French emperor had failed, by destroying the bulk of his opponent's military might close to the frontier.

The Germans had harnessed modern technology to create a fighting method faster and more devastating than any of Napoleon's soldiers could have imagined. They called it *Blitzkrieg* – lightning war. Blitzkrieg relied on the twentieth century's most formidable weaponry – planes, tanks and motorised infantry – using the power of radio communication to strike against an opponent with rapid, well-coordinated blows. The Germans believed that speed and modern technology would always crush their enemies. When they had invaded Poland in 1939 and France in 1940 both countries had succumbed in weeks. Blitzkrieg was now to be unleashed against Russia – and Napoleon's disastrous 1812 campaign was not to be repeated.

'We were following Napoleon's invasion route,' wrote Major General Hans von Greiffenberg, chief of staff of the Germans' Army Group Centre, 'but we did not think that the lessons of the 1812 campaign applied to us in 1941. We were fighting with modern means of transport and communication – we thought that the vastness of Russia could be overcome by rail and motor-engine, telegraph wire and radio. We believed in the power of our battle-seasoned army and its well-honed coordination with the Luftwaffe. Above all, we had absolute faith in the infallibility of *Blitzkrieg*.' 'We were fast,' said Panzer Lieutenant Hans-Erdmann Schönbeck, 'and our tank forces could cover huge distances. And once we broke through the enemy's defences, our orders were not to worry about threats to our right or left but to keep going, deep into Russian territory. We would strike his rear installations, communication units and supply depots. It was a new way of fighting – highly mobile and flexible – and it was difficult to anticipate. It brought fear and panic to our opponents.'

Some remained doubtful. War against Russia was a step into the unknown. The country was vast, and with Britain still undefeated, war was being opened up on two fronts. But the stunning German successes in the first few days assuaged the sceptics. Ulrich de Maizière, an officer in the 18th Panzer Division, had put his own fears behind him: 'Our initial victories were utterly exhilarating,' he admitted. 'I had wondered how we would supply our troops once we penetrated deep inside Russia. But now I put these concerns aside. Our advance was rapid, and the speed we were moving at made everybody feel supremely confident. I was convinced that the campaign would be over by the autumn.' Philipp von Boeselager, an officer with the Wehrmacht's 86th Infantry Division, added: 'We were going forward so quickly. A heady optimism swept through the ranks. We genuinely thought Russia's fate would be decided in six weeks.'

When a belief becomes a certainty, one loses the sense that it began life as a point of view, one which events might prove wrong. And when that certainty becomes internalised, it removes all thought of a plan for alternative outcomes. In the opening days of the war with Russia, one German soldier observed euphorically:

> I predict that the swastika flag will be flying over the Kremlin in Moscow in four to five weeks, and that then, after we have destroyed Russia, we will have time to deal with England. It is no secret that we aim to reach Moscow in a month with our invincible army. We only need to wage another blitzkrieg. We only know how to attack: at them, at them and at them again – in cooperation with our heavy weapons. Fire, cordite, iron, bombs and shells – all will rain down on the Russians. That's all that is needed to give us the title 'fastest soldiers in the world'.

'Our ground forces have completely surprised the enemy,' Wolfram von Richthofen observed. 'The first prisoners say that no one expected our offensive – and as a result we are rapidly pushing forward everywhere.'

Alexander Andrievich was a supply officer for the Soviet Sixth Army: 'The German bombing of our frontier forces was merciless,' he said. 'The weather was ideal for their planes – with long, clear sunny days – and they rained bombs down upon our troops as if they were conducting a military exercise. I came across the remnants of one of our units, close to a forest. There were hundreds upon hundreds of dead. The German attack had been so rapid that most had not even time to get out of their vehicles.' There was one image Andrievich always remembered. 'I saw one of our generals standing by a crossroads. He had come to review his troops, and was wearing his best parade uniform. But his soldiers were fleeing in the opposite direction. He stood there, forlorn and alone – without even an adjutant by his side – while the troops flooded past. Behind him was an obelisk, marking the route of Napoleon's invasion in 1812.'

Stephan Mikoyan, whose father Anastas was Soviet trade minister and a member of Stalin's inner circle, commented: 'Stalin did not believe the Germans would attack us in the summer of 1941 – and he ignored all evidence to the contrary. The rout that we suffered at the beginning of the war was largely his fault.' The Soviet leader had indeed made an astonishing miscalculation.

Warned by a variety of intelligence sources, he should have taken better precautions, for Hitler's invasion had been plotted well in advance. Nearly a year earlier the Führer had instructed Major General Erich Marcks to start planning an attack on Russia, and on 5 August 1940 Marcks drew up a first invasion blueprint. 'The aim of the campaign,' he declared, 'will be to defeat the Russian Army and render the Soviet Union incapable of becoming a threat to Germany in the foreseeable future.' The Marcks plan envisaged the defeat of Red Army forces close to the frontier, followed by a rapid strike against the Russian capital, a hammer blow that would bring down the Bolshevik regime: 'Moscow is economically, politically and spiritually the heart of the Soviet Union,' he stated. 'Capturing it will destroy the cohesion of the Russian realm.'

By 18 December 1940 Marcks's preliminary investigation had matured into a full-scale military directive, codenamed Operation Barbarossa, which now calculated a defeat of the Soviet Union within three months, declaring: 'The mass of the Red Army stationed in Western Russia is to be destroyed in bold operations involving deep penetrations by armoured spearheads.' This was blitzkrieg in action, and once Russia's land armies had been obliterated, German troops would move forward and seize Moscow. 'The capture of this city,' Hitler's high command emphasised, 'will give us a decisive success – both politically and economically.'

This unequivocal statement that the Soviet Union would be defeated within three months shaped the planning of Operation Barbarossa. It was intended as a summer campaign, anticipating that by the second week of October, when the weather usually began to change in Russia – with torrential rain, and also the first snow – military operations would effectively be over. This rapid timetable distanced the 1941 invasion plan from its predecessor in 1812. The terrible disintegration of Napoleon's army had begun after he started his retreat from Moscow in the latter part of October – a fate that could not be repeated.

Napoleon had also initially hoped to destroy Russia's armies close to the frontier, but after the capture of Smolensk in the middle of August 1812, with his quarry still eluding him, the

French emperor had made Moscow his principal military objective. The Germans – with three invading army groups totalling
nearly three million men – were invading with far greater forces
than Napoleon's *Grande Armée* of 600,000. But in June 1941 the
Germans, like their predecessors, were well aware of Moscow's
crucial importance.

Philipp von Boeselager emphasised this point: 'For us, Moscow
was the spider in the web – the transport, commercial and political
hub of Russia. We understood that once you took Moscow you
would control the whole country.' In the first few weeks of the
war, this objective did not seem so very distant. Gerhard Dengler,
an officer in the 23rd Infantry Division, remarked: 'In those early
days of success the musical conductor of our military orchestra
had already composed a special march for our entry into Moscow.
It was rehearsed for the expected victory parade in the Russian
capital.'

The assumptions of German officers and soldiers were echoed at
the highest level of command. Field Marshal Günther von Kluge,
commander of the German Fourth Army, said: 'Moscow is both
the heart and head of the Soviet system. Besides being their capital, it is also an important armaments centre. It is the focal point
of the Russian rail network, particularly for those lines that lead
to Siberia.' Kluge believed that the main thrust of the campaign
should follow Napoleon's route in 1812: 'The Russians are bound
to throw in strong forces to prevent the capture of their capital,' he
remarked. 'Our armies should therefore advance with all strength
possible along the Moscow road, via Minsk and Smolensk. We
must aim to capture the Soviet capital before winter sets in.'

Kluge believed the capture of Moscow would be the culmin-
ation of the campaign. It was a view shared by the commander of
the German Army, Field Marshal Walther von Brauchitsch, and
his chief of staff, Colonel General Franz Halder. On 3 July 1941,
with Hitler's war against Russia less than two weeks old, Halder
was contemplating the successful encirclement of a mass of Soviet
divisions at Minsk. He wrote: 'I think I am not exaggerating when
I say that the campaign against Russia has been won in fourteen

days.' The Germans were convinced that the military power of the Soviet Union would dissolve after these first frontier clashes, and in their wake the Wehrmacht would move forward easily and occupy Russia's capital.

Medical orderly Vera Yukina recalled conditions in a Soviet field hospital near Smolensk. 'What we saw turned people's hair grey overnight,' she said:

> The enemy's planes were bombing our military formations at will. We heard that many of our soldiers had been killed, and more and more wounded began arriving at the hospital. Some were brought in military vehicles, some were carried in carts and some were even crawling on their hands and knees, covered in blood. We dressed their wounds, and the surgeons removed shell fragments and bullets – and with little anaesthetic remaining, the operating theatre resounded to men's groans, cries and calls for help. We quickly ran out of beds and had to put up a large tent and lay out the newcomers on the bare earth. We tried to evacuate some of them to hospitals further from the front, but although the trains were marked with the Red Cross the Germans were methodically bombing them.

Yukina then said: 'The worst thing was that our troops kept retreating. Did our field commanders want to lure the Germans all the way to Moscow, and then destroy them – just as Napoleon's army had been destroyed in 1812? But Napoleon did not have the Luftwaffe.'

Fourteen-year-old Ivan Nikitin lived in the centre of Moscow. On 7 July his father, a railway worker at the city's Yaroslavl Station, came home looking worried. 'He sat down in the kitchen with my mother,' Nikitin recalled, 'and through the half-open door I was able to hear most of the conversation. My father described how a large contingent of NKVD [Soviet secret police], some in uniform, some in plain clothes, had arrived at the station, roped off an entire platform and then loaded a special train with a secret cargo, which was then driven off at high speed.'

A friend of Nikitin's father – one of the station's administrative staff – confided to him that Lenin's tomb had just been evacuated from the Mausoleum on Red Square and the sarcophagus put aboard that train, bound for some unknown destination. He warned of NKVD orders that any railwayman who accidentally witnessed the scene was to be immediately sent to the front – at this stage of the war, an almost certain death sentence. Ivan Nikitin was left dumbfounded. 'Lenin no longer on Red Square?' he mused. 'Of course, nothing had been said about this on the radio – it would be far too provocative, suggesting there was no longer the will to defend Moscow.'

The next day Nikitin ran over to Red Square and made his own inspection. He found there were no longer any queues for admission; instead, the Mausoleum's doors were now firmly closed. Everything else seemed normal. Under the Kremlin's bell tower the guards were still leaving their sentry posts and making their parade steps to the Mausoleum, but Nikitin suspected this was an elaborate hoax. He could not get the image of the closed doors out of his mind, and wrote:

> For the Soviet people Moscow, the Kremlin and Lenin's Mausoleum represent the heart of our homeland and the wellspring of our patriotism and fighting morale. The soldiers at the front and the workers in the hinterland feel calmer and safer knowing that Comrade Stalin and his government are staying in the Kremlin and the body of Lenin lies in the Mausoleum below. But now I know differently.

German troops were advancing rapidly. 'We have now marched some 400 kilometres eastwards,' Alois Scheuer wrote on 12 July from Army Group Centre's northern wing, 'over dusty dirt roads, through forest, swamp and moorland, past places where bitter battles have taken place, scattered with war debris of all kinds and innumerable dead. Impatiently we continue our advance.' Corporal Scheuer and his comrades in the 197th Infantry Division were soon confidently noting the remaining distance to Moscow.

One of the troubling and yet most prescient features of Napoleon's 1812 campaign had been its cruelty. It degenerated into carnage and savagery, with no mercy being shown to prisoners of war on either side. One of Napoleon's generals, Count Philippe de Ségur, described how thousands of captured

Russian soldiers died in makeshift camps, receiving no provision or care:

> These unfortunate people were left to die of hunger in enclosures where they were confined like brute beasts. This was barbarous – but what else could we do? Exchange them? The enemy rejected the proposal. Release them? They would then have publicised the distressed state our army was in and, joined by others, would have returned to pursue us. In this mortal warfare, to give them their lives would have been sacrificing our own. We were cruel from necessity.

In 1941 the war in the east began without a framework of rules to guide it, since neither side had chosen to recognise the Third Geneva Convention of 1929, and its articles concerning the humane treatment of prisoners of war. Soviet hatred of the invading foe was more than matched by German contempt for the Bolshevik ideology and by Nazi race propaganda, which regarded the Slavic peoples as *Untermenschen* (sub-human) and sought to create *Lebensraum* (living space) in the east for an Aryan master race. When the Wehrmacht invaded Russia there were no proper guidelines for the treatment of Red Army prisoners. Commissars – political instructors – were to be taken out and summarily shot. Reprisals would be allowed against the native civilian population for acts of violence or sabotage.

On 25 June a regiment from the Wehrmacht's 23rd Infantry Division reported an incident near Bialystok that seemed to confirm the Nazis' prejudice. In an act of desperation, a white flag was misused by Red Army soldiers, who after waving it in surrender continued to fire on German troops. Six men from the division were shot in the back, and this flagrant breach of one of the most basic rules of war provoked a savage response. The German divisional commander, Major General Heinz Hellmich, decreed the following day that the white flag should be disregarded by his entire force – and for twenty-four hours no quarter was given to the enemy.

Wilhelm Schröder was a radio operator with the German 10th Panzer Division. On 3 July he wrote in his diary: 'A tough fight arose with the Russians. At the end of it, all the prisoners were herded together and shot with a machine gun. This was not done in our presence, but in a clearing behind us. However, all of us heard the firing and knew what was going on. I am deeply worried – I detest this kind of behaviour.'

A few days later Schröder witnessed a massacre of Russian wounded: 'I was standing amidst a mass of wounded enemy soldiers. My comrades and I were ordered to dig a burial pit. What followed was absolutely horrifying.' Schröder remembered a particular moment before the men were shot: 'A heavily wounded Russian soldier, still able to support himself on one elbow, asked me for a cigarette. I gave him one, and also a light – but even this little favour was commented on with disapproval by those standing beside me.' Schröder believed that Hitler's brutal race doctrine lay behind these actions.

In the summer of 1941 some Germans clearly recognised that brutality could quickly become counterproductive, causing a breakdown in army discipline and forcing their opponents – no longer able to surrender – to fight with desperate determination. Lieutenant Fritz-Dietlof von der Schulenburg, an officer with the German 23rd Infantry Division, commented: 'Obviously there is a threat to discipline if our people start to bump off the enemy on their own initiative. If we permit this we descend to the level of the SS.' With this remark Schulenburg strikingly distanced the Wehrmacht from the deliberate cruelty of SS soldiers, who saw themselves as ruthless enforcers of the Nazi ideology of racial supremacy. He continued emphatically: 'The Russians must only be shot in battle or upon the order of an officer. Anything else removes all constraints of conduct and allows baser instincts to run riot.'

On 28 June the commander of the 47th Army Corps, General Joachim Lemelsen, wrote:

I am repeatedly finding out about the shooting of prisoners, defectors or deserters, carried out in an irresponsible, senseless and criminal manner. This is murder. Soon the Russians will get to hear about the countless corpses lying along the routes taken by our soldiers, without weapons and with hands raised, despatched at close range by the shots to the head. The result will be that the enemy will hide in the woods and fields and continue to fight, out of fear – and we will lose countless comrades.

On the same day Robert Rupp, an officer with an advancing motorized unit, witnessed the results of a mass execution near Minsk: 'Many Red Army soldiers whom I saw lying there had been shot with their hands raised and no weapons, often not even a belt. I saw at least a hundred like this. They say that even an emissary who came with a white flag was shot down. They also shot the wounded.'

These early incidences of cruelty were sporadic rather than wholesale, but they were troubling nonetheless. This ruthless clash of ideologies was starting to spawn a vicious brutality. Hans Meier-Welcker, a staff officer with the German 251st Infantry Division, was worried by the violence being unleashed, remarking: 'We often find Russian officers shooting themselves rather than surrendering to us.' Meier-Welcker, a decent soldier, was concerned that the German killings were already becoming counterproductive. He was also ready to pay tribute to his foe, acknowledging: 'The Russian stands out from other fighters as the most courageous opponent we have yet met in this war.'

General Gotthard Heinrici concurred with Meier-Welcker. He too was struck by the war's terrible destructiveness, writing to his wife on 4 July: 'The war in Russia is incredibly bloody. The enemy has suffered losses beyond anything seen in this war yet. The Russian soldiers are told by their commanders that they will be executed by us, so they are reluctant to surrender – and sometimes fire on our soldiers from the rear. This, of course, demands countermeasures on our side, which are harsh. So both sides step things up, and as a result there are masses of casualties.' The spectre of the 1812 campaign was raising its head. Heinrici continued: 'We believe that Stalin will issue an order to destroy everything that could be of use to us as his army retreats. Soon there will be a scorched-earth policy and burnings. It will be just like Napoleonic times.' Heinrici was beginning to feel the vastness of Russia, a vastness that had swallowed up hundreds of thousands of Napoleon's soldiers, adding: 'Then there is the impenetrable nature of the land: everywhere forests, swamps, tall grain – where the Russian can hide. It is not pretty here. And tomorrow we will advance eastwards – into the country's interior.' Yet he held on to his optimism: 'Our opponent has not yet been laid low, but he is badly hit. Russian aircraft have not been seen for days, and this is a great advantage for us.'

On 13 July the German 137th Infantry Division crossed the river Berezina at Borisov. 'Very hot again,' wrote Leopold Höglinger, the radio operator. 'The bridges we have constructed are first class. On the other side of the river, our tanks and infantry are massing.' At this very spot, at the end of November 1812, Napoleon's army had fought a desperate three-day rearguard action – suffering heavy casualties – while their engineers built pontoon bridges across the ice. 'The remains of the props driven into the river bed by the French are still visible when the water is clear,' said General Günther Blumentritt, chief of staff of the German Fourth Army. 'They suffered such appalling losses here.' But these scenes of suffering seemed far away.

After Army Group Centre's victory at Minsk the German advance continued, their forces now pressing on towards Smolensk. Fighting was growing in intensity. 'There are now air battles above us,' Höglinger noted on 16 July. 'We can hear artillery salvoes – ahead, the forest is burning.' The country's reserves of manpower and equipment, and its sheer will to resist, even sporadically, were disconcerting. On the same day one Wehrmacht soldier wrote:

We get ever closer to Moscow. Everywhere there are the same scenes of destruction – much of it the enemy have smashed themselves. It is a cruel war here, for those of our troops who are taken prisoner are shot dead immediately – the Russians act exactly like that. All that you have read about Russia is not exaggerated. The last few days have been tough for us. We were subject to heavy artillery fire – and the enemy did not shoot badly. Although we have penetrated a good distance our opponents lie to the right and left of us and try to cut us off. But now I am lying by a large lake – and have had a moment to bathe and briefly relax. All around is a very beautiful forest – were it not full of Russians.

Although the first encirclement of Russian armies at Minsk was a considerable success, many Red Army fighters continued to resist in a situation that seemed hopeless. Remarkably, a Russian garrison at the citadel of Brest-Litovsk – surrounded on the first day of the war and entirely cut off from help – still continued to defy the invaders several weeks later. After little more than a month's fighting in each case, German campaigns against Poland (1939), France (1940), and Yugoslavia and Greece (1941) had effectively been over. Hopes of a quick Russian collapse, however, were not materialising.

At the beginning of July, Stalin had appointed Marshal Semyon Timoshenko commander-in-chief of the Western Front, and as an able and experienced commander Timoshenko was now making herculean efforts to slow the German advance. He resorted to drastic measures to restore army discipline, setting up catchment areas in the rear of Red Army positions where retreating and leaderless troops were re-formed and re-equipped, and sent back into battle. Fresh soldiers and weaponry were brought in, and strike forces formed to counter-attack and throw the enemy off balance. On 14 July at Orsha new multiple rocket launchers, nicknamed *katyushas*, ['Little Katie' from the popular Russian wartime song about a girl longing for her absent beloved], were first used against the Germans. Timoshenko reported the experiment a success, and production was stepped up. Soviet resistance was stiffening.

Leopold Höglinger's 137th Infantry Division was now fighting in the encirclement battle of Smolensk. On 17 July he noted: 'Our heavy artillery fire has silenced the enemy's batteries and wiped out a column of their troops. The shooting went on all day. We had to repel several Russian breakout attempts.' On 20 July he added: 'Although the Russians are trapped, they have dug themselves in well, and are defending themselves tenaciously.' On 23 July Höglinger saw the 'G' insignia of Colonel General Heinz Guderian's tank and armoured vehicles, as the German Second

Panzer Group pushed forward. 'There has been a tough fight here,' he said. 'On either side of the road one can see the wreckage of Russian planes and tanks.'

On 26 July Höglinger stood on a hill overlooking Smolensk: 'This large, beautiful city lies in front of me,' he wrote. 'But along the horizon are fires and huge clouds of smoke.' The trapped Russian forces west of the city were still desperately resisting. 'All day there was continuous artillery fire,' Höglinger added. 'Our planes are in the sky above us, then Russian bombers.' On 27 July the battle was finally over. 'The Red Army has finally pulled back, and Smolensk is secure. Field Marshal von Kluge and Colonel General Guderian came to our HQ and gave speeches of congratulation.' That night crates of beer were brought up for the troops. It had been a tough fight.

On 28 July Hans Meier-Welcker of the 251st Infantry Division surveyed the countryside around him. Images of farming and summer mingled with evidence of the war's destruction:

A tender blue sky hangs over a green, spacious and open country, with meadows, cornfield, fallow land and farmhouses. There are moorlands, sand, dirt tracks – and burnt-down bridges and graves – with crosses and helmets . . . The villages are burning, and little is spared from the flames. Some of the women kneel before our soldiers, crying hysterically, because we are taking their last cow or chicken from them. We bury our comrades, often by the dozen, and our fellows chase after a flock of helpless geese.

Three days later Meier-Welcker wrote in sadness and frustration: 'If only our people behaved better and showed a little human decency . . . We smash open the farmers' beehives to get at the honey, although by preserving the hives we could get ample for next year, as well as being provided with old stocks of honey. This is predatory stupidity, and by needlessly destroying their homes we release swarms of angry bees to hover around our heads.'

By the end of July the Germans had concluded the battle west of Smolensk, capturing hundreds of thousands more Red Army soldiers and consolidating their hold on the city. They were now astride the motor highway to Moscow, and with the Russian capital only 230 miles away some Germans remained supremely confident. One officer wrote triumphantly: 'You will have heard about the great fight for Smolensk on the radio. It was my proud troops who achieved the breakthrough, who raised the flag for victory. We are but a short distance from Moscow – and as our formations rapidly advance it is as if this Russian city is welded to an iron chain, in the grip of a military power the world has not witnessed before.'

'Now we are past Smolensk,' Karl Fuchs – a tank gunner with the 7th Panzer Division – exclaimed happily. He did not think the campaign would last much longer, and rather than seeing the war as a political struggle against Bolshevism, he invoked the Nazi ideology of Aryan supremacy to justify his claim, denouncing his opponents as racially inferior: 'The war against these subhuman beings is almost over . . . We really let them have it! They are scoundrels, the mere scum of the earth – and they are no match for the German soldier. Not even their biggest tanks can protect them . . . And so we move on to the final battle and victory.'

But for others, prospects of an easy, rapid victory seemed to be fading. Field Marshal von Kluge, commander of the German Fourth Army, was becoming concerned: 'The operational situation is already somewhat mixed,' he said, 'since the Russians are fighting much more skilfully than we allowed for. Hopefully this will not continue all the way to Moscow. Things could get really difficult for us if we were faced with winter fighting. The enemy are doing particularly well against our advance forces, bringing up fresh armoured divisions, and releasing them into combat in a strength we did not anticipate.'

One hundred and twenty-nine years earlier, Napoleon's initial hope had been to bring the Russian armies to battle and destroy their forces before reaching Smolensk. He had never intended to march deep into the heart of Russia. But when the French emperor launched his assault on the city on 17 August 1812, decisive military success eluded him.

Using the precious summer months of 1941, the Germans

captured Smolensk nearly a month earlier than the French army had managed to do. Yet Russia was still not finished, and the campaign remained far from over. General Walther Nehring, commander of the 18th Panzer Division, shared von Kluge's fears: 'The further our armoured spearheads advance into the depths of this country, the more our difficulties mount, while the forces of the enemy seem to gain in strength and cohesion. Also the growing distance between our Panzer forces and the infantry moving up behind is starting to cause us problems. We are suffering increasing tank losses against an enemy who is still numerically superior to us.'

This would not, it appeared, be a lightning campaign after all. Towards the end of July Count Claus von Stauffenberg visited the Wehrmacht's elite tank formation, the Second Panzer Group, commanded by Colonel General Guderian, now stationed between Orsha and Smolensk. Guderian was the creator of the Germans' fast-moving tank tactics. His Panzers had made remarkable progress, but this had come at a price, and some of his officers were worried about the losses in tanks and equipment. Previous German success had been based on the superior mobility of its armed forces. Now, for the first time, serious fears were raised that without this advantage they might suffer the same fate as Napoleon's army.

In conversation with Stauffenberg, Major Georg von Unhold, one of the Second Panzer Group's officers, likened a rapid tank advance to the daring cavalry charges of Napoleon's flamboyant commander, Joachim Murat. Exciting as it sounded, this contained an incipient menace. The turning point in the 1812 campaign had come, Unhold said, during the French occupation of Moscow, when Napoleon's army was no longer able to feed and quarter its horses. Deep in the interior of Russia, with winter approaching and food running out, the loss in horses could not be made good; their absence robbed the French Army of its speed of movement. Then, in the terrible retreat that followed, Napoleon's forces were preyed upon by Russia's dreaded Cossack cavalry.

A month into the campaign – and at a high level within the

German Army – doubts were emerging that a blitzkrieg strategy would be successful against the Soviet Union. Unhold was beginning to dread the sheer size of Russia, and believed that the German high command was expecting his tanks to do too much. 'I am worried that our armoured corps is being hounded to death,' he confided to Stauffenberg, 'in the same way that Murat lost his splendid cavalry in 1812.'

'For the first four weeks of the fighting we barely had time to think,' said Private Heinz Otto Fausten of the 1st Panzer Division. 'But I remember a conversation I had with a friend in my unit, towards the end of July. We asked each other: "Will the Russians really be done for in a matter of weeks?" At the beginning of our offensive we had hammered their forces. But they were still fighting – and we had seen how tough some of their soldiers were, how they were willing to sacrifice themselves to slow our advance. We began to realise that there would be no easy victory.'

Lieutenant Erich Mende of the 8th Infantry Division was also concerned: 'Fighting around Smolensk has been very tough. First our German Panzer divisions broke into the city, cutting off the Red Army soldiers behind them, still defending its western approaches. Our planes dropped supplies on our armoured troops there. But the struggle was very bitter – because elite Red Army units from Moscow were thrown into the battle.' The Soviet Union's capacity to bring in countless reinforcements disconcerted Mende. 'And after the encirclement of the enemy, we have halted,' he continued. 'The troops are becoming restless. "Why aren't we going any further towards Moscow?" they are asking. The city lies little more than 200 miles ahead of us. Our soldiers hope that by the end of August, or early September, we can be in the Russian capital, with the strength of the Red Army largely exhausted.' Fearing that the advance was losing its momentum, Mende now wanted German troops to head straight for Moscow, just as Napoleon had done.

In early August German troops pushed past Smolensk, but they were unable to make further progress. Franz Frisch's artillery battery had reached Yelnya: 'The combat there was the toughest we had yet experienced,' he recalled. 'Our Panzer troops remained optimistic, and started putting up signs showing the distance to Moscow, but we regarded these with wry amusement. The Russians were giving us a really hard time.' Frisch observed the way in which the army hierarchy progressively minimised the soldiers' difficulties:

> When we went to our forward positions, and the situation did not look good – we said so. We did not beat about the bush. We would start our reports with a single word, *Scheisse* – shit – and that meant things were really bad. But our commander did not feel able to use such language with his superiors, so he would say things were 'serious'. At the next level up, it would become a 'problem' that was 'under control'. A level higher, and it was 'a straightening out of the front'. By the time it reached the high command, such expressions as 'a planned withdrawal' and 'a correcting of the front' were then proclaimed as a sort of victory.

Leopold Höglinger's unit was involved in fierce fighting near the village of Kossaki. On 6 August its advanced formations were surprised by a Red Army counter-attack. 'The Russians appeared in considerable force,' Höglinger wrote, 'and after savage hand-to-hand fighting our troops were forced to pull back, abandoning vehicles and tanks.' The enemy was resisting strongly. 'There is shooting in front of us, and behind us,' Höglinger continued. 'Columns of smoke are rising up. The Russians have appeared with artillery and tanks and half the village is burning. What is happening?' he wondered. Shortly afterwards, Höglinger reached a bridgehead established by Colonel General Guderian at Roslavl. 'Guderian stands ready to advance on Moscow,' he noted, 'but as we passed his vehicles, we saw that a quarter of them were captured Russian tanks.' The heavy fighting was taking its toll.

Army Group Centre needed to regroup. While it did so, Colonel General Maximilian von Weichs, commander of the German Second Army, voiced his concerns over the fate of Russian prisoners of war taken after the battle for Smolensk. Violence against prisoners by front-line soldiers had lessened, but Weichs was hearing disconcerting reports of their mistreatment as they were marched to camps in the rear of the German position. He wrote to Army Group Centre's commander, Field Marshal Fedor von Bock: 'I am becoming more and more concerned about this issue. Prisoners captured by us must be ensured proper accommodation and food.' He added: 'The excesses being committed by the guards and security detachments must be fully investigated, and those found guilty punished by court martial. The treatment of Russian prisoners by the German armed forces should be strict but fair.'

In the early days of the war, the Führer had contented himself with threats of destruction against Russia's capital. On 29 June he had looked at a situation map and boasted: 'In a few weeks we'll be in Moscow. Then I'll raze it to the ground and build a reservoir there. The name Moscow must be expunged.' On 8 July Colonel General Halder, the chief of staff of the German Army, noted in his diary that Hitler now wanted to raze Moscow to the ground by bombing. The Führer ordered a massive raid by the Luftwaffe, and on 21 July the German planes went in. 'It was a sea of fire,' remembered Ivan Sokolov, a member of the city's air defence. 'There were flash bombs, incendiaries and bombs which emitted a terrible sound as they hurtled through the air. They were designed to create a sense of terror.'

Yet, faced with growing Russian resistance, the Führer was also starting to have his doubts. On the very same day as this ferocious airborne attack, Hitler began to downplay Moscow's overall importance. His attention was now drawn to the destruction of Leningrad, which he perceived was a vital symbol of the Bolshevik regime, even though diversion of forces would leave only infantry armies to advance on Moscow. It was stated: 'The Führer is not concerned by this, since to him Moscow is only a geographical objective.'

This was an extraordinary comment to have made, for in reality Hitler remained well aware of Moscow's political and economic importance. On 4 August he visited the headquarters of Army Group Centre, which was redeploying its forces after the battle for Smolensk. Its commander, Field Marshal von Bock, was waiting for permission to attack Moscow, but this did not happen. Instead, the Führer hesitated, unsure what course to pursue. His adjutant, Major Gerhard von Engel, was struck by this. 'One sees clearly how indecisive Hitler is regarding the continuation of the operation,' he wrote. 'Ideas and objectives keep changing. One emerges from situation conferences as nonplussed as one went in.' The anticipated short pause in the fighting, followed by a rapid advance on the Russian capital, failed to materialise.

The Germans were now east of Smolensk, with the Red Army flinging more and more troops against them. On 9 August the weather briefly changed. Rain thudded against Hans Meier-Welcker's tent in the 251st Infantry Division. The ground around the German soldiers abruptly turned to a quagmire. 'The roads are suddenly mud, supplies cannot get through and our vehicles cannot move forward,' Meier-Welcker wrote. The rain passed, and the ground quickly dried out again. But there was something disconcerting about the dramatic change in the weather. Meier-Welcker added thoughtfully: 'The east begins to show its true face.'

Hitler's attention now turned south, towards the Ukraine, the city of Kiev and the rich industrial region of the Donets Basin. The Führer was concluding that the destruction of the Soviet Union's industrial strength was a prerequisite for further advance on Moscow. On 10 August General Alfred Jodl, chief of staff of the German armed forces, spoke about the intended change of direction to planning officer Colonel Adolf Heusinger. Heusinger was bewildered that Moscow was no longer the German Army's immediate objective. Jodl responded that Hitler was afraid of history repeating itself: 'The Führer has an instinctive aversion to treading the same path as Napoleon,' Jodl said. 'Moscow gives him a sinister feeling.'

On 11 August Colonel General Halder noted: 'It is increasingly clear that we underestimated the Russian colossus . . . At the beginning of the war we believed that the enemy had about 200 divisions. Now we are counting 360. These forces are not always well armed and equipped, and they are often poorly led. But they are there. When a dozen of them have been smashed, another dozen replace them.'

Finally, on 21 August 1941, Hitler made his decision: the advance on Moscow would be halted and instead German armies would swing south, into the Ukraine. The Führer disregarded the views of the commander-in-chief of the German Army, Field Marshal Walther von Brauchitsch, who had strongly argued for an immediate resumption of the attack on Moscow. Instead Hitler now stated: 'The most important objective to be accomplished before the onset of winter is not the capture of Moscow but seizing the Crimea and the industrial and coal-mining regions of the Donets.' On a number of occasions Hitler had said to his entourage that he did not want to make the same mistake as his 'illustrious predecessor'. Now he felt that he had distanced himself from Napoleon's invasion. By diverting his armies into the Ukraine and denying the Soviet Union the centres of her heavy industry, and making these economic factors the basis for his decision making, the Führer believed that he was fighting the war in a more modern way. As a result, therefore, history would not repeat itself.

The German Army chief of staff, Colonel General Halder, was furious: 'He, and no one else, is to blame for the zigzag course caused by his successive orders,' he said angrily of Hitler. Field Marshal von Bock, commander of Army Group Centre, was equally indignant: 'Turning south jeopardises the main operation,' he exclaimed. But Hitler's arguments impressed many German commanders. Some, alarmed by the Soviet Union's military strength, agreed that the Wehrmacht's war strategy should now include economic targets. General Erich von Manstein, commander of the 56th Army Corps, wrote to his wife on 28 August: 'We will break the Russians' military strength by capturing the centres of their heavy industry and raw materials, so that they cannot effectively equip large army groups any more.'

Others were concerned about the sheer number of enemy troops massing on their flanks. There were nearly a million Soviet troops in the area around Kiev, as Stalin committed more and more troops to a defence of the Ukraine. A number of German

commanders believed that this concentration of forces now constituted a serious threat, one that would have to be eliminated
before an advance on Moscow was resumed. Colonel General von
Weichs, commander of the German Second Army, was a strong
supporter of the turn south: 'Fighting a great encirclement battle
around Kiev, with the goal of the complete destruction of the
enemy forces there, seemed to me at the time a vital pre-requisite
for the overall success of the campaign.' He continued:

> And I still believe that forcing a major battle in the Ukraine before
> attacking the Russian capital was a strategically sound decision. I felt
> it unlikely that Army Group Centre could successfully advance on
> Moscow with such strong enemy pressure on its flanks. And even
> if they had managed to capture the Russian capital, with such large
> enemy forces remaining in the south, around Kiev, I doubted whether
> this would have had the decisive effect that Brauchitsch and Halder
> assumed. The Russians would have continued to fight.

Weichs thought it was crucial to destroy the bulk of the enemy
before advancing on Moscow. Whereas some were content simply
to follow in Napoleon's footsteps, demanding a rapid attack on the
Russian capital, Weichs looked hard at what Napoleon had failed
to do – annihilate the military forces opposing him. At the battle
of Borodino the French emperor had allowed the Russian army,
although badly mauled, to survive intact. It had then regrouped,
and harried his army mercilessly on the retreat. 'The experiences of Napoleon in 1812 give us a stark warning in this regard,'
Weichs concluded.

Field Marshal von Kluge, commander of the German Fourth
Army and an avid reader of Armand de Caulaincourt's history of
the 1812 campaign, shared Weichs's views. He also believed that
the threat on Army Group Centre's flanks should now be eliminated. So did Colonel General Adolf Strauss, commander of the
Ninth Army. All Field Marshal von Bock's infantry commanders
were opposed to an immediate advance on Moscow. And when
the charismatic Panzer leader, Colonel General Heinz Guderian,
also fell in behind Hitler's plan, it was decisive.

Guderian had been an advocate of an immediate push on Moscow, but then became alarmed at the strength of the Russian opposition and also feared that his Panzer forces might be split up and used in piecemeal operations. Hitler astutely offered him a key role in the new offensive, one where all the tank and motorised divisions would be kept under his command. Guderian was completely won over. 'I was received by the Führer,' he wrote to his wife, 'who, as always, was very friendly to me, and very clear about the strategy he wanted me to follow.' Guderian's Panzers would now detach from Army Group Centre and drive south, towards Kiev. Guderian was enthused by the new military operation: 'I left the meeting [with Hitler] well satisfied, and with high hopes,' he concluded. The balance of the war had now shifted. Army Group Centre went onto the defensive, while military operations commenced on its flanks.

On 20 August the German Corporal Alois Scheuer, on Army Group Centre's northern wing, wrote: 'We have taken up defensive positions, on rising ground, in the middle of a grain field. Time passes slowly as we wait in our foxholes. Things are drying out after a heavy thunderstorm, and occasionally our peace is interrupted by salvoes of Russian artillery. But much larger operations are underway elsewhere.' Scheuer became reflective. 'How things will develop beyond that, I do not know. But I believe we are fast approaching a time of final reckoning here in Russia. We must have faith in what is now being undertaken, and trust in our leadership.' On 25 August he added: 'I am sitting in my foxhole, my coat wrapped around me, enjoying the quiet of the morning.' Nearly two weeks later, Scheuer and his men were still occupying the same positions. 'Little has changed in our situation,' he wrote, 'and the Russians opposite us are equally well dug in. It is a gloomy and rainy day – the summer seems to be drawing to an end.'

Further south, the Kiev operation was developing well. The Soviet forces were caught off guard by the shift in the German attack, and Stalin's dogmatic insistence that his armies hold their ground had allowed a massive encirclement operation to be launched. Stephan Mikoyan said: 'Our commanders warned Stalin that the forces defending Kiev were in danger of being trapped. But he refused to allow a retreat. He hoped that Kiev would hold.'

Red Army soldier Peter Braiko never forgot what followed: 'The Germans broke our defences in two places – to the north and south of Kiev – and then pushed fast moving tank formations through the gap in our lines. With extraordinary speed, they executed a pincer movement that caught five of our armies. All of a sudden we were ordered to blow up our defences and retreat eastwards. But it was already too late – the Germans were everywhere.' It was the Wehrmacht's greatest victory of the war, and it created a new mood of optimism among their soldiers and commanders.

'The victory at Kiev made a deep impression on me,' said Hans-Erdmann Schönbeck, an officer in the 11th Panzer Division, part of Guderian's army group. 'When they said "We've done it!" I felt an incredible sense of triumph. It was an overwhelming experience seeing the long lines of enemy prisoners going past.' 'We succeeded, didn't we!' said German tank officer Hubert Menzel. 'We had waged an encirclement battle across distances that we'd been incapable of imagining before.' Suddenly, anything seemed possible again. Colonel General von Weichs also paid tribute: 'I believe this victory was one of the most outstanding operations in the history of warfare, and for the skill in which its strategy was executed it can take proud place alongside such other great encirclement battles of the past as Cannae and Tannenberg.'

For Hitler the encirclement at Kiev was a dazzling success, and with the threat from his flanks summarily removed, his attention swung back to Moscow. Now that military events in the south were proceeding so well, the Führer believed it remained possible to capture Moscow before winter set in. Plans for an assault on the Russian capital were revived. On 6 September, with the Kiev battle still underway, Hitler at last gave his categorical support for an attack on Moscow. In a new directive, he spoke of the opportunity that was now emerging to utterly destroy the Soviet armies defending the Russian capital, then advance on the city. 'To this end,' the Führer stated, 'it is necessary to concentrate all our strength which can be spared from the flanks and moved up in time.' The new operation would be codenamed Typhoon.

The number of German troops assembling for this operation was far greater than that available to Field Marshal von Bock a month earlier. To the north, Leningrad had now been besieged, and Hitler released the armoured divisions of Army Group North to join the forces gathering for Typhoon. These were led by Colonel General Erich Hoepner, who took on an important role in the planning of the new offensive as Guderian was still engaged in the Kiev battle. Hoepner had a clear vision of how the attack should proceed. He wanted a deep encirclement of Soviet armies and reserves, followed by an all-out tank dash to Moscow. Hoepner believed that the Germans should strike fast at the Russian capital before the autumn rainy season set in and fresh Soviet reinforcements could be mustered. He realised that the assault was being launched dangerously late in the year, and that time was of the essence. The risk in this approach was that any failure to encircle the defending armies completely would allow some Russian troops to break out, and harass the advance. Hoepner felt it was a risk that needed to be taken, but others disagreed. Field Marshal von Kluge argued strongly that the offensive should concentrate on a tight encirclement of the enemy forces, and his view prevailed. The German high command believed that if the armies defending Moscow were obliterated, the Russian capital would fall automatically.

On 17 September Hoepner noted: 'Tomorrow I am flying over to see Bock, to discuss my new role. This is a large task. Unfortunately, we are not united in the way we envisage the attack, and quarrels and disagreements are breaking out'. A week later, with the battle for Kiev almost concluded, Hoepner wrote: 'I am driving to Smolensk to discuss the operation with Brauchitsch and Halder. It looks as if it will be launched at the beginning of October. Unfortunately, I have not got everything that was originally agreed – and some of the plans have been changed, in a way that I think is badly mistaken. I will have to live with this disappointment. I still hope we can bring the whole thing to a finish by the end of October.'

The battle for Kiev had been a great German victory, but Hans Meier-Welcker was concerned by the quality of the Russian troops starting to arrive on Army Group Centre's northern flank. Although few, their resilience was disconcerting. 'The enemy have deployed a new Siberian division,' Meier-Welcker noted, 'of a type we have not encountered before. They make particularly good use of the terrain, moving through forests and swampland – areas that we consider impassable – and attacking at night.' His comrades were exhausted, but remained resolute with one last goal before them. 'Our target – Moscow – was now quite clear,' said Hans-Erdmann Schönbeck. 'We had to get there!'

On 28 September Alois Scheuer wrote: 'I have now lived through and experienced a quarter of a year in Russia. It is hard to express it in words. There is much I would like to forget, and never be reminded of again. But I have always tried not to lose hope and to keep my courage up'. Scheuer noted how the nights were growing increasingly cold. His company had been reunited again, in preparation for the new offensive. 'Hopefully, October will bring us better tidings,' he concluded.

Napoleon had entered Moscow on 14 September 1812. But the German Wehrmacht, which prided itself on being 'the fastest army in the world', had fallen behind the French emperor's invasion timetable. It was now launching its offensive on the Russian capital several weeks after Napoleon had actually occupied the city. On 30 September the German newspaper *Völkischer Beobachter* ran an article entitled '1812 and Today'. It anticipated that – whatever the outcome of Typhoon – the war with Russia would not now be over before the winter, as Hitler had confidently proclaimed. It therefore sought to reassure the German people. The article began:

Napoleon's Moscow campaign practically forces itself upon one as a parallel. Friend and foe alike have availed themselves of it, drawing from it positive or negative aspects . . . It is inevitable that winter will one day bring our operations to a halt. But did our troops not spend several winters on the Eastern Front in Russia during the First World War, without suffering privations? True, this time our front will be much further east. However, we can supply our soldiers with whatever they need to survive the winter without harm to body and soul.

The paper then continued:

A people like ours, having the organisational skill to build a network of national highways, a powerful armaments industry and equally powerful armed forces, will have no difficulty organising the battle against the Russian winter. The time has not yet come to speak about the form this winter war will take. One thing can be said without exaggeration: the German Wehrmacht will tide over the Russian winter better than its eastern foe!

2

Typhoon

A T THE BEGINNING of October 1941 Hitler's armies readied themselves for their last great offensive of the year –
Operation Typhoon, the assault on Moscow. On the morning of
2 October the assembled German troops heard an address from
their Führer: 'My soldiers,' he enjoined, 'the conditions have
been created for a final mighty blow to smash the enemy before
the onset of winter. Today begins the last great decisive battle of
this year. We will free the German Reich, and the rest of Europe,
from a menace greater than any since the time of the Huns, and
later, of the Mongol hordes.'

Hitler derided the Russians. 'Now, my comrades, you have seen
with your own eyes "the paradise of workers and farmers" and the
poverty that afflicts it. This enemy does not consist of soldiers but
a mass of beasts.' He then praised the fighting performance of the
Wehrmacht: 'Thanks to your bravery,' he told his soldiers:

> we have succeeded in crushing this opponent's tank brigades, one
> after another, in annihilating countless divisions, in taking countless
> numbers of prisoners, in occupying vast territories – not empty space,
> but those regions from which the enemy was living and from which
> his war machine was being supplied with raw materials. Within three
> weeks his most important industrial regions will be completely in our
> hands. Your names, soldiers of the German armed forces, will be asso-
> ciated for all time with the most tremendous victories in history.

For many, Hitler's proclamation gave the intended boost in
morale. 'Our attack rolls forward,' Leopold Höglinger, radio
operator with the German 137th Infantry Division, wrote in his

diary. 'The Führer's proclamation has confirmed the powerful significance of the battle now beginning. It should bring about the destruction of the enemy and a final victory in the east before the winter.' As the sounds of artillery rolled around him, he added: 'Three infantry armies and three Panzer armies stand ready for this offensive. It will be decisive.'

In his last great campaign of 1941 Hitler had assembled a force of around one and a half million men, four thousand artillery pieces, 1,400 combat aircraft and over a thousand tanks. German army quartermaster Eduard Wagner was exultant: 'Now the operation is rolling towards Moscow. Our impression is that a final, great collapse is imminent and tonight the Kremlin is packing its bags. What matters now is that the Panzer armies reach their objectives. Strategic operations are being defined that once would have made our hair stand on end.'

But some front-line German officers were more pragmatic. Private Wolf Dose had fought his way to Leningrad, where he and his comrades from the 58th Infantry Division were in siege positions around the city. The Soviet forces defending Leningrad were outnumbered, weakened by hunger and short of supplies – but they were still holding out. 'The Führer has told us that the decisive battle in the east is beginning,' he wrote in his diary, 'a battle that will finish off the Russians – but how and where he did not say. I do not believe that the Soviet Union will capitulate. We are, after all, dealing with fanatical Bolshevism.'

Hans Jürgen Hartmann – fighting with Army Group South – shared these reservations. His unit had participated in September's massive encirclement battle at Kiev. The Germans had won a great victory in the Ukraine, but the troops were exhausted. Now there was more fighting to be done: 'The last great decisive battle of the year,' he wrote. '*Mein Gott!* And what is the decisive result supposed to be – Moscow, Kharkov, the Volga? We were so per-plexed by this announcement that we immediately launched into a heated discussion of its staggering claims – and quite forgot to eat!' The following day Hartmann remained sceptical: 'Since the Führer's order we have listened breathlessly to news that a gigantic operation is underway, heard how the first key strongholds have been taken and that everything is going according to plan. But all of us share the same concern – for we know the tremendous resourcefulness of the enemy, an enemy that our leadership has blithely declared "is broken, and will never rise again".'

Hitler had made this dramatic claim at a rally in the Berlin Sportpalast on 3 October, developing the theme of racial superiority laid down in his proclamation to the troops a day earlier. Hartmann and his fellow fighters remained unmoved by the Führer's rhetoric, and the bitter prejudice that underlay it. 'As for the references to the "bestial inferiority" of the Russians,' Hartmann continued, 'was he "bestial" and "inferior" somewhere else? Did we not notice anything because we have been fighting in the wrong place?' These soldiers feared the consequences of underestimating their opponent. Hartmann continued:

> Then there is the propaganda about the 'false Soviet paradise'. True, we have seen with our own eyes the terrible poverty in which so many live, in a country rich in natural resources. But we have also witnessed its ruthless diversion of its industrial capacity into munitions and armament manufacture. Perhaps it is only 'talk' that our enemy is broken and will never rise again. I cannot help myself – I am totally bewildered. Will the whole war still be over before the winter?

Some of Hartmann's comrades clutched at this new hope, despite remaining unconvinced that Russian resistance was nearly finished. They imagined – despite their nagging doubts – that the Führer must have a broader overview, and that he would never say something with such conviction unless he was utterly convinced it was true. 'No leader would make such statements without having complete justification for them,' Hartmann exclaimed, 'that would be inconceivable.'

Hartmann and his comrades – on the northern flank of Army Group South – would now be supporting Typhoon by marching on the great Soviet industrial city of Kharkov. 'But will we be able to reach it?' he wondered. The high command had, after all, announced that the Russians were finished before. 'What happened to the other predictions before this one?' Hartmann concluded. 'It has been said – too often for comfort – that "the enemy will never rise again!" Will this great, long-hoped for offensive finally lead to a decision – or will our campaign end in the same fashion as earlier ones in history? The first snow is expected soon. Napoleon also advanced on Moscow, and even though we are some 130 years in the future, the fate of Napoleon hangs over all of us.'

And yet, on the morning of 2 October the fate of Napoleon still seemed distant. The power of the German attack was overwhelming. Military chaplain Ernst Tewes was serving with the 11th Panzer Division, and he declared:

> What I had previously read about in news bulletins I now experienced at first hand. On the morning of 2 October I learnt the real meaning of hell. I reached a small village where some of our wounded were being tended, but moments later the Russians launched an assault, with rows of their infantry emerging from the edge of a nearby forest. A large number of our own tanks, assault guns and infantry hurriedly rushed into action and a real shooting match began. I was caught right in the middle of it. The enemy got through to the edge of the village and their guns opened up on the vehicle where I was taking cover. I thought we were about to be slaughtered and began to recite the prayer for the dying to the men around me.

Nearby soldiers listened, then brought proceedings to an abrupt close, launching a violent counter-attack that snuffed out all threat from the enemy. The relieved chaplain then wandered safely around the village: 'A few minutes before the shooting I spoke with a young lieutenant – a company commander,' Tewes recalled. 'Now I found him on the ground, just a few metres from me – shot in the heart. We buried him by his guns. Then a truck arrived with three badly wounded soldiers; one of them was bleeding heavily from the stomach and would not last much longer. Nearby, four men were carrying a dead comrade to another grave, freshly dug, by the roadside. All the time, more wounded kept appearing.'

Conditions of brutal fury were being unleashed. 'At 6.00 a.m.

hundreds of guns and rocket launchers sent out a massive barrage of preparatory fire,' Private Heinz Otto Fausten of the 1st Panzer Division recalled. 'At around noon we crossed flattened enemy positions, our river of troops and vehicles flooding eastwards.' The remaining Russian troops resisted with desperate ferocity. 'Combat against the enemy – who fought with sub-machine guns, rifles and even spades – lasted for hours,' Fausten continued. 'We forced a breakthrough by bringing up flame-throwing tanks. We flung oil over their positions – their dugouts and shelters – and saw the terrible result as our tanks opened fire. Russian soldiers ran about in all directions, chaotically, flaring up like human torches.'

The commander of Army Group Centre, Field Marshal von Bock, was delighted by the first day's fighting. He had long pressed for an all-out offensive on the Soviet capital and now his hopes were coming to fruition. 'The Army Group has started its offensive according to plan,' Bock wrote on 2 October. 'We are advancing rapidly – everywhere.' He added: 'The performance of our infantry is quite unbelievable, and I can now throw in our Panzer forces.' Sometimes the German advance seemed almost effortless. Lieutenant Wolfgang Koch and the vanguard of the 18th Panzer Division were bearing down on the Russian town of Orel. As they sped forward Koch and his men played Tchaikovsky's choral music at full volume on the gramophone fastened atop their vehicle. Their attack seemed triumphantly choreographed; the Luftwaffe was bombing ahead of them, they followed up with their tanks and their Russian opponents simply disappeared. 'In the weeks before our attack we constantly saw Russian bombers and fighters,' Koch observed, 'but now they seem to have blown away. Either the enemy is frightened or he hasn't got any planes left, and the last few are being held for the fellows in the Kremlin's towers. Instinct tells us that Russian resistance will soon be at an end. Only fought-out remnants will be left after that, and those can be swiftly dealt with.'

Koch's tank dash towards Orel had been prepared by Colonel General Heinz Guderian earlier than the rest of the offensive and was launched on 30 September. By 2 October this overture to

Typhoon was about to achieve its first success. Yet as Koch's unit closed in on the town his gramophone-record playing exuded brash overconfidence, a state of mind sometimes known as *Siegseuphorie*, euphoria based on a succession of dazzling victories and a belief that anything was possible. 'Guderian was nicknamed "Fast Heinz",' said Panzer Lieutenant Hans-Erdmann Schönbeck, 'and it was an apt personal motto for his tactics. We were fast and could turn up where we were least expected, advancing deep into enemy territory. By the end of September 1941 we had met with success after success – it was a quite overwhelming experience. We became supremely confident.'

But on Typhoon's northern flank Heinrich Haape, serving as a front-line doctor with the advancing German 6th Infantry Division, recalled a more sinister image from that first day. At dawn he accompanied the troops as they raced through cleared paths in the enemy's minefields. Suddenly he glimpsed, in the half-light, a Russian sniper directly ahead of him, hidden in the branches of a tree. Haape flung himself to the ground, remaining there, motionless. Then he realised that the Russian was dead:

> I crept closer to him. His eyes were now only holes. His teeth grinned, yellow-brown, from shrunken lips, shrivelled by the summer heat. Mummified and sunken, his parchment face stared at me. I passed, and saw that his skin had been honeycombed by maggots. His rifle lay at the foot of the tree and his uniform was riddled with countless bullet holes. He must have been a victim of earlier fighting here, caught in his tree by a burst of machine-gun fire. Perhaps others, like myself, had been fooled by the menacing attitude of the corpse and had peppered his lifeless body with bullets.

The artillery opened up, and clumps of earth and tree branches whirled through the air. Haape was briefly lifted up and then thrown back by the impact. He glimpsed his medical orderly, only a few yards away, frantically trying to dig himself into the ground. Haape pressed his face into the churned-up soil. When he looked up he saw a huge shell crater where the orderly had been. There was no trace of the man himself, only a few pieces of his rucksack and some shreds of uniform. He had totally disintegrated.

Haape ran forward, following the clatter of automatic weapons and blasts of hand grenades as the soldiers ahead of him began to clear the Russian defences in hand-to-hand fighting. Haape jumped into the first trench and began tending the wounded. A German platoon worked its way into the rear of the enemy position and opened up with machine-gun fire. Then the soldiers dashed forward as one man, up the nearby hillside to capture their key objective, marked on their maps as height 215. The division's combat journal paid tribute to their fighting performance: 'Infantry Regiment 18 deserved special mention, as facing difficult terrain it conducted a fierce attack over swampy ground, and took the vital high ground on the far side of the river. During this, the regiment lost more than 500 dead or wounded in one day of combat, but through their sacrifice the door to greater success has been opened.' At the end of this day of carnage, however, Haape again recalled the Russian sniper's face. It still seemed an ominous portent.

And yet, it was astonishing how badly the Russians had been caught off guard. They were simply not expecting a major German offensive so late in the year. As masses of German tanks and infantry swept forward there was shock and bewilderment among the front-line soldiers, disbelief and hesitancy from Stalin's high command. At the beginning of October Major Ivan Shabalin, head of the Soviet Fiftieth Army's political section, was stationed north-west of Orel and Lieutenant Koch's Panzers, near the town of Bryansk. Shabalin was apprehensive. 'In each of our divisions I have found the command system ineffective and morale poor,' he wrote in his diary:

Many of our men have been recruited from regions now under German occupation – they are now understandably worried about the fate of their families. And although we have held the same defence line for over two months, there has been scant preparation against an enemy attack and the few measures that have been taken seem hurried and inadequate. At night time, when the Germans conduct their reconnaissance, the men in our forward positions simply sleep. We fail to take any active measures . . . this is a travesty of how war should be conducted – I despair! Someone needs to take hold of this situation urgently.

Alarmingly, on 2 October there was no one on the Soviet side who could take hold of the situation. In July and August 1941 one of the Soviet Union's most able generals and commander-in-chief of the Western Front, Marshal Semyon Timoshenko, directing a united force of defenders, had brought the German Army Group Centre to a halt east of Smolensk. But in September Stalin had sent Timoshenko south to Kiev and split the forces defending Moscow into three separate formations. The Soviet leader had made a terrible blunder – and it left the defence of Russia's capital in a complete mess.

Shabalin's Fiftieth Army was supposed to be part of the Bryansk Front, commanded by Colonel General Andrei Yeremenko; to the north of them, based at the town of Vyazma, was another front, the Western Front of Lieutenant General Ivan Konev, and joining them – to complete an already confused picture – was the Reserve Front of Marshal Semyon Budenny. These Soviet forces, around 900,000 strong, were numerically outnumbered by the German Army Group Centre, and crucially, they had far less air support. There was no effective liaison between their respective HQs and little contact with their forward units. It was a recipe for disaster.

On 2 October Shabalin found himself directly in Typhoon's path: 'A continuous rumble of enemy artillery can be heard,' he recorded, 'and masses of their aircraft are flying overhead – our flak guns are shooting at them constantly. It is clear we are facing a major assault along our whole front, and in many sections our troops have already been pushed back.' Shabalin noticed something strange. 'I expected to be imbued with martial emotions,' he wrote, 'but instead feel only a surprising, hollow emptiness.' The following day he added: 'The situation is chaotic – our signal corps works badly, our command structure likewise. The generals in our neighbouring armies keep to the rear, already making plans for their own escape. We hear that Orel has been evacuated, and that town is 150 kilometres behind our own position – such hopeless disorder!'

Something urgently needed to be done, and on 4 October, despairing of effective orders from Stalin's high command, Shabalin went to see Major General Mikhail Petrov, commander of the Fiftieth Army, to discuss how they themselves might try to check the German offensive. Driving through the village of Dyatkovo the two men found one of their divisional commanders, who claimed he had not received orders and as a result was doing nothing. Next they encountered the division's commissar, who told them he was trying to ascertain the situation on the ground, but as he was heading in the wrong direction Petrov and Shabalin found this difficult to believe. Something was terribly wrong. They kept stopping groups of fleeing soldiers, telling them to about-turn and get back to divisional HQ.

Then the two men halted. A scene of desolation was opening up before them. Gun emplacements and machine-gun posts lay obliterated by German air attacks; forward trenches had been simply blasted to pieces by their artillery. With the Luftwaffe dominant in the skies the remaining Red Army soldiers were constantly forced to seek shelter, and had been unable to counter the enemy at all. In contrast, German infantrymen were so confident that they advanced towards Russian positions walking upright, as if they were on parade.

Shabalin was totally dismayed. 'The division I am with is smashed,' he wrote. 'We have lost contact with the regiment on our right flank, and have no idea if anyone remains alive. The regiment on our left is down to its last twenty men, and the division as a whole can scarcely muster 300. The Germans are making fresh probing attacks and our forces are in total disorder.' Shabalin felt badly let down. 'It was vital that we undertook a counter-attack,' he continued angrily, 'but nothing happened. On both sides, a mass of armies has rolled into battle, but we seem terrified of the Germans. Orel is burning and three Soviet armies are encircled and what is our high command doing? – it sits and "thinks", such is its response to this crisis. I am beside myself with exasperation. What next – are we going to allow the entire front to collapse?'

The Bryansk Front was indeed collapsing and Stalin and his high command seemed paralysed with shock. While they hesitated, unable to believe the news they were hearing, the advancing Germans drove a wedge between Shabalin's Fiftieth Army and Soviet forces further south. That evening Shabalin again met up with Petrov. Petrov, a courageous man and skilful soldier, was totally overwhelmed.

'Petrov discussed matters with me,' Shabalin related, 'and said that Front HQ seemed unable to provide help or clear instructions. He asked, "Are we really supposed to keep shooting people for retreating without permission in a situation like this? It makes a mockery of army discipline." The general then produced a litre of alcohol, and after downing it all fell into a deep sleep.' Shabalin concluded: 'With our commander in such a state we can expect few active measures against the enemy. Meanwhile German tanks are racing towards Bryansk to complete the encirclement of our forces.'

Higher up the Soviet military hierarchy things were little better, for the commander of the Bryansk Front, Colonel General Yeremenko, was himself struggling to master a near hopeless situation. On 2 October, when the German onslaught began, Yeremenko had requested permission to employ flexible tactics against the enemy, retreating where necessary, but Stalin's supreme command had brusquely told him to hold his battle lines. Yeremenko then left his HQ in Bryansk and moved up to his front-line positions to organise a counter-attack against the Germans, but instead ran straight into the advancing Panzers. With no forewarning of the enemy's breakthrough, and suddenly seeing German tanks ahead of him, Yeremenko ordered his car and radio van to reverse off the road immediately, only to find that he had driven straight into a swamp. The general was forced to abandon his vehicle and start walking. At the height of the German offensive the commander of three Soviet armies was left wading through rivers and marshland, completely out of contact with his own HQ and Stalin's high command. Late on the evening of 5 October he reappeared, eventually having hitched a lift from a passing lorry.

After this unfortunate escapade Yeremenko once more tried to get Moscow to authorise a withdrawal. But the commander's run of misfortune had not yet ended. While waiting for a response he heard the clanking of tank tracks. Looking out of the window, he saw to his astonishment that German Panzers were now only a few hundred yards from his command post. Rushing outside, with shells exploding around him, he hurriedly gathered a scratch force of several lorries, three tanks and some infantry from a nearby assembly area. Taking charge of this impromptu convoy, he broke through German lines and sped away. Yeremenko had once again managed to evade capture by the enemy, but other members of his staff had already fled in panic, reporting to Moscow that the HQ had been entirely overrun. Believing Yeremenko dead, Stalin's high command then appointed General Petrov to his position. Their chain of command was dissolving in complete chaos.

For most Germans this stunning start seemed a happy omen. Typhoon had begun in bright sunshine and General Gotthard Heinrici, the commander of the German 43rd Army Corps, was optimistic: 'After our triumph at Kiev, we now stand at the gates of the decisive battle in Russia,' he wrote. 'We hope with confidence that it will also bring us a great success. The overall situation in the east will largely depend on what is achieved by us in the near future.'

The architect of Typhoon, Field Marshal von Bock, was deploying his forces with considerable skill. With three infantry and three Panzer armies at his disposal – supported by the planes of the Luftwaffe's Second Air Fleet – he used his advancing infantry, with massive air support, to pin down the opposing Soviet forces while his Panzers broke through their weakened flanks. His tactics were working brilliantly. General Heinrici's corps – part of the Wehrmacht's Second Army – engaged the Russians along the length of the Bryansk Front, allowing Germany's most able tank commander, Colonel General Guderian, to lead his Second

Panzer Army in a rapid dash to Orel, turning the entire Soviet position. Guderian then drove his tanks behind Yeremenko's armies, cutting off all means of escape.

The shattering impact of Typhoon's first few days seemed to justify Heinrici's hopes of a grand triumph. When Guderian's Panzers reached the town of Bryansk on 7 October, Major Shabalin declared starkly: 'History has never witnessed anything like this defeat . . . We have not seen a single one of our aircraft in the last few days. We are giving up cities with practically no resistance.' He judged that Soviet commanders had irretrievably lost control of the battle, and unaware of Yeremenko's exploits concluded bitterly, 'it is rumoured that these idiots are already on their way back to Moscow.'

A remarkable opportunity was opening up for the Germans. The Soviet regime did appear to be on the brink of collapse, and some Russians even seemed glad that the days of Bolshevism were passing. When Heinrich Haape and the soldiers of the 6th Infantry Division reached the town of Bolotovo, they found its inhabitants friendly and helpful. One of Haape's comrades was struck by this and said with feeling: 'If we give them back what Stalin and the Bolsheviks took away, their old Mother Russia, their church, millions will hail us as their deliverers. And with their help, we could truly conquer Russia. Our victory would be permanent.'

The combat journal of Haape's division was now recording that demoralised Red Army soldiers were starting to surrender en masse: 'One of our artillery officers took some Russians prisoner,' it was noted. 'They told him that the nearby forest was full of troops wanting to surrender. It is only fear of their commissars that is holding them back.'

Yet amidst this heady German optimism, Colonel General Erich Hoepner was feeling uneasy, confiding his doubts to his diary. Summarising the campaign's first five days, he began positively enough. 'The military situation is developing well – nearly 30 Soviet divisions will soon be surrounded,' he stated. Then his tone changed. 'Things have not been done as I have suggested – that much is clear to me – or even more Russian troops would have been seized.' Hoepner, the commander of the Fourth Panzer Group, had wanted a deeper encirclement of Russian forces, one that would have trapped all their remaining reserves as well, allowing his tanks to bear down on Moscow as fast as possible.

Hoepner felt a real sense of urgency about the attack on the Russian capital. He shared the fears of Hans Jürgen Hartmann serving with Army Group South, that when all seemed lost the Red Army was still capable of regrouping and conjuring up fresh reserves, seemingly out of nowhere. They must not be allowed to do this again. And he knew that after three months of campaigning many German units were seriously depleted, their men exhausted and their equipment worn away through constant use. Hoepner also recognised that the logistics for Typhoon – the continued supply of fuel, food and ammunition for German forward units – would soon become a problem as the lines of communication extended, particularly once the weather changed. And it was the approach of the autumn rainy season, which would turn the Russian dirt roads into quagmires within weeks, even days, that worried him the most.

Yet Hitler and the German high command seemed entranced by the encirclement battles, as if the vast haul of prisoners and equipment would bring an end to the struggle by itself. They did not believe that the Red Army had the will or the resilience to keep fighting once these battles were finished. There seemed plenty of evidence for such a view. Stalin had been caught unprepared by Typhoon. After several days of fretful dithering he did make an important decision, recalling General Georgi Zhukov – the Soviet Union's most able commander – from the defence of Leningrad. Zhukov was now given a new mission, to defend the Soviet capital. On the evening of 7 October the general arrived at the Kremlin to find Stalin alone in his office encumbered with a heavy cold. 'A very difficult situation has developed,' the Soviet leader said, pointing to a map of the approaches to Moscow, 'but I can't get a detailed report on the actual state of affairs.' Zhukov was despatched to find out the situation on the ground.

Bryansk was now in enemy hands and its defending armies

encircled, so Zhukov drove instead to Lieutenant General Konev's Western Front HQ, reaching it at 2.30 a.m. The news there was scarcely any better: four of its armies were also surrounded by the Germans. Zhukov phoned Stalin and told him bluntly that there were no longer any troops left to stop the Germans reaching Moscow.

Konev's Western Front had suffered a calamity even greater than that at Bryansk. The Wehrmacht's Fourth Army and Ninth Army had struck against Konev's front-line forces, while two of their Panzer armies turned his flanks. Once again the Germans quickly got behind Soviet positions and Konev rapidly lost control of events. A plea to Moscow to allow a withdrawal met with little success: 'I reported to Stalin about the situation,' Konev recalled, 'and he listened to me, but made no decision. Communications were disrupted and further conversation ceased.'

Faced with the threat of four of his armies being encircled, Konev pulled the commander of the Soviet Sixteenth Army, Major General Konstantin Rokossovsky, out of the battle line, ordering him back to Vyazma to organise a counter-attack. But Rokossovsky's efforts to rebut the Germans proved as ill-starred as Yeremenko's had been. There was no time for reinforcements to be sent; instead, when Rokossovsky arrived at Vyazma he learnt to his consternation that German tanks had already entered its suburbs. Rokossovsky got out as fast as he could.

As the Soviets rushed about in confusion, the Germans bearing down on Vyazma were fighting with confidence and cohesion. Major General Wolfgang Fischer's 10th Panzer Division had broken the Desna river line on the first day of Typhoon, seizing vital road and rail bridges and pushing past the remaining Russian forces. Exploiting his initiative, Fischer continued his advance by the light of the full moon and on the following day had already reached the town of Mozalsk, 40 miles behind the Soviet positions. Fischer's Panzer charge built up momentum, overtaking unsuspecting Red Army columns still moving in the opposite direction. The bewildered Russians surrendered to him without resistance. Struck by the confusion of the enemy troops, Fischer disarmed his prisoners and sent them rearwards without even bothering to give them a military escort.

Fischer maintained his rapid pace, and when twelve Russian trucks smashed into his column, just ahead of his own vehicle, he remained unperturbed. The division's combat journal recorded that all staff officers were engaged in the fight that followed, Red Army vehicles were quickly disarmed and thirty Soviet prisoners captured. By 6 October Fischer's force was closing in on Vyazma and with fuel running low and fresh Soviet forces in the area, he struck quickly. Noticing that the town's defences were weak, he launched an attack that same evening. At 7.15 p.m. the airport was seized; two hours later Fischer's men broke into Vyazma's suburbs forcing the Soviet commander, Rokossovsky, to flee in the opposite direction. It was an astonishing success.

Rapid, well-coordinated armoured warfare was the hallmark of German blitzkrieg, their devastating 'lightning war', and it still seemed that the Russians were unable to counter it. On 7 October, when the German 7th Panzer Division arrived from the north and linked up with Fischer, a shocked and bewildered Konev realised that most of his armies had now been trapped. All he could do was to relay these gloomy tidings to General Zhukov. Zhukov, taken aback, then tried to ascertain the situation at Marshal Budenny's Reserve Front. He was told that some of Budenny's force, hurriedly gathered together and with little military training, had disintegrated in panic and the whereabouts of the remainder was unknown.

Zhukov decided to find out for himself. As he drove on through the night, searching for the Reserve Front commander, a dense fog descended over the countryside. Alarmingly, when Zhukov eventually reached Budenny's HQ there was no sign of its commander and no one seemed to know where he was. When Zhukov finally tracked him down he found the Soviet marshal in a state of collapse, only able to repeat, again and again, that he had nearly been captured by the Germans. He had lost touch with his staff for three whole days during the crucial opening phase of the battle.

Zhukov was witness to a catastrophe. The twin encirclement battles of Bryansk and Vyazma had left three quarters of a million Red Army soldiers surrounded. It was the Wehrmacht's greatest success of the war with Russia. As Zhukov was learning of the calamitous state of the Western and Reserve Fronts, General Petrov took up 'temporary command' of the Soviet armies encircled around Bryansk. He was less than enthusiastic about his new post. He recalled that another Soviet commander, General Dmitry Pavlov, had been executed by Stalin at the beginning of the war for failing to hold back the Germans. It seemed an unfortunate precedent. 'Now our high command will shoot me too,' he told Major Shabalin on 7 October. 'Why say that?' Shabalin responded in surprise. 'The threat is implicit,' Petrov said carefully, 'in the phrase "temporary command of the front". As things stand, I have no idea what is happening to our armies – I cannot find out the strength of my forces, or even where they are.'

The Germans speeding past Bryansk were better informed. General Heinrici's forces sealed off Petrov's Fiftieth Army, separating it from the two other armies of the Bryansk Front, then pushed on to the town of Kaluga. On 8 October Heinrici wrote triumphantly:

> The enemy was totally surprised by our latest attack. Since our preparations took place out in the open, one would have thought this scarcely possible, yet the Russians knew neither the time of the assault nor its direction, and my army corps – after breaking through their positions on the first and second days of the battle – was able to advance without opposition. The struggle is far from its end, and I expect the encircled enemy to try and break out from these pockets with desperate courage. But I believe the Red Army has been knocked out and will quickly lose the remnants of its forces defending Moscow. At the end of the month Russia will be without a capital.

The same day German soldier Heinrich Larsen sent a letter to his wife: 'Victory over the Red Army will be ours,' he declared emphatically. 'The mighty Führer has promised to end this campaign victoriously before the beginning of the winter. My darling, your wish for a successful end to the war will be fulfilled soon.

Moscow, the stronghold of worldwide Bolshevism, will fall in a few days and the remainder of the Russian forces will be annihilated together with their capital . . . Maybe when you read these lines, the war in the east will be over.'

Larsen's letter – and its sweeping prediction that Moscow would fall within days – was again a product of the *Siegseuphorie* sweeping the German Army. It was an inflated sense of invincibility, for there were warning signs that the Russians might still be capable of rallying, if given an opportunity. In a clash near Mtensk on the Orel-Tula motor highway, Guderian's advance formations were briefly disconcerted when the Red Army employed a new design of tank, the T-34, and counter-attacked vigorously. Guderian's troops were shaken by the speed and armoured strength of this vehicle, which was far superior to their own tanks. Although the T-34 was not yet available in large numbers, the Wehrmacht's intelligence had been entirely unaware of its existence.

Private Wolf Dose and his comrades besieging Leningrad were impressed by Typhoon's progress nonetheless. 'In the evening a special communiqué came through,' he wrote on 8 October, 'announcing that five of our armies are advancing on Moscow, and that we can expect the complete destruction of the city. This news is particularly pleasing for us. Should we succeed, the Russians will be reduced to flying in reinforcements for Leningrad from strongholds beyond the Urals.'

On 9 October Shabalin saw the first snow falling. It soon turned to rain. On the roads north of Bryansk, a mass of Soviet cars and lorries were struggling to escape the Germans, and endless columns of soldiers were retreating. At 1.30 p.m. they all came under heavy artillery fire and Shabalin's fellow army staff rushed off in panic, only to run straight into a traffic jam of vehicles. Four German planes then appeared, bombing and strafing at will. Shabalin recorded grimly: 'Our army is in a tragic situation: we no longer have any idea where the rear is, or where the front line is to be found – it is impossible to tell any more. And we have suffered such terrible losses. We are trying to salvage what we can, and our remaining vehicles are jam-packed with equipment; every soldier is carrying something, even strips of plywood. But all the time the ring around us closes.'

On 9 October General Georgi Zhukov was formally appointed head of the Western and Reserve Fronts. Stalin had recognised his earlier mistakes and placed all his military resources under a unified command. Zhukov's mission was simple: to try to save Moscow. But he had desperately few soldiers at his disposal. By gathering the remnants of armies that had escaped encirclement at Vyazma and those trickling out of the Bryansk pocket, Zhukov could scrape together a mere 90,000 men. The Germans outnumbered his forces by odds of nearly 15:1, a horrifying situation. The Soviet commander planned to hold a fresh defence line at Mozhaisk, 65 miles west of Moscow, but somehow he had to buy time to bring fresh reinforcements into the battle line. If he failed, Moscow would fall.

Karl Fuchs's Seventh Panzer Division, advancing on Vyazma from the north, had helped seal off the Soviet armies in the pocket. 'My tank crew and I are itching to prove ourselves once more in battle,' he declared. Their exploits were now being broadcast on German radio. On 9 October he noted: 'For the time being we are resting in a Russian blockhouse. The enemy did not believe that we would attack at this time of year, with the cold weather setting in – now the last hour of Bolshevism is near.'

At the end of Typhoon's first week Field Marshal von Bock surveyed the fruits of a colossal victory. On 9 October he noted happily that 'the pocket at Vyazma is shrinking more and more, and the number of prisoners and war material captured by us steadily growing'. The following day he added that 'breakout attempts in the area south of Bryansk have also been contained'. Believing that the remainder of these defenders would quickly surrender, Bock initiated the second phase of his campaign and on 12 October ordered an all-out push on Moscow.

Even the sceptics were swallowing their doubts. 'We are hearing astonishing stories about our successes,' Hans Jürgen Hartmann wrote that same day. 'Overtaking motorised columns call out to us with quite incredible news, the slaughter of countless enemy soldiers before Moscow. The whole front is surging eastwards. "Ivan" is clearly groggy – and one last punch will probably knock him out of the ring. What an unbelievable conclusion!'

Yet Colonel General Hoepner, about to spearhead the assault on Moscow, remained concerned. He wanted more troops for the attack, and was frustrated that some of his best Panzer units were still bogged down reinforcing the Vyazma encirclement. 'I am angry about this,' he wrote. 'I want to use all my forces – independently of the Vyazma operation. My Panzers should be allowed to keep pushing on, maintaining the initiative and pursuing the enemy eastwards.' Hoepner knew that to achieve the kind of knockout blow Hans Jürgen Hartmann and other German soldiers were hoping for, his maximum strength would be needed to break the last Russian defences.

But elsewhere this sense of urgency was completely lacking. News of Bock's advance on the Soviet capital had prompted a wave of euphoria among Hitler's entourage – considerably removed from the realities of the front-line fighting – and this dizzy mood soon spread. On the evening of 12 October German newspapers proclaimed the imminent fall of Moscow. The *Völkischer Beobachter* even announced in huge, glaring headlines: 'The great hour has come – the eastern campaign has ended!' Such blatant triumphalism made Bock uneasy. Believing Hitler poorly advised over this, he contacted army high command and said sharply: 'There you go with your premature announcements. Are you not aware of the real situation here? Neither the pockets of Bryansk or Vyazma have yet been liquidated. They will be. Meanwhile, kindly refrain from proclaiming victory beforehand.' He was asked for a date when Moscow could be made safe and secure; there were even rumours that Hitler wanted to make a triumphant entry into the city alongside columns of marching German troops. 'Hitler will be informed in good time,' Bock responded.

On Bock's northern flank, leading elements of General Hans-Georg Reinhardt's Third Panzer Group sped forward at a pace the Russians seemed unable to anticipate. 'We were racing ahead,' Heinz Otto Fausten recalled:

when we were suddenly told to pull off the road and switch off our engines. We saw a column of Russian tanks and artillery rumbling along in the opposite direction, heading towards the front. They had no idea that we had advanced so far. We were told to give chase, and we swung back onto the road and pursued the unsuspecting Russians. Radio instructions came over our intercom, 'Faster, faster!' We passed a forest's edge, open ground, the forest again, and then something exploded right over our heads. Braking hard, we saw the flash of a Russian gun nozzle in the incline below us. But our commander had summoned an air strike against the enemy, and this was the first and last shot they fired against us. Plane after plane swooped down on the forest, bombing the hapless Russians – and their tank brigade simply disintegrated before our eyes.

Fausten's 1st Panzer Division had captured Zubtsov, on the river Volga 120 miles west of Moscow, on 11 October, and that night he and his fellow soldiers lay on a hill above the town watching the white attack flares lighting up the sky, their flickering glow reflecting in the water of Russia's holiest river. On 12 October the Panzers took Staritsa on the Volga north of Zubtsov, and then received a dramatic order to seize Kalinin, the north-western bastion of Moscow's defences. It was nearly 50 miles ahead of them.

The first snow was falling as Fausten's company raced along the road to Kalinin. 'We were rolling forward non-stop,' he recalled. Russian resistance was collapsing all around them:

Along the sides of the road were lines of fleeing enemy soldiers. They were no longer digging in and such obstacles that remained on the roadway we easily pushed out of the way. We indicated in sign language to the astonished Russians that they should drop their weapons and march westwards. There was a risk that some of them – once our tanks had gone past – might flee into the forest. But as darkness broke we received a quite incredible order – only to shoot in an emergency!

It seemed as if the Red Army had lost the will to fight. On the morning of 14 October the Panzers of Fausten's company closed in on Kalinin:

We dashed on, through scenes of total disorder. Red Army command-ers swore at us from their vehicles, believing that we were Russians fleeing from the front. Enemy vehicles cut into our column, joined us for a while, and then, realising our identity swerved off again. It was all quite incredible. We reached Kalinin without any losses, having amassed an astonishing array of booty – hundreds of Russian trucks and artillery pieces – on our 100-kilometre raid.

To the south of Moscow, Günther von Kluge's Fourth Army had seized Kaluga, and Heinz Guderian's Second Panzer Army captured Mtensk north of Orel. German armies were form-ing a menacing arc around the Soviet capital and Bock now felt Moscow within his grasp. He mobilised forces for a fresh advance in the centre, along the Smolensk–Moscow motor road, the Soviet capital's main transport artery. It looked as if the remnants of Russian resistance were about to cave in.

'Almost all routes to Moscow are open,' General Georgi Zhukov declared, 'and we cannot prevent the surprise appear-ance of enemy armoured formations before our capital. We must quickly assemble forces from wherever we can.' But where was he to find them? Zhukov's daughter Ella later said: 'In 1941 my father never gave anybody the slightest indication – not even his family or closest aides – that he doubted that Moscow would be held. However, deep inside, he was not sure whether the city could be saved. He told me this himself, afterwards. But at the time he could let no one know this.'

Seeking, therefore, a new defence line to hold off Bock's assault, Zhukov gambled that the soldiers in the Bryansk and Vyazma pockets would continue to resist, tying down German troops who could otherwise be used in the push on Moscow. The Germans expected these Russian troops to surrender en masse, but remark-ably, many kept on fighting.

Major Shabalin had faced disaster before, in the early days of the war, when he was attached to a rifle division close to the frontier. The Germans had smashed Soviet positions, leaving the division broken and leaderless and surrounded by Panzer troops, but Shabalin had gathered its shattered remnants together and

fought his way out of trouble. On 12 October 1941 Shabalin
was once again thrown entirely on his own resources. He and
his fellow army staff had undertaken a night march to reach the
shelter of a little village at Boyanovichi, north of Bryansk. They
had some breakfast and Shabalin tried to snatch a couple of hours'
sleep, but he was woken by a German bombing raid; all around
him the village huts were burning. Defiantly, he determined to
shave – despite the enemy shells crashing down – and drank some
tea, then joined the hurried evacuation. At 1.30 p.m. Shabalin
reached a cemetery on a nearby hill and surveyed the scene
below him. 'I saw the myriad puffs of German mortar fire,' he
remembered, 'as they pulverised our chaotic exodus. There must
have been more than a thousand of our vehicles, in three lanes,
desperately trying to move along the highway.' A staff meeting
was hurriedly convened to 'reorganise army transport' but as it
began three Red Army cavalrymen rode up and reported that
enemy troops were fast approaching. 'Again, things collapsed
in disorder,' Shabalin recorded, 'as our staff attempted another
messy retreat. As we withdrew, bullets whistled around us;
shooting could be heard everywhere. And then I got separated
from everybody else. Our entire war council ran off – and I was
left alone in the forest.'

The following day Shabalin gathered leaderless Red Army soldiers together and continued to try to break out of the pocket. 'I
did not sleep all night,' he wrote:

> It is wet and cold and we are moving terribly slowly – all our vehicles
> are bogged down on the muddy roads. We tried to push some of
> them forward with tractors, but with no success – they remained
> completely stuck. More than fifty cars had to be abandoned in ground
> that resembled a quagmire; about the same number are stuck fast in a
> nearby field. At 6.00 a.m. the Germans opened fire on us – a continu-
> ous bombardment of artillery, mortars and heavy machine guns – and
> it went on all day. The enemy is pushing us ever closer inside the ring.
> I cannot remember when I last slept properly.

The remorseless German advance was designed to break the
mental and physical strength of the enemy, until any act of

resistance seemed utterly futile. Werner Lacoste was an artillery spotter with the German 79th Infantry Division, and also an
accomplished artist. As the encirclement battle of Bryansk drew
to a close, he took advantage of a lull in the fighting and a little
late autumn sunshine, and returned to the combat zone – now
completely deserted – to sketch some hayricks:

> I was completely absorbed in my work and enjoying the stillness of my
> surroundings, when suddenly I heard a noise from one of the heaps of
> hay. I got up and went to investigate. To my surprise I discovered a
> Red Army soldier was hiding there – he seemed just as taken aback as
> I was. He clambered out and brushed himself down. I wanted to con-
> tinue my drawing before the light faded, so I simply pointed him in
> the direction of our artillery battery – about 1,000 metres away – and
> told him he should go there to be taken prisoner. I thought nothing
> more about it and carried on with my work. Then there was more
> rustling, and another three Red Army soldiers emerged from the hay.
> Again I directed them to the battery. They all duly turned up and
> were then taken to a prisoner collection point. They could have just
> as easily overpowered me, or simply run off.

Yet, other Red Army soldiers continued to fight. At Vyazma,
where more Soviet armies were surrounded, the men had been
ordered to break out in groups but the Germans had a strong line
of Panzer divisions blocking their path and the Russians were
running out of supplies. 'The situation of our encircled forces
has worsened sharply,' Lieutenant General Mikhail Lukhin, commander of the Soviet Nineteenth Army, wrote. 'There are few
shells, bullets are running out and there is no food left. We are
eating horseflesh, and whatever the local population can provide.
Medicines and bandages are used up. All our tents and makeshift
dwellings are overflowing with the wounded.'

Tank gunner Karl Fuchs's 7th Panzer Division was repelling
these desperate Soviet attacks. On 12 October he recorded: 'The
alarm sounded and our tanks moved out. Russian tanks and support troops wanted to break out of our ring. Once the fog lifted
from the valley, we really let them have it with every barrel.
Tanks, anti-aircraft guns and the infantry fired on everything

in sight. And once the main body of our company arrived, we destroyed their remaining forces. We had no losses at all.' Fuchs concluded proudly: 'I think that this battle around Vyazma is the last flickering moment of a once powerful Russia. For days now the enemy has been trying to break out of our iron encirclement, but all his efforts have been in vain.'

Horst Lange was among German troops moving to Vyazma to reinforce this cruel blockade. He was struck by the eerie desolation of his surroundings: 'We saw primitive little foxholes and piles of bloated Russian corpses – their faces tinged blue and green. The soldiers' guns were still in their hands. Next to them – inert and indifferent – a mass of prisoners were repairing the road. We passed a burnt-out village with only the traces of fences and some scattered garden plants showing that houses once stood there. Our convoy moved on, past lines of scorched tree stumps, pushing up a cloud of fine brownish dust.' A particular image lodged in Lange's mind: the charred remnants of a Red Army soldier, hanging out of a partially destroyed truck. It reminded him of photos he had seen the previous year at a German archaeological exhibition. They showed corpses excavated from Pompeii after the eruption of Vesuvius in AD 79 – victims overwhelmed by an overpowering force of nature.

Ahead, in the next valley, another village was burning. An old man on crutches struggled along the road; a shy, starved seventeen-year-old girl wandered lost and disorientated. Lange was no ardent Nazi and showed flashes of compassion for the Russian people, but his comments were still underscored by an abiding contempt for their way of life. He thought communist posters were 'bright, loud and without an iota of taste', Bolshevik propaganda 'philistine', and saw 'few intelligent faces' among the ever-growing throng of prisoners. Lange was dismissive of Soviet efforts to improve the country's lot. 'The delusion of progress,' he wrote scornfully, 'as the enlightened doll-folk, mass-produced and identically carved, bask in some notion of the "general good".' In contrast, the might of the German war effort was reassuring to him. 'The ceaseless, uninterrupted flow of our reinforcements,'

Lange observed, 'the orderly marching columns . . . the tangible motion and function of our machinery, organised down to the last detail': these forces were now astride the tarmac road running from Smolensk to Moscow, and their progress towards the Soviet capital seemed irresistible.

Yet, on an excursion away from the hubbub of battle, Lange was briefly disconcerted. On a whim, he climbed the hill to Vyazma's old cathedral. The snow lay heavy on the ground and jackdaws flew screeching around the towers. Inside, the building lay still and quiet. Its windows were boarded up and a wooden floor had been built over the flagstones for grain storage; the sacks were piled up in the corners. 'An insult to the grandeur of the room,' Lange thought angrily. He noticed scattered agricultural implements; a soldier's dirty cap; the chain on which a candelabra had once hung, lying broken on the floor. The stone font remained, and then, as he glanced upwards, above the debris of the Bolshevik regime, he saw painted angels still adorning the walls. An odd sense of foreboding drove him outside. Perhaps, in defending their Motherland, the Russians were fighting for something older than Bolshevism after all.

Overwhelmed by the German attack, Stalin's regime hid its confusion beneath a procession of vague news reports. 'We were abandoning one city after another,' Olga Freidenberg wrote, 'but official bulletins – so avidly, so anxiously awaited – grew more and more laconic. The more each of us was worried about the news, the less of it we were given.' The press was unable to make any mention of the peril hanging over Moscow until 14 October, when a government-released statement finally referred to the fighting around the capital: 'After many days of bitter battle, in which the enemy suffered huge casualties, our troops left Vyazma,' the report said tersely. The encirclement of masses of Red Army soldiers was simply too demoralising to mention.

Lines of Soviet soldiers were being force marched to the rear by the victorious Germans. On the evening of 14 October twenty-one-year-old Zoya Zarubina was summoned to the Kremlin. Zarubina's stepfather, Leonid Eitingon, was a leading NKVD

official and a trusted security adviser. A year earlier he had master-
minded the assassination of Stalin's exiled rival, Leon Trotsky, and
Zarubina herself was a skilled linguist, working on intercepted
German intelligence documents. Now she was given a rather different assignment. A Wehrmacht newsreel had been captured –
filmed only a few days earlier, on the front line – and Stalin wanted
to watch it in his private cinema with army chiefs and heads of
government. Zarubina was asked to translate the commentary.
'There was an ominous silence,' she remembered, 'as the small
audience gathered and took its places':

> The film sequence opened with a triumphal fanfare of music and shots
> of German tank men and infantry waving jubilantly at the camera.
> Then we saw masses of Red Army prisoners being marched away,
> in seemingly endless columns. When the commentator announced
> the number of Soviet troops killed or captured there was an audible
> gasp in the room, and one army commander close to me gripped the
> seat in front of him, rigid with shock. Stalin sat in stunned silence. I
> will always remember what appeared next on the screen – a close-up
> of our soldiers' faces. They were just young kids, and they looked so
> helpless, so utterly lost.

Zarubina was struck by the mood of despondency in the private
cinema. She believed that Stalin and his ministers had already
decided to abandon the capital. 'We knew that key buildings had
already been mined,' she said, 'and NKVD suicide squads were
prepared for a last-ditch defence of Moscow's approaches. No one
thought the Germans could be stopped.'

On 15 October German tank gunner Karl Fuchs declared: 'The
battle of Vyazma is over and the last major Bolshevik troop formations have been wiped out. I will never forget my impressions of
this destruction. From now on, Russian resistance will be minor –
all we have to do is keep rolling forward.' Fuchs added: 'Our duty
has been to fight and free the world from this communist disease.
One day, many years hence, the world will thank the Germans
and our beloved Führer for our victories here in Russia.' German
intelligence reports and aerial photographs confirmed Fuchs's jubi-
lation. By their estimation hundreds of thousands of Russians lay

dead and over 600,000 had already been captured, with the tally still rising. Further resistance in such dire circumstances seemed impossible and almost everyone assumed that the Red Army was finished. Luftwaffe commander Wolfram von Richthofen flew low over the north-eastern edge of the Vyazma pocket: 'There are horrific scenes of destruction in the places where Red Army soldiers have made unsuccessful attempts to break out,' he reported. 'The Russians have suffered a total bloodbath. Piles of bodies, heaps of abandoned equipment and guns are strewn everywhere.'

The full might of Bock's victorious army group converged on Moscow. One flank was poised to strike against the capital from Kalinin in the north-west; another was pushing towards Tula from the south-east. German army doctor Heinrich Haape, moving forward with the 6th Infantry Division, declared resoundingly: 'The steel ring that is tightening on Moscow will be the greatest pincer movement of all time.' Haape, normally careful and cautious in his assessments, was intoxicated by the prospect of imminent victory.

But on 15 October Heinz Otto Fausten started to feel something was wrong. His battle group and 1st Panzer Division, which had seized Kalinin in a dramatic raid the day before, was now expecting to advance on Moscow. The Russian capital – 100 miles to the south – should have been the target of all its future operations. Quite incredibly, they were sent north – in completely the opposite direction. The men were bewildered, and their confusion only increased when, after driving for about 20 miles, they received a radio message giving them fresh orders. It was from Army Group North, stationed outside Leningrad. The 1st Panzer Division was now told to execute a pincer operation to help straighten out the Leningrad Front.

'We had worked hard to get into this position,' Fausten recalled, 'and this sudden about-turn made little sense to me. We were losing too much time, and I wondered if an opportunity was slipping through our fingers. I needed to say something, to voice my doubts – which we never normally did in my company. I went over to a comrade and said to him: "This is not the way our troops should be used." He nodded in agreement, and quoted the military maxim: "Always keep to the main objective – never be distracted from it."'

Others shared Fausten's concern. Carl Wagener was on the operational staff of the Third Panzer Group. 'With the capture of Kalinin, a great tactical opportunity had opened up for us,' he wrote:

> We now held the cornerstone of Moscow's defences and could strike immediately at its poorly protected northern flank. The city lay at our mercy with roads still firm, little more than one day's drive away. Instead our Panzer forces, and the Ninth Infantry Army, which was coming up in support, was ordered to strike at an insignificant town, Torzhok, more than a hundred miles *north* of Kalinin. We listened to this new assignment from army high command with a sense of complete astonishment. We realised that they had to consider the entire eastern front in their deliberations. But surely everything should be subordinated to the highest goal – Moscow?

'The history of warfare usually demonstrates one cardinal principle,' Wagener continued:

> that success almost always goes to the side that amasses a major superiority of forces at the critical moment. And yet – unbelievably – at this vital moment we did not apply the maximum concentration of strength against the weakest point of the enemy. Our Panzer Group should have immediately been thrown against Moscow's last defences. Instead, the aims of the great offensive became splintered and fragmented.

Hitler and the German high command had become more and more ambitious and – in a state of elation – were losing touch with the realities on the ground. After the victories at Bryansk and Vyazma they were now resuming military operations in the north, around Leningrad, and in the Ukraine, around Mariopol and the Black Sea. They also began withdrawing army units and air support from Army Group Centre for refitting in western Europe. And they *still* intended to capture Moscow. Wagener recalled the proverbial warning: 'He who tries to seize everything at once ends up with nothing at all.'

Colonel General Hoepner's Fourth Panzer Group was now preparing to move against Zhukov's main defensive position. Hoepner wanted his strike against Moscow to be fast and hard, and Walther de Beaulieu, his chief of staff, was working tirelessly to gather as many motorised units as possible – but many of these were still elsewhere. Would the remainder be enough? 'The enemy's weakness, and the gap in his defences, needed to be exploited immediately,' Beaulieu wrote:

> But we had at most four motorised divisions which could be used in the attack. And Panzer Group 3 was not astride the adjacent motor highway to Moscow, to support our offensive, as we had wanted and suggested, but instead had been diverted north of Kalinin . . . We gathered what we could at Gzhatsk, on the main Smolensk-Moscow road. Opposing us, further along that same road, Zhukov was hastily fortifying a defence position ten miles west of Mozhaisk, on the battle-field of Borodino. It looked as if Napoleon's costly victory in 1812 was once more to be replayed.

Hoepner intended to use some of his forces to outflank Zhukov's position. Then, on 15 October, came the deterioration in weather conditions that he had feared. Torrential rain turned dirt tracks into quagmires, and plunged German army vehicles into a sea of mud. 'It took two days and nights to cover ten kilometres, if you could travel at all,' Hoepner wrote in frustration. 'Our supplies were cut off – ammunition, fuel for our vehicles, bread soon became worth their weight in gold.'

Suddenly, these difficulties were being felt all along the German advance. Military chaplain Ernst Tewes observed: 'Since yesterday we have had continuous sleet and snow. Our men are suffering – the vehicles are not properly covered and winter clothing has not yet arrived. We are struggling to move along terrible roads.' Heinrich Haape's division was experiencing similar difficulties. 'The troops hauled and pushed, the horses sweated and strained – at times we had to take a brief, ten-minute rest from sheer exhaustion,' he wrote, 'then back to the transport, our legs in black mud up to the knees – anything to keep the wheels moving.'

Hoepner had anticipated this problem, yet the majority of German commanders were taken by surprise. 'The weather has thrown a spanner in the works,' General Heinrici noted in frustration, '*which nobody expected* [my italics] – it is becoming a real inconvenience for us. No one back home could imagine the state the roads are in now. A thick mush runs several feet deep on their surface and is then pushed like a wall of mud in front of cars until they no longer can move. We only have a fraction of the transport space that we need and in such conditions, more and more of our motor vehicles are breaking down.'

For a commander of Heinrici's ability to describe the Russian rainy season as unexpected was quite astonishing. How could the formidable German military machine fail to foresee this, and the effect it would have on their motorised formations? Intoxicated with success, they were losing touch with reality.

The weather was also disastrous for the Soviet forces in the Bryansk pocket, hampering any chance of their breaking out of encirclement. The men were forced to abandon their vehicles and continue on foot. On 15 October Major Shabalin wrote:

> The Germans are everywhere – incessant gunfire, mortar and machine-gun exchanges. I wandered around, seeing heaps of dead bodies and the most unspeakable horrors – ghastly evidence of the enemy's bombardment. Hungry and unable to sleep, I took a bottle of alcohol and went out into the forest. I fear our total destruction is imminent. Our army is beaten, its supply train destroyed and I am writing this by a bonfire – we have lost all our officers and I am surrounded by a mass of strangers. Our military strength has simply dissolved around us.

Both sides were becoming badly affected by the rainy season, which was rendering many roads impassable. When Stalin inquired why Kalinin had been lost to the enemy, Soviet quartermaster General Andrei Khrulev blamed the weather for a catastrophic breakdown in supplies. A shortage of transport planes had prevented air drops to marooned defenders, so Khrulev suggested that horse-drawn wooden carts should be used to bring ammunition and food to these Red Army soldiers. 'We are living in a technological age,' Stalin responded sarcastically. But wagons and carts were now employed en masse, because no motor vehicles could get through.

Hoepner now abandoned all subtlety and concentrated his armour in a wedge, intending to smash through the Russian defences. To oppose him, Zhukov was frantically deploying all the troops he could find. On the evening of 15 October Nikolai Nechayev's artillery battery drew up near Rayevsky Hill, a prominent landmark of the battle in 1812. Nechayev and his troops were moved to see it, but they were also worried about their inadequate artillery support and lack of infantry. 'How are a few anti-aircraft guns supposed to stop masses of German tanks?' one man complained bitterly.

But more and more Russian tanks, artillery and infantry were arriving. Zhukov made it clear that there could be no retreat. 'We were thrown into battle near Borodino,' said Boris Baromykin of the 32nd Rifle Brigade, 'issued with rifles picked up from the fighting, many of which were still encrusted with blood':

> We were ordered to line up, and there, in front of us, they put a soldier from one of the Central Asian republics – apparently he was guilty of having retreated without permission. The poor fellow was standing just a couple of metres from me, peacefully chewing a piece of bread; he could only speak a few words of Russian and had no idea what was going on. Abruptly the major heading the military tribunal read out an order, 'Desertion from the front line – immediate execution', and went up to him and shot him in the head. The guy collapsed in front of me – it was horrible. Something inside of me died when I saw that.

Baromykin admitted: 'Our retreat from the Germans had been chaotic. We had been like a herd of desperate cattle – the only thing holding us together was fear that our commanders would shoot us if we tried to run away.' This was the mindset of Russian soldiers in the early days of Typhoon, a fear of being shot for desertion. But at Borodino a remarkable change was about to take place.

On 16 October Hoepner arrived on the field of Borodino to encourage his men forward. He was surprised that the Red Army was holding its ground with such determination. 'For the first time in the war, the number of Russian deaths far exceeded the prisoners we were taking,' he noted. Borodino's defenders were fighting and dying where they stood. Yet final German victory still seemed tantalisingly close. 'Villages were burning,' Hoepner recalled, 'colouring the low clouds with a blood-red light.' He had heard the reports of panic in the streets of Moscow. 'The approach of our tanks and infantry was bringing terror to the Russian capital,' he continued. 'Its people were fleeing, its factory equipment was being destroyed. Looting had begun. The Soviet leadership was preparing to leave the city.'

Moscow on 16 October did indeed appear on the verge of collapse: the city's underground had stopped running and many of its factories had abruptly closed. 'Rumours of the proximity of the Germans spread like wildfire,' Stephan Mikoyan recalled, 'alongside the news that major industries had been evacuated and the city's most important buildings mined. This sparked a general panic.' And journalist Nikolai Verzhbitsky vividly remembered how that sense of panic mounted as the roads filled with refugees and the roar of artillery could be clearly heard in the distance: 'Red Army soldiers are being marched off in different directions,' he wrote in his diary, 'some not even in proper uniforms, but there is only fatigue and bewilderment in their eyes – they have no idea where they are going.'

Ordinary citizens were equally confused. *Pravda* had not come out that day and there was no concrete information about military developments, only alarming rumours. People milled about on the streets seeking reassurance, and Verzhbitsky jotted down snippets of their conversation:

'Why is no one coming on the radio and telling us something – be it bad, good, anything,' one man complained. 'We are all left in a total fog.'

'So, are we going to be celebrating the October Revolution?' someone asked plaintively.

'Haven't you heard?' a woman answered. 'The Germans have taken charge of the festivities. They are bringing candy and will be handing it out on Red Square – go help yourself!'

North of Bryansk, Major Shabalin and his band of soldiers continued to resist the Germans. Conditions were desperate. On 16 October Shabalin wrote: 'Again I spent the night in the forest – I have not had bread for three days. There are lots of soldiers here but no officers. Throughout the night the Germans bombarded us with all kinds of weapons. At 7.00 a.m. we got up and marched northwards. The gunfire continued. During a brief halt I managed to wash my face and hands. It is horribly cold and damp.'

During the morning it rained; at midday the rain changed to snow. German artillery fire forced a halt for several hours, but Shabalin and his men, wet through and freezing, eventually reached a deserted village. The brave Russian troops were holding together in adversity, determined to breach the encirclement rather than surrender to the enemy. That evening they gathered wood, scavenged for food and risked lighting a fire. For a brief moment the horror of war was forgotten as the men dried their clothes, shared cigarettes and put up makeshift tents. Shabalin and three comrades then went to find some straw to sleep on. On their return they saw, through the snowy drizzle, a road through the forest. A German military convoy stood along it, the lorries stationary, its soldiers watching and waiting.

Astride the Moscow-Smolensk highway, Borodino's defence was being coordinated by Soviet Major General Dmitry Lelyushenko. A courageous and skilful tank commander, Lelyushenko had already given Guderian's Panzers a rebuff at Mtensk on 6 October and was now thwarting Hoepner, using small groups of the new T-34 tanks and recently developed multiple rocket launchers alongside his infantry. The Germans brought up more tanks and their own multiple-barrelled mortars. One SS lieutenant described the ferocious slugging match that followed:

We stood beside the main road, in a position protected by woodland, and watched the enemy moving his tanks into position. Our own artillery opened up. Meanwhile our infantry was pushing forward, north of the highway, in bitter, costly fighting. Then a firefight began of an intensity I had never before experienced. Suddenly I heard the characteristic sound of the Russian rocket launchers . . . I dived behind a tree, and witnessed the horrible yet strangely beautiful spectacle of the bursting rockets as they impacted. The smell of the powder smoke and the gloomy black-red-violet light from the tulip-shaped shell bursts were something I shall never forget.

Suddenly, all hell broke lose behind us. Our own rockets were being launched. The ear-shattering racket had to be heard to be believed. It mixed with the crash of the incoming Russian rounds. It whistled, thundered, hissed and roared with the discharge and impact of artillery, machine guns and mortars. The effect was dreadful.

Hoepner was determined to finish the Russians off. On the evening of 16 October German forces got around the flanks of Lelyushenko's position and hammered his defences with air strikes. Then Hoepner threw in his tanks and infantry. Lelyushenko ordered up his last reserves, but thirty German tanks had broken through his lines and were speeding towards his command post. Lelyushenko led out his entire staff, officers, soldiers and orderlies – everyone armed with Molotov cocktails – and fought off the Germans. He was seriously wounded, and in a lull in the fighting he was carried unconscious off the battlefield. His men resisted with even greater determination.

'German tanks were rolling over our trenches,' Soviet soldier Makary Barchuk remembered, 'and their machine gunners were moving up behind them. They wanted desperately to make a final breakthrough. And they used psychological tactics – taunting us through loud-hailers, and playing the sound of weapon fire all around us through their speakers. A few of our men had had enough, stood up and began to walk towards the enemy. But we shot them down, and carried on fighting. We were not going to let the Germans through. And when it was no longer possible to hold our positions, we regrouped and formed up behind new ones.'

'When our commissars had told us that we would inherit the

strength of those who had defeated Napoleon,' Boris Baromykin said, 'something changed within us. We began to think about Moscow, and about our responsibility to defend the Russian capital. It was our city – and we did not want the enemy to seize it. We resolved to make a stand.'

Late on this same evening of 16 October a special train was readied at Moscow's Kazan Station. Stalin and his government were about to leave the city. 'A train had been prepared to take Stalin out of Moscow,' Stephan Mikoyan acknowledged, 'and he actually turned up at the station, walked along the platform, prepared to board it and then paused. Stalin turned and said to Molotov and my father [Anastas Mikoyan, the Soviet trade minister], "Go, you go, both of you – I'll just stay here a while." My father was livid. "If you stay, I am staying as well," he retorted. Everyone then returned to the Kremlin.'

However belated, this was a genuinely courageous decision. The prospects of holding the city still looked bleak, but within days order had been restored in Moscow, fresh forces sent out to oppose the Germans and, most importantly, reinforcements summoned from Siberia. For the Soviet leadership to have come so close to flight, then decided to hold on, constituted a turning point.

Georgi Osadchinsky had been training cadets at the Alma Ata machine-gun school when special instructions arrived. He recalled:

> We were quickly assembled and an order from Stalin was read out. It was blunt – we were told that Moscow was in grave danger and special 'strike forces' were being formed up for its protection. Ours was the 35th Rifle Brigade – some three thousand soldiers, cadets from Alma Ata and Tashkent, and veterans from the wars with Japan and Finland. The Brigade was well-equipped with heavy machine guns and mortars; the men were given semi-automatic rifles and plentiful supplies of grenades. On 19 October we began three weeks of intensive combat training – at the end of it we would be sent to defend Moscow.

Throughout Russia's hinterland similar forces were being gathered. Stalin was taking a calculated risk. A few years earlier there had been a war with Germany's ally, Japan, whose forces had occupied Manchuria and then invaded the Soviet Union. They had been defeated, but on the outbreak of war with Germany the Japanese army of nearly a million men was again mobilised close to the Soviet frontier. Denuding Siberia of troops might encourage a fresh attack. Yet intelligence reports reaching Stalin indicated Japan was planning to strike against Britain and America in the Pacific, and with the Siberian winter already setting in, would be unlikely to move against him.

Stalin therefore made a crucial decision, recalling the Siberian divisions guarding his eastern frontier and mobilising special strike forces from the region's military academies, then moving them westwards along the Trans-Siberian railway. Having decided to stay in Moscow, Stalin wanted to provide Zhukov with the reinforcements necessary to defend the capital. But these would take at least three to four weeks to arrive, and this precious time would have to be bought in blood, fighting a desperate rearguard action against the Germans.

On 17 October Hoepner still had not broken through at Borodino. The fighting was savage. When his soldiers captured villages and defence positions the Red Army counter-attacked and drove them back. 'The Russians no longer have a recognisable army,' he wrote, 'so should not have the capacity to conduct a successful defence here. Yet the formations opposing us – the Siberian 32nd Rifle Brigade and some tank units – have proved remarkably effective.'

Also on 17 October mass surrenders took place in the Bryansk pocket. But Shabalin and his men refused to give up. They kept marching, pressing on through the freshly fallen snow, glittering in the morning sunlight. Eventually, they found an abandoned field kitchen but there was no food in it. At noon they reached a forest clearing and saw German soldiers ahead of them, blocking their route. There was a volley of fire and then the enemy unleashed an artillery and mortar bombardment, forcing the Red Army soldiers to pull back. That evening they crossed a railway bridge, searching for straw for their night camp, and exchanged shots with another

German patrol. 'Are we reaching the limits of our endurance?' Shabalin wrote. 'The enemy is simply too strong – and no one is intervening to help us.'

The following day they moved on, through desolate marshland. They were still determined to breach the German blockade. 'Everyone has just one thought,' Shabalin wrote, 'to find a way out.' That evening they stopped, lit a fire and shared the little food they had found, making a soup from a piece of meat and a few potatoes; Shabalin was able to shave and dry his clothes. Everyone was working together instinctively, as a team. As they sat by the fire Shabalin, an ambitious NKVD officer responsible for army education, realised that he no longer needed to give political lectures or issue instructions to the men around him. The comradeship binding his group of fighters together was enough in itself. And as Shabalin realised that, he felt a remarkable peace of mind.

On 19 October Boris Baromykin's 32nd Rifle Brigade finally pulled back from Borodino, after four days of bloody fighting. 'The Germans kept trying to finish us off,' Baromykin remembered:

> They knew that we were the last defence force before Moscow. Their artillery was constantly shelling us, and their planes hovered overhead, bombing and machine gunning our retreating columns. As we moved down the Smolensk-Moscow highway their tanks were hard on our heels. But we resisted doggedly. We frequently turned our guns and fire point blank to beat off their pursuit. We counter-attacked against their infantry.
>
> The retreat was a living nightmare. Human guts hung from the trees, where soldiers' bodies had been blasted by the sheer force of the explosions. The snow around us was soaked red with blood. There was an all-pervasive, pungent smell of unwashed male bodies, hardened, encrusted blood and burning. To slow the German advance, we set light to everything, so that the enemy would not have it. We were determined not to let them through.

On 19 October Major Ivan Shabalin wrote his last diary entry: 'All night long we have been marching – through rain, across marshlands, in the pitch dark. I am soaked through to the bone.

My right foot is now badly swollen and it is very difficult to walk.' At 4.00 p.m. on 20 October Shabalin's small force was finally destroyed as it attempted to break out from the Bryansk pocket. The Germans recovered his diary from the heaps of slain. Shabalin and his men had demonstrated remarkable resilience in a near-hopeless situation. To undermine such resilience, the Germans needed to treat their captured prisoners humanely, and thereby encourage others to surrender. But they seemed incapable of doing this.

German artilleryman Josef Deck's motorised unit – part of the 17th Panzer Division – drove past the residue of the Bryansk encirclement: 'We passed endless columns of prisoners, starving, exhausted, dying men – some falling before the wheels of our cars into the snow, others, dull and apathetic, in rotting clothes, collapsing as they marched. Again and again we had to move the dying to the side of the road. The ever growing pile of bodies on the roadside began to form a grim embankment, rising on either side of us, veiled in white by the falling snow.' Some Russians carried a little horsemeat and some rough bread, and in small groups they pulled away from the main column and into the forest, making fires to warm themselves. Their smoke-stained, blackened faces – from which the whites of their eyes stared eerily out – seemed to Deck to resemble medieval masks of the devil. They held horses' heads over the flames, cupping the fat running out and devouring it greedily. Others disappeared, perhaps to join the partisans. No one made much effort to stop them. 'It grievously damages our cause if we do not feed the prisoners we have captured,' Deck said starkly.

A few of the Russians, half crazed with hunger and cold, now shoved threateningly against Deck's vehicle, forcing him to shoot over their heads to clear a way forward. He and his comrades took pity on two of the desperate men clinging to the truck's running board. They found out their names, Andrei and Nikolai, and their destination – a prison camp further west – and resolved to help them reach it. But after a few miles their vehicle broke down. They made some temporary repairs, and then slowly moved off

again, managing to reach a deserted peasant hut at the edge of the
forest by nightfall. For a short while the war was forgotten. Andrei
– a mechanic before the war – worked on the vehicle, while
Nikolai, who spoke a little German, kept guard over it. Then
Andrei rolled a cigarette. Three German soldiers and two Russians
enjoyed a smoke together. The following morning they attempted
to rejoin the column of prisoners.

'As we closed up towards it,' Deck remembered, 'following
its route westwards, more and more bodies could be seen, lying
frozen in the snow, agony and suffering caught in their features.'
These men had fallen, and too weak to pull themselves up, had
been trampled to death by the mass coming up behind. 'There was
hardly a face that had not been disfigured,' Deck recalled, 'either
by the cold or wounds.' When Deck's motorised unit reached
the camp, and bade farewell to Andrei and Nikolai, its sole field
kitchen had already closed and there was no food available for the
thousands of assembled prisoners.

The strategic picture was changing. Colonel General Hoepner
felt utterly thwarted by the weather, and also by the desperate
tenacity of the Russian soldiers. On 19 October he wrote from
his HQ at Gzhatsk, west of Borodino and the Mozhaisk defence
line:

> I have been stuck here for the last six days. With the roads in such a
> terrible state we can only move forward slowly. And the resistance
> from Moscow's defenders has been far stronger than I expected. The
> Russians have brought up a fresh division from the Far East and thrown
> new tank brigades, containing hundreds of tanks, into the battle – it is
> quite incredible. I had a really tough fight on my hands at Mozhaisk,
> on the main motor highway to Moscow, where the strongest defences
> are. The Russians here fought with remarkable courage.

Radio operator Wilhelm Schröder's 10th Panzer Division
reached Mozhaisk that same evening. 'I was impressed by the
beauty of the church,' Schröder recalled, 'which, standing in
the snow-covered town at twilight, formed a wonderful picture,
its outlines etched against a stark winter sky. All around it, the

buildings were in flames.' But the German soldiers arriving in the town were exhausted. 'Tired and fought out, we entered Mozhaisk,' remembered Helmut Günther, a motorcycle rider with the SS *Das Reich* Division. 'We knew now that there would be no easy advance to Moscow, and that somewhere ahead of us, the Russians would make another stand.'

German situation reports expressed surprise at the increasingly strong resistance from the enemy. One Wehrmacht commander, faced by the Soviet 316th Division commanded by General Ivan Panfilov, spoke of 'well-motivated soldiers' who were putting up 'a surprisingly tough fight'. On 20 October Field Marshal von Bock left his headquarters at Smolensk and moved up towards the front line. He wanted to see for himself the difficulties his units were now facing. Bock was taken aback by what he discovered, noting with concern: 'It is truly incredible. Even the supposedly first-class roads are practically impassable. Repairing them – and also the bridges that the Russians have blown up – is so hindered by the mud that the task is almost impossible. Even if a single supply truck gets through the men consider this an achievement.'

Bock also saw the horrific state of Red Army prisoners being marched westwards: 'It is a ghastly sight. Totally starved and half dead, these unfortunate men slog along, barely able to move one foot after the other. They beg for scraps of food. Countless dead lie along the road . . . I discussed this awful situation with my commanders, but it is impossible to help them.' 'We are being told the most gruesome things about the thousands of Russian prisoners being marched to Smolensk,' radio operator Leopold Höglinger wrote in his diary. 'They are being treated like animals.'

German soldiers' belief in a quick, final victory was now rapidly disappearing. 'How much longer is this all going to last?' Harald Henry wrote on 20 October. 'There has to be a stop soon – we can't take much more of this.' 'It has been raining again,' tank gunner Karl Fuchs wrote on the same day, 'and the white cover of snow has turned dirty brown, and mud and slush are everywhere. Frequently the vehicles slip and slide, and get stuck. We have lost all sense of time . . . The landscape here is bleak and desolate.'

Hans Meier-Welcker, slowly moving forward with the German Ninth Army on Typhoon's northern flank, recorded: 'For the last three days we have had icy winds and snow. Yesterday it thawed again – and the roads became thick with mud. It is a huge effort to push on in these conditions. Our route is lined by dead horses that have broken their legs or collapsed through sheer exhaustion.'

On 20 October Private Gerhard vom Bruch of the 6th Panzer Division complained: 'More and more time is being lost – and we are suffering endless halts. During the day the snow thaws somewhat; in the night it freezes again, and fresh snow sweeps over the flat countryside. Was it merely an illusion that we would be able to defeat this Russian colossus in just a few months?' On the 21st Bruch added: 'We are making painfully slow progress.' A day later he continued: 'The whole division is now split up – and we are still trying to reassemble it.' 'Was it merely an illusion?' Bruch had asked, and there was indeed an air of unreality in the failure of the German high command to anticipate the autumn weather, the supply difficulties, the exhaustion of their soldiers, and above all, the capacity of the Red Army not only to keep fighting but to fight with exceptional steadfastness and courage.

The German 78th Infantry Division was struggling through the mud in support of the offensive. On 22 October the troops pushed on towards Mozhaisk in worsening weather. The condition of the motor highway was now so bad that the majority of motor vehicles could no longer use it. During the afternoon the divisional HQ sent out the following message: 'Highway completely congested. Do not attempt further progress – halt and find quarters, then report the status of battalions. Wait for a new order – do not try to send out messengers.' The supply situation, in particular the shortage of fuel, was growing serious. Trucks that had been despatched to Smolensk days ago had not yet returned. When the division finally reached Mozhaisk on 25 October, it found the road surface had totally disintegrated. Guns sank into the morass up to their hubs. Remaining vehicles became hopelessly stuck. The horses, which had not received hay or oats for days, chewed on tree bark, snapped at the straw on the roofs of huts and then sank down, exhausted, in the mud. Food trucks were also stuck fast and no rations were getting through to the men.

The 78th Division had begun suffering an alarming increase in casualties. One of its regiments had to be disbanded, and amalgamated with the others. No one had expected the Russians to fight so hard. From the map room the German position still looked imposing, but front-line soldiers were growing increasingly discouraged. 'The military situation should still be very favourable to us,' Gerhard vom Bruch wrote in some puzzlement on 26 October. 'Kalinin, on our left flank, the cornerstone of any attack on Moscow, is firmly in our hands and our leading divisions are only 60 kilometres from the Russian capital. We hear the wildest rumours, that Stalin has already fled the city and that within a few weeks the Soviet state will be brought to its knees. But in reality, things seem rather less rosy.' Lieutenant Walther Schaefer-Kehnert of the 11th Panzer Division put it more bluntly: 'For weeks they had been trumpeting in Germany that we had already won the war. That's what the *Völkischer Beobachter* actually announced. Our troops were furious. They said: "They should come and take a look for themselves!"'

German anger and frustration began to be vented on the Russian civilian population. On the night of 27 October Robert Rupp and his company, part of Guderian's Panzer forces, were ordered to the village of Mikhailovka. 'We were told to fan out on the left and right of the road. Anyone seen acting "suspiciously" was to be shot immediately. Civilians would be strung up as a warning to others. Mikhailovka itself would be set on fire. The reason: partisans had attacked five soldiers in the countryside nearby – a second lieutenant and a private had been killed and another man wounded.' On receiving these instructions Rupp felt his face go completely pale. 'Destroy the whole village – isn't that an overreaction?' he asked his company commander. 'It is a valid reprisal,' was the curt reply. 'It will act as a deterrent.' Rupp's heart was pounding as he moved back along the road with his fellow soldiers: 'We saw troops ahead of us leading some of the cattle away. A number of men were already running towards the village carrying ammunition and spades. I guessed that the spades would be used to dig mass graves. Then I heard sounds of gunshot and of children screaming. I realised we were about to commit a massacre.'

A woman with five children huddled, petrified, by one of the huts. Behind her, on the straw, two villagers lay dead. Rupp called out to her in Russian and after considerable hesitation she came over. 'I warned the woman what was going on and told her she had to get out as quickly as possible. She and her children fled.' Most of the inhabitants were not so lucky.

Half of Rupp's company was despatched to the far end of Mikhailovka, quickly encircling the village. An informer had told the Germans that weapons for the partisans were stored in a railway building. Nothing was found there. But the mood of the men was ugly. 'It's just as well the Russians sleep by their stoves,' one said. 'It makes our job easier.' Soldiers ran through the village tossing hand grenades onto its straw roofs. Mikhailovka began to burn. The fire soon spread, until the whole village – more than fifty houses – was in flames: 'We heard the terrible roaring of the cattle, the shrieks of women and children – and then the cries faded away,' Rupp remembered. The men congregated around a field kitchen on the village outskirts. Military vehicles were parked by it. There was an uneasy silence. Then someone came over and told them they were to move off. 'We drove away from the village and behind us the sky was glowing dark red. How many survived that fire I do not know – but I later found out that the sole remaining inhabitant of Mikhailovka was one old man.'

On 29 October an irate Hitler summoned Bock's Fourth Army commander, Field Marshal von Kluge, to his headquarters in East Prussia. When Kluge returned the following day he reported: 'The Führer finds it difficult to believe the written reports from Army Group Centre concerning manpower shortages, supply difficulties and the impassable roads. He is very disturbed that Moscow has not yet fallen and is amazed that we did not foresee all of the contingencies.'

Hitler could not countenance the fact that in the terrible autumn mud battered Russian defenders had somehow held off the might of the German Wehrmacht. Moscow had won a vital reprieve. The fighting – with so much at stake – was ugly and cruel. 'In a desperate situation,' Boris Baromykin said, 'we at last felt the iron determination of our commander, General Zhukov, to withstand the enemy':

> The slogan 'Moscow is behind us!' became a reality as we defended the city, and the mood among our soldiers changed. Dull resignation was transformed into a fierce hatred of the Germans. We resolved to meet violence with violence. Once, towards the end of October, the enemy pushed us out of the village we were holding and began shooting us down. But we regrouped – then took the village back. We seized five of the German soldiers and literally ripped them apart with our bare hands, our teeth, anything – one man was even using a table leg to smash a skull in. We killed those men in a frenzy of hatred.

Colonel General Hoepner felt baulked of his prey. He wrote on 30 October: 'The roads have become quagmires – everything has come to a halt. Our tanks cannot move. No fuel can get through to us; the heavy rain and fog make air drops almost impossible . . . After our great victories at Vyazma and Bryansk we are now stuck in the mud.' But Hoepner still hoped that the city could be taken. 'Dear God,' he implored, 'give us fourteen days of frost. Then we will surround Moscow!'

The frost, which would harden the roads and allow the Germans to move forward again, was on its way. It would come perilously late in the year, and would find the fate of Russia's capital still lying in the balance.

3

At the Gates of Moscow

IN EARLY NOVEMBER 1941, as German armies remained coiled around Moscow, one Wehrmacht officer felt a sense of foreboding. At the beginning of the month platoon commander Robert Rupp wrote a long, troubled entry in his diary: 'I am making frequent visits to a neighbouring family,' he began. 'The mother tells me that three of our soldiers were quartered in her home, and that they raped her seventeen-year-old daughter. First they chased the mother out of the house, and then they put a pistol to the daughter's head and forced her to submit to them. The women went to the town *Kommandant,* who sent out a security detachment immediately, but the soldiers had already fled.'

Rupp was staying in the Russian town of Orel about 200 miles south of Moscow. There were already severe food shortages there. Two of Rupp's comrades returned from a field hospital in the rear of the German positions, telling awful stories about the plight of Red Army prisoners, herded together like animals and suffering from appalling hunger. German soldiers and military police were behaving with mindless brutality:

A sergeant flogged one young girl who was merely handing tomatoes to some of the prisoners through the camp fence. The soldiers who are detailed for guard duty are being begged by many of the Russian wounded to shoot them and put them out of their misery, and some actually do it – this is happening all day long. A civilian, who was carrying a jug of water over to a prison wagon to pass around the thirsty men, was shot in the face. From open wagons – in the freezing cold – young Russian medical orderlies are carried out, already sick, and deliberately left on the station platform for days. One of these girls, a nurse, offered the soldier on duty 100 roubles if he would shoot her immediately!

Rupp looked out along the street. A civilian had been strung up with a placard around his neck, announcing that he had been caught helping the partisans. Rupp felt a sudden emptiness within him.

It is difficult to describe precisely the attitude of German soldiers to their Russian enemies. Some were clearly upon a journey from humanitarian values to callous indifference or worse. Others, faced with the suffering of the prisoners of war, were travelling in the opposite direction. Not every individual shared the attitudes of Hitler, that this was a racial war to exterminate an inferior enemy. Some may have learnt these ideas at this time. Others may have held them, and then rejected them, appalled by what they witnessed. Testimonies conflict and the picture is confused and changeable.

Rupp's concerns were shared by some German commanders. At the beginning of November General Georg Thomas wrote: 'The commander-in-chief of the army needs to raise the condition of Russian prisoners of war with the Führer himself, before it causes us real problems.' With the reactions of decent soldiers like Rupp in mind, Thomas added: 'It is already having an unfavourable effect on the morale of our troops.' The general seemed, however, to have less interest in the 'unfavourable effect' that the brutality of German soldiers would have on the Russian civilians who witnessed these atrocities.

Conditions in Russian territory occupied by the Germans were becoming more demeaning for the native population. Nina Semonova lived in the town of Rzhev, 130 miles north-west of Moscow, captured by the advancing Wehrmacht in mid-October. She wrote in her diary on 1 November:

The Germans have now taken over our whole house. An interpreter is there as well. He tells us: 'Do not appear in the passageway if a German officer is entering or leaving the building.' Everyday conditions worsen. We had saved a few scraps of food – a little butter, a small amount of meat and some white bread. Naturally, everything has now been stolen from us. A collective has been established here – but we will get no share of it.

Some German soldiers arriving from the west to take part in the Wehrmacht's renewed offensive against Moscow were shocked by the devastation that greeted them. Wilhelm Pfeiffer had reached Vitebsk, north-west of Smolensk, in early November. His radio signals unit had paused there, before moving closer to the front: 'Once we crossed into Russia, burnt-down villages were every-where,' Pfeiffer wrote in his diary, 'but the amount of destruction in Vitebsk is extraordinary. I am spending hours struggling through its rubble-strewn streets. Standing at the top of the hill, I gaze at a landscape of ruins. Fire-blackened chimney stacks – the remnants of burnt-down houses – rise upwards, towards the sky, as far as the eye can see. And what has happened to all the civilians?'

Seventeen-year-old Vera Kalugina was one of the surviving inhabitants of the town: 'That November the Germans were boasting: "Moscow kaput, Stalin kaput – the war is nearly over!"' Kalugina remembered:

Everything became gloomy and sinister. Although Vitebsk was a large town, I felt there was no longer enough air to breathe. There was nothing at all to eat. If you went out to the market in order to buy or barter something, German security police would arrest you. They seized young people for no particular reason and deported them to Germany. We had to remain inconspicuous, as if we hardly existed at all.

You had to have documents of identification for everything. If you wanted to cross the bridge, and go out of the town, or even if you just went out in the street, you always had to present your papers. I saw how they strung a young man up, right beside the town hall, because he had not got the right identity pass with him. And they would come into our homes and make random inspec-tions of our papers. It was deliberately degrading. We lived in a constant state of tension. I did not feel I was living a human life – it was an animal existence.

Occupying German troops in Vitebsk may have bragged 'Moscow kaput', but the Wehrmacht forces poised before Russia's capital nearly 300 miles to the east were no longer so jubilant. Instead, with winter fast approaching, the men were becoming uneasy. On 3 November Heinz Otto Fausten received the Iron Cross. 'My commanding general congratulated me,' Fausten recalled, 'as I was the first ordinary soldier he had given the award to. Then he looked at me for a moment, and added softly: "Get back safely with it!"' Driving back through Kalinin, Fausten passed a ruined factory – roofless – with snow drifting into the outer compound. More than a thousand German soldiers were there, kneeling. A priest was standing in front of them. To his astonishment, Fausten realised that they were receiving a general absolution, a religious ceremony in which those who repent are released from blame for their wrongdoing.

Fausten's 1st Panzer Division had regrouped north-west of Moscow. Hellmuth Stieff, staff officer with the German Fourth Army, was stationed along the Nara river, west of the city. 'Since yesterday we have had frost,' wrote Stieff on 5 November, 'and – thank God – the worst of the mud is over. Before this happened, it was impossible to think about continuing the attack. Now we must retrieve our vehicles, which are scattered everywhere, and sort out our supply situation. It has been so frustrating to become stuck so close to our goal – scarcely 60 kilometres from Moscow.'

Colonel General Hoepner was to coordinate the last great push on Moscow. 'We are waiting to move forward,' he wrote on 5 November. 'But although we had frost yesterday, the temperature will need to be colder to harden the road surfaces . . . For our new attack, at least ten days' supplies will be necessary.' The general added in frustration: 'Our high command continues to set unrealistic objectives – they have no idea of the situation at the front.'

The Nazi leadership was in fact aware of the critical lack of winter clothing, and trying hard to conceal this fact from the German population. Joseph Goebbels sent the following report to the press:

Necessary winter clothing for the troops – furs, driving coats and warm underwear – is lying in railway depots ready to be delivered. Distribution is being rendered difficult by the transport situation and delays are unavoidable. In the meantime, it would be better not to refer to this issue at all. When choosing pictures, particular care must be taken. Our soldiers must not appear poorly equipped. For example, we do not want photos of Russian prisoners wearing coats, when their German guards have none.

While the Germans readied themselves for one last attempt to take the Russian capital, the Soviet leadership was standing fast in the city. On 7 November Stalin resolved to hold the traditional parade on Moscow's Red Square, marking the anniversary of the Bolshevik Revolution. The decision was taken at the last minute. 'We only heard about it the previous evening,' remembered Soviet soldier Ivan Barykin, of the 154th Marine Brigade. 'The parade was brought forward by two hours – starting at 8.00 a.m. – because of fear of an enemy air attack, and our troops went straight to the front.' Yet it had enormous symbolic importance, demonstrating to the entire country, and to the world, that Moscow *would* be defended. In his speech to the Red Army force Stalin astutely appealed to Russians' love of their Motherland, invoking 'the example of our illustrious ancestors', heroes such as Alexander Nevsky, who had defeated the Teutonic knights in the thirteenth century. The Soviet leader recognised that communist zeal would not be enough to defeat the new invaders; the country would have to be mobilised in a genuinely patriotic struggle. He was also fully prepared to match Hitler's brutality: 'If the Germans want a war of extermination,' he declared, 'they can have one.'

And evidence of that brutality was growing. On 9 November Robert Rupp decided to visit a prisoner-of-war camp at Mtensk: 'What I saw there was harrowing,' he stated:

Early in the morning they bring out the work detail, flogging them, and raining blows on their heads, before leading them away. At noon and in the evening a tiny amount of food is available for these unfortunates. It is horsemeat, which stands out in the open in large vats. The prisoners come with makeshift canisters, some hammered out from their helmets. They beg for more – they are so desperately hungry. Yet the horsemeat is scarcely edible. At night, they sleep on wooden slats, in a side annexe exposed to the open air – and it is already very cold.

Most of them are sick – and many have chronic stomach pains. Some attempt to patch up their boots by winding wire around them; others try to make gloves from pieces of rag and string. All have lice, for there is no provision for washing or changing clothes. I found a supply officer and described the prisoners' condition and we immediately got into an argument. I learnt that some clothes were available – but they had been left in storage and not distributed.

In a derelict factory room, there is a long trough and one dripping tap. Rats scurry around it. This is the prisoners' sole source of drinking water.

Rupp added: 'These conditions are an absolute disgrace. There is not an iota of compassion here.' He made a final trip to the camp hospital: 'It is situated in a large ruined hut, where the wounded lie on the bare earth. Someone is having a foot amputated. An old man begs me to allow him home – he wants to be properly cared for.' Rupp concluded: 'This day has profoundly shaken me.' Shortly afterwards he wrote to his wife: 'Only rarely do I weep. Crying is no way out when you are standing amidst these events. The feelings of guilt and shame are too deep'.

The frost was hardening the roads, and the German Panzers hoped soon to advance once again. On 10 November Nina Semonova wrote in her diary: 'A sunny day. I carried my baby daughter outside, to get a little fresh air. A German officer appeared. He boasted that they had already occupied Moscow and Leningrad. I remained silent.' Once again, there was a widening gap between the sentiments of troops occupying towns such as Rzhev, and therefore distanced from the actual fighting, and those on the front line. Here, the inactivity was playing on soldiers' nerves. 'The men are becoming listless and apathetic,' wrote Hellmuth Stieff on 11 November. 'We have a frost now, and temperatures have fallen to below −10 degrees Celsius, though we still do not know when the attack will start again. We are ready to try for this one last goal.' And then Stieff echoed the complaint of Hoepner: 'Our high command continues to issue wholly unrealistic orders, and we have not yet been properly resupplied with ammunition and fuel.'

The growing gulf between front-line perceptions of what was feasible and the views of the German high command was beginning to worry Stieff seriously, and he returned to it, declaiming: 'For us, their attitude is utterly incomprehensible. They devise their objectives in the map room, as if the Russian winter did not exist, and our troops' strength is still the same as when the campaign started in June. However, winter is now on our doorsteps, and our units are so burnt out that one's heart bleeds for them. Soon we will be unable to attack anything at all – the men desperately need rest.'

Such frustration was now widespread. 'When we talk about the war,' Lieutenant Ludwig Freiherr von Heyl of the 36th Motorised Infantry Division wrote from Kalinin on 12 November:

we are all of the same opinion: that the official army communiqués are largely exaggeration, that the Russians are in many respects an equal opponent to us and an opponent from whom we can learn something. For despite our series of victories, they are in no way broken, they continue to resist strongly against the whole German army, and an end to the campaign may not be reached before the winter. In a larger sense, the war has reached a critical stage.

Further major advances are no longer possible because of the difficulties we are having with our supplies. I personally believe that by December we will no longer be able to conduct large-scale military operations at all, and – although much remains unpredictable – we will then have to switch to a protracted defence. But no preparations are being made for such an eventuality.

We have not lost our courage or resolve, but a little realism from time to time would do no harm here. For the last three days, temperatures have dropped steadily, from −5 to −20 degrees Celsius, with light snow. The thought that the real winter is yet to come is a sobering one.

Heyl's unit had received some reinforcements, but was still under strength, and in particular had not made good its losses in officers. 'Yesterday our very competent second lieutenant was killed,' Heyl continued:

> He died in of all places the Corps command post in the centre of the city – it received a direct hit.
>
> This is no gentleman's war here, but more of a brutal pillaging raid. One becomes totally numb. Human life is so cheap – cheaper than the shovels we use to clear the roads of snow. The state we have reached will seem quite unbelievable to you back home. We do not kill humans, but 'the enemy', who are rendered impersonal – animals at best. They behave the same way towards us.

For Heyl and his comrades, the only way of coping with the war's horror was increasingly to close off all human feelings. Alois Scheuer, whose unit was scarcely 50 miles from Moscow, took the same view: 'The war in Russia, and all its consequences, are truly terrible,' he wrote. 'One must cut off from all decent feelings and thoughts. We have to fight the enemy to the death, and now hunger and cold are added. One must harden oneself to bear it all.'

'We have to fight the enemy to the death,' Scheuer had written, while Heyl emphasised the Bolshevik ideology lying behind the ferocity of his opponents: 'It is frightening how little store the Russian sets on an individual life,' he concluded. 'Twenty years on the "soul mill" of Bolshevism have ground this into the national character. It can be the only explanation for the fierce fighting that we are now experiencing.'

However tough the fighting, the prospect of ordering a temporary halt was unpalatable to Hitler. He had frequently boasted that the war in the east would be over before the winter. Now he prolonged the campaign, hoping for a last great triumph. He had seen a report of the SS security service, which stated: 'Large sections of the German population are disappointed that Bolshevism has not been crushed as quickly as had been hoped, and that the end of the eastern campaign is not yet in sight . . . The halt in the advance on Moscow is a matter of particular concern, all the more so since it was reported several weeks ago that German troops were only 60 kilometres from the Russian capital.'

Hitler now hoped that the capture of Moscow would improve the popular mood in Germany and reawaken the conviction that the Wehrmacht was invincible.

Hans Jürgen Hartmann and his comrades in Army Group South, however, had been sceptical all along of the Führer's predictions that Russian resistance would quickly collapse. Now they were becoming deeply afraid. Towards the end of October they had fought their way into Kharkov, 200 miles east of Kiev, and they now expected the entire front to take up winter quarters. Instead, rumours circulated that Army Group Centre was to make a last push on Moscow, and were greeted with dismay. As Hartmann wrote:

> Even if no one speaks of it, all of us are feeling a heavy weight, that presses down on the soul, as time and time again we think about the advance on Moscow. We know from the Wehrmacht news bulletins roughly where our troops are and where the *Schwerpunkt* [the focal point of the fight] will be. If at Moscow, which is even colder than it is here, our tanks and pulling vehicles do not have glycerine and proper coolant, and as a result receive the same surprise that we have just had, then it is 'Goodnight!' to our chances.

Hartmann reflected further on this last desperate offensive:

> At this very moment, our attacking forces will be situated in a host of nameless villages, with overworked engines constantly running in the terrible cold. Our front is already overextended, and basic supplies will be even scarcer than here. We know the cost of having to do constant maintenance work, around the clock, cleaning gun parts and warming artillery barrels in steam so that they will still function properly. Ahead of these soldiers there will be little left to eat, and if supplies of food no longer get to them they will have to forage for whatever they can find.

He felt the same foreboding that had afflicted others:

> All in all, as I look eastwards, and see the grey, forbidding November clouds which sweep towards us, I fear we have become dangerously

overstretched. The frost that we see each morning is tracing on our buildings and equipment a terrible warning for us. It was the winter that broke old Napoleon. We always believed that we were superior to him. But maybe that was make-believe. At the end of it all – then as now – perhaps everything hangs on the simple workings of fate.

As Hartmann wrote these words, thousands of German soldiers were preparing for a last-ditch assault on the Russian capital. Horst Lange's 56th Infantry Division was among them. 'We are to push forwards again,' he wrote, 'past Kalinin and the Volga before we take up winter quarters.' Lange and his comrades found the marching arduous, for the snow-covered tracks had frozen over, the ruts were stone-hard and an icy wind swirled around the struggling infantrymen. The landscape was disorientating. 'Our marching rhythm is regularly interrupted,' Lange wrote. 'We get lost in this wintry world, stand about in the freezing cold and then move forward again. Our second lieutenant, who has the map, has no idea where we are, and has gone over to the next village, which has appeared – indistinctly – between folds of snow drifts. He is going to ask for directions.'

To their relief, the men finally reached the main Smolensk-Moscow highway, and pushed on towards the town of Gzhatsk, where Colonel General Hoepner had organised his offensive against Borodino a month earlier. Lange found his surroundings bleak and depressing: 'A small, dirty town,' he commented, 'with the houses mostly destroyed and two large churches lying in ruins. One has completely burnt down. I hate this grey, monotonous landscape, yet find myself caught in its all-encompassing, hostile grip. We trudge past a hill, dotted with large windmills, whose enormous sails turn slowly. The surrounding villages are crammed with soldiers and Luftwaffe personnel. It is beginning to snow again.' Lange felt uneasy. He saw around him evidence of partisan operations – bridges and causeways had been blown up, and the column frequently halted while new ones were constructed. 'They are trying to disrupt our supplies ahead of the offensive,' he thought. Then the way ahead was blocked by a narrow ravine, and negotiating a crossing point Lange's boot slipped on the icy ledge. He fell straight through the ice into the freezing water below.

Eventually, Lange stumbled into his living quarters for the night. 'I spoke to the inhabitants in broken Russian,' he continued. 'They want to know when this war is going to end, which is only too understandable, since they now have German soldiers billeted on them eating their last reserves of bread.' He looked around him: 'Torn rags on the floor, rickety furniture and the detritus of former prosperity – holy pictures, metal icons and a large mix of photos, with Tsarist and Bolshevik soldiers coexisting peacefully together on the wall. They all show the same tough, courageous faces.' The following morning the troops pushed on. Spruce forests seemed to hover above the greying horizon as a damp chill sank into the men's bones. Lange found the time passing in a kind of trance: 'The constant marching in these conditions creates a sort of drunkenness,' he observed, 'where reality starts to dissolve. Physical sensations are strangely heightened, while the normal train of thought becomes more and more disjointed.'

Every morning, as the soldiers awoke at an unnaturally early hour, with all outside still cloaked in darkness, they sang: to rouse their sleeping comrades and to steel themselves against the cold. Their improvised refrain created a sense of unity out of the awful conditions they were facing: they were all in this together. Yet it also hinted at an unfolding tragedy, one that the men were beginning to sense instinctively. Their high command remained oblivious to its approach:

> The frost has turned this land to ice
> Winter is fast approaching,
> The sun has shrunk, summer slunk away –
> And shivering, we are marching.
> Shivering in whirling snow and freezing night
> The dead fields are a ghostly white
> As onwards we are marching.
>
> On a long and never-ending road
> Our infantry is embarking.

85

The fog comes down, the wind lifts up
And howls, as we are marching.
Our skin grows cold, our blood does race
We feel our heartbeat's frantic pace
As onwards we are marching.

So step by step we struggle on
A frozen landscape passing.
We've never known such bitter cold
When through this snow we're marching;
We cry out in rage, we curse and swear
But there never is an answer there
As onwards we are marching.

The way back home we no longer know
And in Russia, have no hope of finding.
With iced-up rifles and frozen guns
Further and further are we marching.
The snow clouds above the sky do fill
The cold most earthly things would kill
But onwards we are marching.

While Lange and his comrades were marching towards the front, German generals were now debating whether to continue the offensive. A growing number of them believed that a halt should be called, and any further attack on Moscow postponed to the spring. Colonel General Maximilian von Weichs, commander of the German Second Army, on the southern flank of Army Group Centre, was a strong advocate of this course of action: 'We all had hoped that the frost would harden the road surfaces again,' Weichs wrote. 'However, I know from my experience in the First World War how quickly winter falls here – and it is far more extreme than in central Europe. I doubted whether the operation against Moscow was still feasible this year, and suggested instead that a defence line be built before the drop in temperature made digging difficult, so we could hold our positions during the winter months and continue the operation in the spring. This option was rejected – and I was accused of not supporting the offensive any more.'

Hans Meier-Welcker – on the staff of the 251st Infantry Division, part of the Ninth Army on Army Group Centre's northern wing – was also reassessing the situation: 'The fallacy of the war against Russia was the belief that the Soviet Union would collapse internally after our first military successes,' Meier-Welcker wrote. 'But even at this current stage of the war, there is no sign of this. And since the hope of a rapid internal collapse has proved a mirage, we are in a quite different situation. We no longer know how to master our opponent.' After this frank acknowledgement Meier-Welcker continued:

> Another mistaken belief was that our great October offensive would bring the whole campaign to a victorious conclusion. But we have dangerously underestimated the enemy's resources. In mid-October we believed – very prematurely – that the combat strength of the Red Army was broken. However it is quite amazing how quickly the Russians have created new armies. They have brought up fresh reinforcements – and are now conducting their defence with considerable skill.

Meier-Welcker believed that prospects of success were fading fast: 'We are facing a growing supply crisis, which is affecting not only my division but the whole Army Corps. Rail links are inadequate, and as the roads have been impassable to motor vehicles for several weeks, we have received scant supplies of fuel, ammunition and food. We have had to abandon many of our vehicles, economise on ammunition and rely on what the troops and horses can carry forward.' He concluded: 'The supply situation is undermining the attacking potential of the entire Army Corps.'

When these concerns were conveyed to the Army's high command they reacted defensively. Weichs was dismissed as the commander of the German Second Army, but his replacement, General Rudolf Schmidt, was even more forcefully opposed to a resumption of the attack on Moscow. On 13 November he warned: 'The number of losses due to frostbite is now rising steadily. Our troops are still largely without winter clothing. Many have stuffed newspapers into their boots – their footwear is worn and defective and gloves are sorely missed.' Schmidt continued:

> In respect of winter clothing, the Quartermaster General is grievously at fault. Things are determined by weather conditions at the front, not the temperature in Germany, and the temperature here is now dropping below −11 degrees Celsius. Our men are often out in the open at night, where many lie, stand or sit — and then have to fight the following day.
>
> The thoughts of our higher command seem rose-tinted. They are hiding in a world of false optimism and completely overlooking the operational problems we are facing. Our leaders cannot face the fact that the army is no longer in a position to continue this offensive. Our battalions — already under strength — have been reduced from 500 combatants to fewer than 60!

Schmidt finished: 'The troops have had no chance to rest or recover, are suffering from the worsening cold and are quite at the end of their tether. Once the strength of our forces drops below a certain point even the sharpest orders will have little effect. *We have reached this point now.*'

In response, it was trumpeted that the Russians themselves were almost at the end of their strength. But this boast had been made too many times before. 'Do we really know for certain that only a few enemy divisions are left facing us,' Private Gerhard vom Bruch wrote on 12 November, 'and that after that the road is clear to Moscow — and who knows what other cities? We are quartered in a poor village east of Kalinin, close to the motor highway, waiting for supplies to reach us before starting yet another offensive.'

At a crucial meeting of army staff and the German high command at Orsha near Smolensk on 13 November such concerns were minimised. The commander of the German Army, Field Marshal von Brauchitsch, had suffered a mild heart attack three days earlier, so the meeting was convened by the army's chief of staff, Colonel General Franz Halder. Although Halder invited discussion, he presented the advance to Moscow as a fait accompli. He simply announced that the offensive would continue, regardless of any difficulties, making clear that he spoke for Hitler as well as army high command, and closing proceedings by saying emphatically that it was 'the Führer's wish'. Halder himself was strongly in favour of the attack on Moscow, and he knew that the commander of Army Group Centre, Field Marshal von Bock, supported the plan. Opposition was brushed aside.

There were only enough supplies available for German troops to reach the Moscow-Volga Canal. The rest would be delivered 'later'. General Hermann Geyer summarised the attitude of the high command in a letter to his officers: 'The positive aspects of every situation must always be recognised and emphasised. The enemy's problems are greater than ours. And in such difficult situations a soldier can often do more than his best, more than seems humanly possible. Success often comes at the last minute, and can hang upon a single thread. Often one realises later that, given a last push, the opponent would have fallen over.' The German Army, it seemed, was supposed to advance on sheer willpower.

The last offensive would primarily be conducted by the Panzer groups to the north and south of Moscow. Luftwaffe commander Wolfram von Richthofen's 8th Corps would provide the air support. 'In order to achieve success before the onset of winter,' Richthofen wrote, 'we must move forward with our maximum strength. We only have a short time to pursue this attack.' Richthofen was aware that the Russians were bringing up fresh reserves and the general morale of the attackers was not good. If the Red Army was to be knocked out, it would have to be hit hard and fast.

'The cold is ever-present,' Gerhard vom Bruch wrote on 13 November, 'but we are in good heart that soon we will leave this barren place. The frost has overcome the mud, and made the roads to some extent passable again, but now we must try and protect our vehicles against the cold. We start up our tank engines several times each night.' The following day Bruch wrote: 'We are now awaiting instructions to move against the Volga reservoir and the Moscow canal. We are reassured, again and again, that these will be our last orders before the winter. Our task will be to secure a bridgehead south of the reservoir and dam.' The bridgehead would point like an arrow straight into the heart of Russia's capital.

The push on Moscow from Army Group Centre's northern flank was assisted by a blunder from Stalin, who ordered that his own forces in the region launch a pre-emptive counter-attack on 14 November. Although the Soviet leader had decided to stay in Moscow, he was nervous about the resumption of the German offensive. When General Zhukov protested that this small offensive was unlikely to succeed, and would simply use up scarce reserves, Stalin overruled him. Major General Rokossovsky commented bitterly: 'The supreme commander knew well enough what the situation was. What he was thinking of when he gave the order to attack, I do not understand even today. Our forces were very limited, and we were given no more than a single night to prepare'. Rokossovsky's troops were soon in trouble, and many were quickly encircled. Then the Germans began their own advance. On 15 November Private Bruch's 6th Panzer Division set off. 'The beginning of our last great raid,' he wrote, 'along the main highway from Kalinin to Moscow. We set off at noon, driving eastwards, in a newly formed battle group.'

But German infantry forces were struggling to hold their present positions, and could offer little assistance. Colonel General Adolf Strauss, commander of the German Ninth Army, advancing on Army Group Centre's northern flank, was entirely unenthusiastic about the new attack. He was a quiet, careful commander of the old school, holding to notions of military honour even where these were being eroded by the actions of Hitler and the German high command. He was also aware that there were too many problems in the area his troops had recently occupied to consider further activity. But Luftwaffe commander Wolfram von Richthofen was unimpressed by Strauss's leadership at this critical time: 'The Ninth Army's commander is unduly passive,' he wrote. 'His inertia is quite unbelievable.'

Strauss committed three of his divisions to clear Soviet troops from the area between the Ivankovo Reservoir, also known as the Moscow Sea, and the Volga Reservoir, but did nothing further.

He maintained his view that an attack was misconceived. On 16 November he drew up a long memorandum, ignoring the assault on Moscow and instead declaring: 'Unjust and unfair treatment of the Russian population is creating problems for our troops and will only extend the duration of the war.' Strauss warned that the majority of Russians were well aware of the catastrophic conditions in the POW camps, the serious food shortages in areas under German occupation and the growing instances of violence and robbery directed against civilians. He continued: 'The condition of prisoners in camps near us is particularly bad, and the food supply is not even being maintained at a subsistence level.' Strauss acknowledged that the sheer numbers of prisoners was a problem, particularly as relatively few men were available to guard them, but emphasised: 'Random and unjustified killings must not be tolerated. Such actions are unworthy of German soldiers and are causing untold damage.'

Strauss's views failed to carry the day. When objections were raised against one directive – namely, the use of weapons against unarmed Russian prisoners was now to be considered lawful, regardless of circumstances – Field Marshal Wilhelm Keitel, head of the German Armed Forces, responded: 'Criticisms of the new directive reflect the soldierly concept of chivalrous warfare! But what we are dealing with here is the destruction of Bolshevism. Consequently, I approve of the measures as ordered.' The 'measures as ordered' were of course nothing more than an incitement to murder. While some Germans were repelled by them, others fell under their dark spell.

Meanwhile, whatever the misgivings of the infantry commanders, the Panzers were pushing forward. On 16 November Colonel General Hoepner threw fresh forces into the attack. He struck at the junction point of two of the defending Soviet armies, the Fifth and the Thirtieth. His aim was to get a Panzer force onto the Volokolamsk–Moscow highway and outflank the Russian position.

'The German attack on 16 November was very difficult for us,' General Zhukov admitted. 'The enemy was driving forwards,

heedless of losses, in an attempt to break our lines before Moscow.'
Tank brigade deputy commander Anatoly Shvebig was more
explicit. 'The 16th of November was a calamity. Many of our
forward units were surrounded by the enemy, and Rokossovsky
himself was desperately trying to avoid encirclement. The Germans
got onto the road from Volokolamsk to Moscow and we had virtually nothing left to stop them with. My own brigade was down
to its last two operable tanks.' On this day there was a brief resurgence of the German bravado that had dominated the early days
of Operation Typhoon. 'We seized two Wehrmacht officers who
had strayed too far ahead of their advancing forces,' Shvebig continued, 'and they seemed confident of victory. They kept saying:
"Moscow is kaput!" They regarded their capture as some kind
of temporary mishap. That evening the enemy began bombing
our retreating troops.' But some Russian units were fighting with
remarkable tenacity.

Opposing Hoepner's thrust were the troops of General Ivan
Panfilov's 316th Division. At the end of a day of intense fighting
Panfilov wrote to his wife: 'You will hear on the radio broadcasts
and in the newspapers about the heroic deeds of my soldiers and
officers. I believe we have earned that praise. It is an honour to
defend our capital, and all our men are aware of it. They are true
patriots – and are fighting like lions. They have just one thought,
to destroy the Germans without pity and never let the enemy into
Moscow.'

Major General Rokossovsky visited Panfilov's command post.
The combat there was ferocious. 'The German attacks began
with heavy artillery and mortar fire, supported by air attacks,'
Rokossovsky recalled:

> Bombers circled overhead, diving in turn and dropping bombs on
> our infantry and artillery positions. Then groups of tanks, followed by
> sub-machine gunners, were flung into the battle . . . The tanks con-
> tinued to advance, regardless of losses, halting occasionally to blast at
> our anti-tank batteries. Some of them churned about, with damaged
> tracks, or began belching smoke, others pushed on, and managed to
> reach our trenches, before they were put out of action.

Rokossovsky was struck by the fighting spirit of these troops, and was encouraged to regroup and reorganise his own defence. 'I began to believe,' he said, 'that the Germans might not reach Moscow.'

On 16 November a group of Panfilov's soldiers made a stand against the Germans at a small railway crossing at Dubosekovo. It was said that they were inspired by the slogan 'There is nowhere left to retreat – Moscow is behind us!' An anti-tank platoon destroyed a number of enemy tanks, and held off superior German forces for several hours. Soviet propaganda later inflated this episode into a heroic legend, where twenty-eight Red Army soldiers fought to the last man. The details were incorrect. The group were not wiped out but forced to withdraw that same evening, and their commander and commissar were temporarily suspended from their posts for retreating without permission. But there was heroism in the reality of the event, nonetheless.

Many Red Army units were forced to keep fighting where they stood. However, Russian troops were also powerfully motivated. 'In mid-November, when the German offensive resumed, and our forces were suffering terrible losses, iron discipline alone would not have kept our soldiers going,' said Red Army soldier Dmitry Vonlyarsky. 'It was a desperate patriotism, a love of our Motherland, that held us together. The resolve to defend Moscow to the last man sprang from that.' Anatoly Shvebig agreed: 'We no longer had anywhere left to retreat to,' he exclaimed. 'If we pulled back any further, the Germans would get into Moscow. To stop them, we had to stand and fight where we were – and fight to the death.' On 19 November the German Army Group Centre noted that the enemy was putting up an increasingly tough defence, 'to the point of self-sacrifice'.

On the same day, General Panfilov died at his command post. In recognition of his courage, his division was awarded the Order of the Red Banner and the title of a Guards Division. Rokossovsky noted that the slogan 'Moscow is behind us!' was now spontaneously taken up by his whole army.

The German 5th Panzer Division was pushing along the Volokolamsk-Moscow highway. Colonel General Hoepner had praised the fighting performance of these men, but they were confronted by increasingly stubborn opposition. On 19 November German Private Graf Castell described the struggle to take a Russian stronghold at Denikovo:

> We moved up to new positions, ahead of our infantry, close to the edge of the village. Russian artillery immediately became very active. At 3.00 p.m. we received the order to move forward. But as we went into the attack we found that enemy engineers had destroyed part of the road ahead of us and blown up the bridge. The Russians had strongly fortified the station building and our orders were to push round it, cut the defenders off and get the railway line into our possession as quickly as possible. But as our tanks turned off the damaged road, several ran straight into a minefield. The enemy's artillery now found its range. We tried to get round the village, driving our tanks and armoured support vehicles along a gully. But, at the end of the day, the station was still in Russian hands.

Rokossovsky described the ingenuity of the Soviet defenders: 'Whenever the enemy was unable to bypass our defences, he concentrated his tanks en masse, and supported the attacks with heavy artillery and mortar fire, and air bombardment. We countered them by manoeuvring our gun batteries and tanks, which intercepted the Germans, sometimes at point-blank range. Our engineers would travel with them, planting mines along the expected route of the enemy's advance.'

Colonel General Halder, the German Army's chief of staff, was dismissive of such efforts. 'The enemy has no more reserves, and is in a far worse predicament than we are,' he wrote in his diary. 'Our stronger will is prevailing.' But German soldiers' unease was growing. On 19 November Hellmuth Stieff recorded: 'Our winter clothing is only trickling in – a few gloves, woollen vests and hats. God knows when the rest will come! The supply situation should have been resolved weeks ago. It is an extraordinary mess, and we are supposed to be "the best armed forces in the world". The boots and trousers of many of our soldiers are completely ripped and torn, and some are only wearing canvas shoes or just tying leggings round their feet for protection.' He continued: 'The last few days have been particularly tough. West of Serpukhov the Russians brought up five new divisions and attacked our eastern flank. We only just fended off an enemy breakthrough – which would have cut our army's vital transport artery, the Medyn-Moscow road – with the help of artillery and air strikes.' Then Stieff declared:

> I am frightened by what might happen here. We have no more reserves, and fresh reinforcements will not arrive before the spring. We are poorly equipped for winter and have no prepared positions – and the enemy is becoming increasingly active. Hopefully the snow will soon put a stop to the fighting and allow our troops to get some rest, otherwise we are heading for disaster.
>
> We have got ourselves into a fine mess. And it is infuriating to hear the nonsense our propaganda people churn out. It is astonishing how many fairy tales they are making up. They deride the Russians, again and again. It is as if they are deliberately tempting fate.

German infantryman Ernst Jauernick echoed Stieff's concerns:

> We have now begun the last great raid on Moscow – but we lack almost everything. We have not yet been assigned winter clothing, and our motorised units have no lubricating oil. We receive little in the way of food. In the autumn it was the mud that was our enemy, but this cold may finish us off completely. Our poor horses are being pushed to the very limits and are suffering horribly. We can no longer offer them straw to lie on or hay to eat. They get ice-cold water to drink and have to nibble on small branches we gather from the forest. At night they have little shelter from the freezing cold, often having to lie with their bellies in the icy snow.

Jauernick then said with feeling:

> The cold – and the gruelling forced marches – are pushing us to the edge of insanity. Everything is frozen. If we want bread we must chop it into bits with a hacksaw and then put the pieces in our trouser pockets so that they can thaw out. To combat the lice

we make fires from forest brushwood and then take off our clothes and hold them over the smoke. What that feels like, in temperatures well below freezing, is hard to describe. Exhausted and miserable, we are advancing on Istra, the last Russian defence position before Moscow.

On the same day, artilleryman Gerhard Bopp witnessed the execution of a German deserter:

We have moved forward to Bolotovo past wrecked enemy tanks and heaps of Russian soldiers. The cold is growing worse. In the village are many of our dead – and one more grave will soon be added. An execution squad of nineteen men is about to shoot a German soldier for running away from his unit.

The man stands upright, his eyes downcast. The officer reads the judgement out. The divisional priest speaks a few words, and then both men step back. The officer gives the command: 'Fire!' and a volley of shots rings out. The soldier falls slowly backwards. The officer and priest move forward again, and as the man is apparently still alive the officer gives him the 'mercy shot' with his pistol. He is then buried in a hollow, without honour.

Bopp stood there, shocked, and then felt pity for the occupant of the nameless grave. After everyone had gone, he took a picture of it.

German troops around Leningrad with Army Group North were already in winter quarters. On 20 November one of these men – Hans Braukmann – experienced something remarkable. 'The area around our position was so churned up it sometimes felt as if we were crossing a large sandpit,' he began:

Yet on one journey, struggling through troughs of snow, a shot-up tank came into view, and then, behind it, one of the most astonishing vistas I had ever seen. I was reminded of a skilful depiction – in stucco – of a winter landscape. But this was far more astonishing.

On my left was a triangular shaped house, a ruin; in the centre – on a sloping rise – a misshapen tree. On the right were remnants of a burnt-down farmhouse, and behind them the northern lights shone, intensifying their outline. Everything glimmered, as if transcendent. I forgot the danger of whistling shells or enemy rifle fire. The scene was framed in a shade of luminous silver. Gazing at this winter picture, framed by the ruins, it seemed possible to rise up above the world and fly joyfully to the furthest star. Tragically, our human endeavours are moving in a very different direction.

On the same day one of Braukmann's fellow soldiers with Army Group North, Wolf Dose, described with clinical precision the collapse of a Russian prisoner of war, kept on minimal food rations in a work detail outside Leningrad:

Today I watched one of the prisoners, one of the hundreds that are dying here every day. He had been gathering wood, but was too weak and exhausted to throw it back into the bunker. He tripped and fell, and lay for a while in the frozen snow, at −20 degrees Celsius. He recovered somewhat. Perhaps he realised that he could get into the warm, by the stove, in the dugout. He lifted himself up. But the cold had a strange effect on him. He threw himself forward with such sudden vigour that he landed right on top of the stove. He just lay there, stunned, his skin burning away. Someone managed to pull him off and laid him on the ground. His head was resting on some of the wood he had gathered; his charred hand was soldered onto one of the pieces. He groaned quietly. His breathing was slow and uneven – for a long time he did not move.

However, the time came for the prisoners to return to the camp. Dose continued: 'Someone roughly pulled him up. Because of the shock of this sudden movement, he emptied the contents of his intestines into his trousers, which swelled up and burst. I saw his thin, distended abdomen covered in blood, excrement and remnants of clothing.' The Russian seemed no longer of this world. 'His eyes stared into empty space. His face had a strange blue-green hue. The other prisoners were forced to carry this man back to the camp in a greatcoat. Once there, one only hopes that a quick shot will bring his misery to an end.'

This was Dose's conclusion: 'There is a fact I always return to. In the Great War more than 200,000 German soldiers died in Siberian prisoner-of-war camps. Now a Russian has died, one of the many who are dying at our hands. So much blood has been spilled . . . Russia, a country full of cruelty, must be cruelly treated.'

Dose was housed in a warm bunker. The troops of Army Group Centre, however, were still advancing. 'They say that the campaign will end before the onset of real winter,' a soldier of the 31st Infantry Division wrote on 21 November, 'but I do not see much sign of this happening. It is best not to set one's hopes on miracles. Even if we capture Moscow, I doubt whether this will finish the war in the east. The Russians are capable of fighting to the very last man, the very last square metre of their vast country. Their stubbornness and resolve is quite astonishing. We are entering a war of attrition – and I only hope in the long run Germany can win it!'

Luftwaffe commander Wolfram von Richthofen felt the power of the attack waning. 'Our air activity is lessening,' he wrote, 'and everywhere objectives are being redefined, to save time and unnecessary losses.' But he had not given up hope. 'We are still moving forward,' he said. 'The Russians have brought up a substantial number of new divisions and armoured forces,' Colonel General Hoepner wrote on the same day. 'They are using prepared defence positions very well. The fight is getting bogged down in a series of local engagements . . . it cannot really be called a military operation any more. Frostbite is causing us as many losses as casualties fighting the enemy. We have to deplete our frontal strength, and guard our flanks against Russian tank attacks. My Panzer troops are doing all that is humanly possible.'

Stalin had signed a brutal new decree, demanding that a scorched-earth policy be put into effect to hinder the German advance. The Soviet leader's Order No 0428 stated that: 'All inhabited locations up to a distance of 40 kilometres from the German troops are to be destroyed and burnt to ashes. This objective is to be accomplished by the air force, artillery fire and reconnaissance teams armed with petrol bombs. Each military regiment is to have a team of volunteers to burn down or blow up inhabited locations. Those who excel themselves in such tasks are to be nominated for government awards.'

Colonel General Franz Halder, chief of staff of the German Army, remained optimistic. On 22 November he declared: 'Field Marshal von Bock has taken charge of the battle for Moscow from an advanced command post. With enormous energy he drives forward everything that can be brought to bear . . . The northern wing of Army Group Centre still has a chance of success, and the troops are being driven relentlessly to achieve it.' Army Group Centre's commander was fixated by the prospect of capturing Moscow. During the summer of 1941 Bock had repeatedly argued the case for an all-out assault on the Russian capital. The city now seemed within his grasp. At a staff meeting it was noted: 'Our commander expressed his hope that the enemy – in contrast to the earlier battles around Smolensk – now has insufficient forces at his disposal to maintain a successful defence. The new reinforcements from Siberia would quickly bleed away.' Bock, like Halder, saw the campaign as a question of will, and believed that the last battalion could still decide the issue. His own reservations – a fear that the attack was too thin, and was lacking in depth – were set aside in his fanaticism.

But this was a dangerous strategy. Bock's nickname was 'Der Sterber', 'the Grim Reaper', for throughout his career he had been fascinated by the idea of glorious death on the field of battle. In one speech he had even declared: 'The ideal soldier fulfils his duty to the utmost, obeys without even thinking, thinks only when ordered to do so and only desires to die an honourable death, killed in action.'

Bock pushed his men forward ruthlessly. *Time Magazine* wrote of his last offensive: 'In the winter of 1812 Napoleon retreated from Moscow, but in the winter of 1941 von Bock expects to take the city. Furiously determined, "Der Sterber" is disdainful of hardships. Bock looks like a man dying through some mysterious process of internal combustion. He is gaunt, and his eyes have the baleful stare of windows in a bombed-out house. A highly competent general, he believes with an aggressive religiosity in dying, if necessary, for the honour of the Fatherland.'

German soldiers listened to such declarations with dark, wry humour. Bock was aloof and distant, and struggled to build a rapport with the men under his command. Talk of an 'honourable death' or a 'heroic death' did not strike a happy chord with men short of supplies and struggling against the all-consuming cold. 'There was now a constant battle against the elements,' Peter Biewer recalled, 'and going outside to relieve oneself became quite an operation. It was necessary to run for the door, and then stamp out a circle in the frozen ground, so as not to sit with a bare behind in the snow. It was quite a victory to do one's business unhindered, for there was always the danger of being caught by a lurking Russian sniper, or a chance mortar explosion. We used to say – with our commander's stirring injunctions in mind – that to meet one's maker in such a fashion would indeed constitute a true "hero's death".'

The shortages in supplies were leading to widespread theft from the civilian population. On 22 November Nina Semonova wrote in her diary: 'Soldiers have taken our last remaining food: a pouch of grain and some potatoes. Mama complained to a German officer, and was told abruptly, "The German soldier never steals!" Outside in the yard, one of those she had reported struck her a sharp blow.' Three days later Semonova noted: 'The troops have now plundered our clothes store.'

General Hans-Georg Reinhardt's Third Panzer Group was still making progress. On 23 November German troops captured Klin, on the Moscow-Leningrad highway, and pushed on south towards Solnechnogorsk. Soviet Major General Rokossovsky once more had to pull his forces back and establish a last defence line, only 22 miles from Moscow. The Red Army was running out of space. But the fight for Klin – conducted by the Germans through costly frontal attacks rather than enveloping manoeuvres – had cost them serious losses in men and equipment.

On 24 November German Lieutenant Erich Mende said:

The terrible overcrowding of the prisoner-of-war camp at Vyazma has now been relieved by sending many of the prisoners westwards, towards Smolensk, in long marching columns. Moscow Radio had already – in numerous broadcasts – referred to the terrible conditions in this camp, and the International Red Cross had demanded the right to inspect it. Our high command seemed alarmed by this, and suddenly ordered the evacuation of most of the POWs, in conditions unworthy of human beings. To add to the misery of the remainder, the Russian Air Force mistakenly bombed the camp at night, after the prisoners lit fires in order to save themselves from freezing to death. Temperatures have now dropped to −20 degrees Celsius.

Nikolai Obryn'ba had been kept for weeks in a transit camp near Vyazma: 'We were not fed or given water, and the camp was open to the elements. The camp had been built on a potato field, and we survived on leftover scraps, which we dug out of the cold earth. Here for the first time, I saw young, healthy men dying of starvation.' One morning the prisoners gathered behind the barbed wire as tanks and vehicles rolled past. The Germans were advancing again. One of the troops called out cheerily in Russian: 'In two weeks we'll be in Moscow!' Obryn'ba looked up at him – and was utterly taken aback by what he saw. He wondered whether he was hallucinating through lack of food: 'The soldier was smiling and waving,' he remembered, 'but just for a split-second I saw him as a dead man – a corpse with no eyes.'

There had been a brief uplift in German spirits as Hoepner's tanks advanced in the first days of the resumed offensive, and some soldiers clung to this thinning strand of hope. But, as the advance slowed, more and more succumbed to growing pessimism. Lieutenant Kurt Grumann's 87th Infantry Division was suffering increasing casualties. 'Our men are dejected,' he wrote on 24 November. 'Fierce fighting is raging around us – and every day our strength diminishes. Two weeks ago there were 70 men in our company; now there are only 40. Some are already beginning to reckon when their turn will come.'

On the evening of 24 November Erich Mende's unit briefly halted at Vyazma to celebrate the birthday of their battalion commander. Casualties among the 8th Infantry Division had become so great that the majority of the men were returned to France, but Mende's 84th Infantry Regiment had been retained in Russia, and was now ordered forward to support the Moscow offensive. The large, yellow-painted stone house they had assembled in was nicknamed by the Russians 'Napoleon's House'. There was a legend that the French emperor had stayed there on his advance towards Moscow. But the mood of the Germans was sombre. Conversation was dominated by stories of the mistreatment of Russian prisoners, now being marched towards Smolensk. 'At least we are no longer responsible for what is happening,' one man said uneasily. His companions remained gloomy. 'We knew that Napoleon, after the battle of Borodino, fell prey to a series of misfortunes,' Mende related. 'Fires broke out in Moscow, and his army began to disintegrate around him. We had won a victory of our own, at Vyazma, and for a while we believed it a far greater success than Napoleon's. But now we wondered if we might suffer a similar fate.'

These Germans were struggling to reconcile their adherence to the values of the Nazi regime with their human response to the sight of so much suffering. Others, it appears, had shut off all emotional engagement and descended into barbarism. This was witnessed by Nikolai Obryn'ba and his fellow prisoners, now marching westwards: 'Our column stretched out, people walked clasping each other, trying to support the exhausted,' he remembered. 'Vehicles flashed by full of Germans, roaring with laughter and pointing their cameras at us. Near a river-crossing I thought I heard someone beating a mattress. It was a motionless prisoner, spread out on the ground. Two Germans were sitting on his legs and head, while a third battered his body.' The Russians were starving. Some threw themselves on the corpses of horses, trying to tear off chunks of frozen meat. Obryn'ba recalled a succession of images: 'Shreds of bodies scattered along a street, water-filled grave ditches, burnt-out huts and charred and scorched animals.'

'We are still pushing forward,' Colonel General Hoepner noted on 25 November. 'The Führer is apparently following my progress with particular interest. However my troops are suffering terrible hardships and are close to complete exhaustion.' Hoepner clung to his belief that the offensive might yet succeed, if his push towards Moscow was supported by the infantry of Field Marshal von Kluge's Fourth Army. Hoepner sought a coordinated final assault: 'We will need to play all the strings of our instrument to have a last chance of success,' he stated.

Difficulties were mounting on Army Group Centre's southern flank. 'We are only nearing our final objective step by step,' Colonel General Guderian noted, 'in icy cold and suffering from an appalling supply situation.' His soldiers felt the same way. 'In the last few days our losses have grown steadily,' artilleryman Josef Deck wrote. 'The Russians are counter-attacking incessantly. They want to win Yefremov back from us, because it has a large, well-equipped hospital which we captured mostly intact. And in that hospital, wards are filling up with the bodies of our soldiers. Because of the terrible cold we are losing people daily, in this war without leave, without proper rest, without winter clothing, that is taking its toll on all of us.' Yefremov was 180 miles south of Moscow. When German forces had captured the town on 22 November, 1,500 of their wounded had immediately been brought into the hospital there, with thousands more arriving over the next few days. Deck continued:

> Why our strength is being frittered away in this 'ice-hell', where our tanks and vehicles have to be warmed up by lighting fires underneath them and our radios are now constantly failing, no one can say. The Russian forces are becoming increasingly active. They are far better able to withstand the snow and ice. Their units have white snow covers, waterproof jackets and trousers and felt boots made of sheepskin. And they have special lubricating oil for their automatic weapons. They can adjust to these terrible nights, which begin in the afternoon at around 3.00 p.m. when the light begins to fail and only end the following morning at around 10.00 a.m.

Each night Nikolai Obryn'ba and his fellow prisoners marching westwards stopped in specially erected enclosures, fenced with barbed wire. Thousands of Russians, dying of cold and hunger, were abandoned along the route, many finished off with machine-gun fire. Obryn'ba remembered the grim morning ritual, enacted each day before the column moved off once more: 'Before each new march, guards with sticks lined up on both sides of the column and the command: "All run!" would be given. We ran – and blows rained down hard upon us. Then, after several hundred metres, we were ordered to stop and wait in the biting cold, while those too weak to reach this point were shot by the guards. The convoy then continued.'

Their German captors had descended into utter inhumanity. Meanwhile, Army Group Centre's progress slowly continued. 'Yesterday we took Istra,' radio operator Wilhelm Schröder of the 10th Panzer Division wrote on 27 November. 'My unit was the first into the town. We were greeted by an unpleasant amount of enemy artillery fire. We did not sleep much that night – the Russians counter-attacked stubbornly. Today things look different – the town is completely in our hands . . . What we all want to know is, what now? Will we continue to advance on Moscow?'

Istra was only 30 miles north-west of the Russian capital, but the second phase of the Moscow offensive had been launched with only two weeks of supplies. These were now running out, leaving German soldiers increasingly frustrated and angry. Hans Meier-Welcker recorded in his diary: 'Veterans of the fighting on the Eastern Front in World War One are saying that supplies were much better organised at that time. We are making a last push on Moscow, but we have not got enough food, ammunition or fuel.' The German high command attempted to reassure its soldiers by saying that things were far worse for the Red Army.

Lieutenant Erich Mende's 84th Infantry Regiment had left Vyazma and was marching east, to join the attack on Moscow. On its journey local people told the men more about 'Napoleon's House'. It was considered unlucky, and all those who stayed in it apparently suffered misfortune. One of the occupants, Lieutenant Schimmel, a supply officer, panicked at this news, and to the troops' considerable amusement insisted on being doused with holy water and having the sign of the cross made over him. The following day the laughter died away when the medical unit – who had also stayed in the house – were all killed in a Russian artillery strike. When Schimmel also died shortly afterwards the troops began to ask themselves: 'Coincidence, or curse?'

The idea that one is cursed – at a time when morale is fragile or on a knife-edge – has enormous power. Something the rational mind might ordinarily dismiss can take on a life of its own in conditions of such stress and hardship. The fear that Napoleon's curse had come to rest upon the German Army was rendered tangible by this disturbing incident.

The day of 27 November was a critical one for the German offensive. The 7th Panzer Division reached Yakhroma 37 miles north of Moscow, and seized the crossing over the Moscow-Volga Canal. Dmitry Vonlyarsky's 71st Marine Brigade, part of the First Shock Army of Soviet Colonel General Fyodor Kuznetsov, was flung against the German bridgehead, with orders to recapture it, whatever the cost in lives. But the brigade was under strength and poorly equipped. 'The fighting was awful,' Vonlyarsky said. 'We were given some old rifles and a few grenades – and then ordered into the attack, against well-fortified German machine-gun positions. There was hardly any artillery or air support. Unsurprisingly, we suffered enormous losses.'

It was rumoured that Kuznetsov's First Shock Army consisted of workers from Moscow's factories and recently released criminals from the city's jails. The men lacked proper uniforms and had practically no weapons. General Reinhardt of the Third Panzer Group reported to Bock that the defence of the Russian capital might be close to collapse. Hans-Georg Reinhardt was a tough, aggressive Panzer commander, who was determined to keep pushing forward. 'I was struck by his mental strength,' Wolfram von Richthofen wrote, 'and his single-minded concentration on the task at hand.' But Reinhardt had underestimated the resources and the resilience of the Soviet state. Stalin was ruthlessly buying time for Moscow's defence. Although the situation looked bleak for the Red Army, more reinforcements were on their way. Bock believed there was an opportunity to break through. He wanted to cross the Moscow-Volga Canal in strength and surmount the last major obstacle in front of the city. A push by Reinhardt would be coordinated with an attack from Hoepner's Fourth Panzer Group and the northern wing of Kluge's Fourth Infantry Army.

But time was running out for the Germans. Freshly equipped Siberian forces were arriving in Moscow. There were still not many of them, but their presence acted as a huge morale booster for the city's defenders. Georgi Osadchinsky's 35th Rifle Brigade briefly stopped in the Russian capital, and then marched north, along the Moscow-Leningrad highway. On 27 November the men could already hear sounds of fighting ahead of them: 'The horizon glowed red from the burning,' Osadchinsky recalled, 'and there was a heavy rolling sound in the distance, where the battle was taking place. We knew this was our last line of defence. The Germans had taken Solnechnogorsk, on the Moscow-Leningrad highway, and were pushing towards our outpost at Kryukovo. But the main weight of their thrust was further east, aiming to capture Krasnaya Polyana and Lobnya, and then break across the Moscow-Volga Canal. If they succeeded, the road to Moscow would be open.'

A group of civilians clustered around the soldiers. They had been queuing for bread for hours. A young girl approached Osadchinsky, her face blue with cold. She offered him a piece of her bread. Osadchinsky hesitated: he could not take food from a hungry child. But the girl was insistent: 'Take the bread, soldier.' She looked straight into Osadchinsky's eyes. 'Do not let the Germans into Moscow!'

The company swung forward, and the civilians moved out of their way. Osadchinsky gazed at the hellish light ahead of him. He wondered whether anyone could survive in that inferno: 'There, in the fire and smoke, our soldiers were dying. The German advance was inexorable.' Suddenly, Osadchinsky's company swung off the highway, marching north-east. They were heading towards Lobnya.

Russian aircraft were making their presence felt, frequently attacking German positions. 'Enemy fighters and bombers are increasingly active,' Private Graf Castell of the 5th Panzer Division wrote on 28 November, 'and they have quickly found where our tanks and armoured support vehicles are located, making low altitude flights over our lines with weapons blazing, regardless of the risk to their own planes.' Castell's unit was forced to move under cover, with tanks and vehicles camouflaged. More time was being lost.

Colonel General Hoepner formed units from Wilhelm Schröder's 10th Panzer Division into a spearhead, allowing these troops also to advance on Moscow from Istra to the north-west. But the Germans were desperately short of men. 'The assault continues – but in what conditions!' Schröder wrote on 29 November. 'The enemy's tanks are inflicting enormous losses. Many of our companies have fewer than ten men left – my own is down to one officer and seven men. And in the fierce cold, we are losing more and more of our comrades to frostbite.' Private Graf Castell tentatively removed his boots: 'I had worn them continuously for the last fourteen days of the offensive,' he noted. 'The socks were rotting. I rubbed my feet with snow, but worryingly there is very little feeling in them. I put some canvas shoes on – and put the boots on top of our vehicle's running engine to dry out. Our hobnailed boots are little use in such conditions.'

The attack on Moscow inched forward. 'My most advanced forces are now only 25 kilometres from the city,' Hoepner wrote on 29 November, 'but the Russians are bringing up fresh forces from all sides.' On the southern flank, Guderian's advance had also slowed. On 30 November Josef Deck watched the night sky. 'As far as the eye could see, the horizon was wreathed in flames. The Russians, using incendiaries, are creating a "dead zone" before us. Their engineers are following the precedent of Moscow in 1812.' As Guderian's offensive struggled forward, Panzer Lieutenant Wolfgang Paul wrote perceptively: 'The summer had carried us forwards. The autumn gripped us fast, with its tough, unyielding mud. Now the winter wished to expel us from the country altogether. We have blundered, mistakenly, into an alien landscape with which we can never be properly acquainted. Everything is cold, hostile and working against us.'

Late that November Paul's regiment – part of the 18th Panzer

Division – moved along the frozen motor highway with its assembly of German tanks, French trucks and captured Russian support vehicles. Thick snow lay on the ground, and as the column closed up, packs of wolves emerged from the surrounding forests and began to follow it. Ahead lay the Russian forces, still retreating, but now fighting with a desperate ferocity. 'For the first time in the campaign we began to fear them as soldiers,' Paul continued. 'Here was an enemy who could turn on us if given the opportunity. And our strength was dwindling. We have overreached ourselves. We are struggling with homesickness, malfunctioning equipment and the savage instincts which this cruel eastern campaign have awoken within us.'

One evening Paul and his fellow soldiers reached a village lying close to a river. They were exhausted, physically and mentally. That night they crossed the river, expelled the Russian defenders on the other side, laid out mines and set up firing points. They snatched some sleep in one of the huts. The following morning the wind changed direction. Paul and his fellow soldiers heard the sound of gunfire, still distant, but moving closer. They guessed that fresh Russian forces were approaching, intent on recapturing their position. Paul and his fighters explored the small village and on its far edge they found some outlying houses still held by the Russians. With a counter-attack imminent, these had to be cleared without delay and Paul and his men worked fast. They surrounded the huts, tossed inflammables onto the straw roofs and set them alight. The last house would not burn. It would have to be stormed in hand-to-hand fighting. Paul and his men crept forward in the snow. Fifteen metres from the house they stopped and waited. The men gripped their hand grenades. Then, in the lull, Paul experienced a sudden sense of the alien land around him.

He was a brave soldier, who had taken part in many hand-to-hand fights with the enemy and received medals for his courage. 'I possessed an instinct for survival in dangerous action,' he said frankly, 'where life and death always hang by a thread. But I could not find any understanding of this brutal war. The landscape in which our men lived and died – where death came quickly and often – remained a mystery to me. I never could remember the names of any features of its terrain, although I tried, again and again. The Russian words simply would not stay in my mind. Perhaps, on some level, I drew back from any real engagement with Russia. But in this brief interlude, I felt a deep sense of the land around me.'

Paul returned to the task in hand. He gave the signal to move forward, jumped up – feeling the snow falling from his coat – and ran towards the house, unpinning his hand grenade. His men followed. Paul flung the grenade towards the door, ready to charge in after it. But at that very same moment, the door swung outwards. There stood a Russian soldier, who in the same second had also unpinned his hand grenade and thrown it.

Momentarily, time seemed to stand still. 'We faced each other,' Paul remembered, 'with two live grenades already flying through the air. And in that moment I saw his fur cap, then his face – a pale, unshaven face, frostbitten, very much like my own – a damp, runny nose, ears partially covered by his cap, and trickles of saliva running from his mouth. He had just been eating something. And I saw the rage in his face, the sheer hatred.'

Paul's instinctive reaction was to dive for the ground. He overrode it: 'I kept looking into the man's face. And as I held my gaze, I no longer saw an enemy soldier in front of me. I was looking into the face of another human being – a human being as certain to die as I was.' Paul was transfixed. 'I did not throw myself into the snow nor jump to one side. I stood absolutely still. And in that moment – that seemed to last an eternity – I saw how the Russian was also looking at me, as if he too had become dislocated from his surroundings and discovered another world. I saw how he bent his head forwards, as if he wanted to greet me. Then a grey cloud began to rise around his feet.'

Paul felt the searing pain of grenade fragments ripping into his body. Yet the grenade itself had missed him. His Russian opponent began to fall. 'He toppled like a tree, faster and faster, hitting the ground with terrible force.'

Guderian's forces were still able to gain local successes against the enemy. 'We have put three days of tough combat behind us,' wrote General Gotthard Heinrici of the 43rd Army Corps on 29 November:

> We have broken a cornerstone of the Russian defensive positions south of Aleksin, and are moving towards Moscow again. The first day saw extremely hard fighting. In the middle of one clash, when the outcome still lay in the balance, our aerial reconnaissance warned us of the approach of a Russian column 15 kilometres long, which was moving towards our flanks. Our depleted regiments were only able to withstand this onslaught, after forming up a protective screen at the edge of the forest, with the utmost difficulty. We temporarily halted our own action and were prepared to pull back – then fresh reports reached us that our lines were holding. We renewed our attack and broke through. Now the whole Russian front around Tula is in jeopardy.

The situation hung on the edge of a knife. Heinrici was increasingly aware of the risk in continuing the offensive. 'The Russians are fighting with unbelievable ferocity,' he continued:

> Their artillery causes us heavy losses, as do their mines, which lie in rings around their positions. I have one of their new devices in front of me now: it is a small wooden box, about 20 cm long and 5 cm high, which can easily be hidden under the snow. They are inflicting many casualties. And our infantry had again to lie for hours in the snow, without adequate protective clothing, under hostile enemy fire, on ground frozen up to a metre deep. Some of our soldiers were stuck in a snow-covered field for over 10 hours without being able to move. Three of these men actually froze to death.

Field Marshal von Bock began to realise that Guderian's forces could no longer reach Moscow from the south. He concentrated his efforts to the north and west of the city. On 29 November he ordered the 7th Panzer Division to abandon the bridgehead at Yakhroma, 37 miles north of the Russian capital, where fighting had intensified, and instead began to move his forces towards the small town of Krasnaya Polyana, further west. Bock wanted to get his Panzers across the Moscow-Volga Canal at this point – only 20 miles from Moscow. As German tanks advanced on the capital, he planned to send in Kluge's Fourth Army in support. He hoped this would at last break the Russian defenders.

Horst Lange's 56th Infantry Division was struggling through a seemingly endless forest. The troops were to support this last attack, and cross the Moscow-Volga Canal at Krasnaya Polyana. They were marching as fast as possible, only being allowed short breaks. 'We are being pushed to our very limits,' Lange wrote. 'Our remaining transport vehicles are stuck fast in the deep snow. We are not handing our Russian prisoners over to the collection points any more; we are keeping them with us to help carry the supplies. The forest is swathed in white. We find a solitary house, where we can halt for a few hours.' Lange felt the urgency of the war suddenly recede:

> An old man came to greet us. He lived all alone in this vast forest. It was like something out of a fairy tale. We sat with him, a single oil lamp illuminating the darkness. But we had an interpreter – and we were curious about him. Others had fled, but he did not want to leave his house. And as we listened to his story, the old man wandered about the room, growing increasingly animated. He spoke to us about Russia in Tsarist times, about life, luck and fate, and showed us pictures of his wife and daughter. As he talked, I felt a remarkable sense of peace and continuity, of life outside this war.

The following morning the troops resumed their march. 'The enemy artillery is opening up,' Lange continued. 'We are getting closer to the front. We pass Russian emplacements, bunkers, tank traps, and see the bodies of their soldiers – their grey complexions, with a greenish hue, are encrusted in dark red blood. The corpses have been plundered by our soldiers and are without trousers or boots. Signs of battle are everywhere: charred ruins, broken remnants of weapons and scattered shell fragments.' It began to snow again. 'We are seeing more and more horrendous things, glimpsing terrible images,' Lange said. 'Truly, we are entering the underworld.'

Later that evening the German soldiers finally reached their 'quarters', crossing a river and entering a nameless little town, heavily damaged by the war. The streets were icy, and men and horses slipped and fell in the darkness. Some collapsed in sheer exhaustion. More and more troops appeared, searching for accommodation: 'In the cold and darkness one sensed a growing fury,' Lange wrote. 'There was a lot of shoving and jostling, a clamour of angry, loud voices. Hunger, cold and fatigue welled up. Our army appeared on the brink of mutiny – barely retaining its former discipline and purpose.' The troops crammed into buildings and then turned on their radio sets. There was a sudden silence, and then a musical refrain could be heard. An ice-cold wind was blowing outside – but the men's thoughts were elsewhere. It was 9.57 p.m. 'All of us were listening to the radio – a German song on the radio.' It was Lale Andersen, singing 'Lili Marleen'. Infantryman Heinrich Rotard recalled:

> At the end of November 1941, in temporary shelters and dugouts shrouded in snow, our soldiers heard on the radio for the first time the song, 'Lili Marleen'. The news spread like wildfire. We tuned into the German service on Radio Belgrade, where the song was played every evening just before 10.00 p.m. And as we listened to Lale Andersen's refrain, for a brief moment we were taken away from the bitter fighting, the cold – and the death that was all around us.

'We first heard that song on the approaches to Moscow,' German officer Josef Bailer added. 'Everyone was talking about it. "You must hear it!" someone said to me. So we tuned our radio transmitter to Radio Belgrade, and listened – completely captivated.'

The song had a chequered history. It was originally written as a poem to a lost lover by a German infantryman in the First World War, but only published, many years later, in 1937. Its imagery and emotion caught the attention of Norbert Schultze, a musical composer for Nazi propaganda films, but its debut was hardly auspicious: at first, vocalist Lale Andersen didn't want to sing it, and when she did, propaganda minister Joseph Goebbels vetoed the song, believing it was far too melancholy. Then, in August 1941, an employee of the German military radio station at Belgrade discovered it among a crate of old records and began playing it. German soldiers loved it, and soon it was being transmitted every evening, just before the programme came off the air at 10.00 p.m.

In 'Lili Marleen', a soldier recalls meeting his lover under a lantern, by the barracks gate. The song is melancholy, with a military beat, a little like a march, lying beneath its romantic lyrics. Later, on campaign, the soldier thinks back to their fleeting love and wonders who might take his place, should he never return. The last verse runs:

> *From my quiet existence, from this earthly pale,*
> *Like a dream you free me, with your lips so hale,*
> *When the night mists swirl and churn*
> *Then to that lantern I'll return*
> *As once Lili Marleen*
> *As once Lili Marleen.*

'A dance of death lingers between its bars,' Goebbels had complained. On the approaches to Moscow, it was this 'dance of death' that gave the song such haunting power.

On the night of 30 November, Lange and his fellow soldiers stepped outside their makeshift accommodation and looked up at the sky. 'We knew we were very close to the front,' Lange recounted. 'Tomorrow we would reach the motor highway at Solnechnogorsk and soon we would be fighting at the Moscow-Volga Canal. Hungry, tired and cold, with aching feet, it seemed there was no end to our suffering. Yet as we stood there, star after star came out, lighting up the heavens. We stayed, transfixed. As the stars shone, high above us, they cast a most wonderful light.' Platoon commander Robert Rupp could not sleep that night. 'I think about death often,' he wrote. 'The most important thing is to face it without fear.'

Georgi Osadchinsky's 35th Rifle Brigade was digging in between Lobnya and the village of Kiovo, 18 miles north of Moscow. 'We had laid out mines around our positions,' he recalled, 'as mortar salvoes thudded around us. The Germans were only a few kilometres away, at the village of Ozeretskoye, where the 2nd Moscow Rifle Division was engaged in fierce fighting. The flames and smoke were clearly visible in the night sky. The division was suffering heavy losses, and was unlikely to withstand the Germans much longer.' Osadchinsky knew the crucial moment had come. 'We no longer had a continuous line of defence, only isolated strong points. The enemy was pushing forward with advance units of the 2nd Panzer Division and 106th Infantry Division.' If the Germans broke through between Lobnya and Kiovo they would reach the Moscow-Volga Canal, and the city would be at their mercy.

This push forward drew upon the last reserves of German strength. Under their last attack, the Russians were hurrying to bring up reinforcements. Osadchinsky complained to his commander, Lieutenant Vorodeyev: 'Why have we dug in here, where we cannot support the Moscow Rifle Division?' 'We are dug in here, where we are ordered to be,' came the irritable reply. Then Vorodeyev relented. He looked at Osadchinsky, and explained: 'The Germans will break through tonight – and if we join the Moscow Rifle Division, we will be unable to stop their tanks and armoured support vehicles. We do not have enough artillery, and the ground is low-lying – the enemy will simply manoeuvre around our positions and overrun us.' Vorodeyev paused. 'And we have to hold them, until fresh reinforcements arrive. There are no other regular units in place to stop the Germans. If we fail, they get into Moscow.'

The final defence position had been chosen carefully. A high railway embankment prevented the Germans from using their tanks to outflank the defenders. Their armour would be funnelled towards fortified points at Lobnya Station and the outskirts of the village of Kiovo. These approaches had been heavily mined and were covered by anti-tank batteries. 'The Moscow Rifle Division is fighting to the death,' Vorodeyev concluded. 'We will make our own stand here. The enemy must not pass.'

Early on the morning of 1 December the Germans broke through the remnants of the Soviet Kalinin Front. Their tanks were now on the motor highway. They quickly captured Krasnaya Polyana and brought up their artillery units. They were now in range of Moscow. Bock instructed Kluge's Fourth Army to attack from the west, and ordered his Panzers across the Moscow–Volga Canal and into the city. Georgi Osadchinsky and his fellow Red Army soldiers stood in their way. The men waited in their dugouts and trenches. At noon German tanks appeared outside Lobnya Station. The crisis point had come.

4

The Tipping Point

'I T IS THE beginning of December 1941,' Panzer Lieutenant
Gustav Schrodek wrote in his diary. 'We are so close to
Moscow. The Russian capital is in our sights. Will we reach it?'
Schrodek's 11th Panzer Division – part of General Reinhardt's
Third Panzer Group – was moving along the Moscow-Volga
Canal, on the northern outskirts of the city. The Panzer troops
were approaching Moscow's suburbs. 'We are unbelievably close,'
Schrodek repeated. 'I saw a sign saying "Moscow – 18 kilo-
metres". The capital is so near we can almost touch it.'

German soldiers felt that the capital was within their grasp. 'We
are now only a stone's throw from Moscow's suburbs,' Private
Gerhard vom Bruch wrote on 1 December. 'We are passing
the outermost stops of the city's bus service. We know we have
reached a critical moment. Either the Russian is genuinely at the
end of his strength, and we will defeat him, or our advance will
peter out.' However, Bruch's 6th Panzer Division scarcely resembled a tank formation any more. 'Apart from one or two assault
guns, we have no more armour piercing weapons,' Bruch continued. 'We are all becoming infantry.' The few remaining vehicles
were unable to make further progress, for the Russians had blown
up the road ahead of them. 'It will take considerable repair work
to bridge it,' Bruch said uneasily.

The Russian capital was now within firing range of German
heavy artillery. 'One of our batteries was less than 20 kilometres
from Moscow,' said Lieutenant Walther Schaefer-Kehnert of the
11th Panzer Division. 'It meant that we could shoot right into the
city. This really lifted our spirits. We were like little boys, yelling

to each other, "We're firing at the Kremlin!" Our gun crews took turns, firing continuously, and the barrel's recoil mechanism became so hot that the paint melted.' On the morning of 1 December, Karl-Gottfried Vierkorn of the 23rd Infantry Division believed that he had even caught sight of the Kremlin. 'I remember looking through the field telescope,' Vierkorn said. 'The night had been clear, and at sunrise I could see the suburbs of Moscow, and beyond them, what seemed to be the golden towers of the Kremlin, gleaming in the sunlight.' Whether Vierkorn had actually seen the Kremlin or not, the sense that it was so close deeply moved German soldiers. 'It galvanised our troops,' said Ekkehard Maurer, an officer in the same division. 'Some felt a fresh surge of optimism – they still hoped to be in the city in a matter of days.'

When Heinrich Haape and his fellow soldiers from the German 6th Infantry Division drove along the Moscow-Leningrad highway on 1 December, the men joked about sightseeing in Red Square. Haape recalled the snow falling quite heavily as they left the town of Klin, and headed south, to the most advanced German positions. 'The sky was leaden, and visibility was limited,' he wrote. 'Everything seemed oddly quiet. It was as if the air was filled with a strange music, almost inaudible – but full of expectation.'

They drove on, past hoardings bearing images of Stalin and Lenin. Many of the buildings along their route were burnt-out shells, and most of the civilian population had fled. Haape's division followed the tracks left by two German heavy lorries, and occasional Wehrmacht sign boards showed they were still on the right road. A regimental command post came into view. They had reached the German front-line position, and they stopped and chatted with the soldiers there. 'Moscow is so near,' one said. 'One more push and we will be there – and it will all be over. Surely we can't be denied it now!' Opposite lay a Moscow tram station, and Haape and a comrade walked over to it. 'There was a deathly silence,' Haape remembered:

In front of us was the tramway shelter, and telegraph poles, pointing all the way to the great city beyond the curtain of snow. There was no movement around us as we stopped, and stared at the wooden seats. I saw a bin attached to the wall, felt inside and dragged out a handful of tickets. The Cyrillic letters spelled out 'Moskva'. On the spur of the moment, I took them as a keepsake. Then we trudged back to our vehicle. My comrade broke the silence, speaking for both of us: 'The city must fall, yet . . . I wonder . . .' We reversed the car, and headed back along the motor highway. The snow was falling a little more heavily now.

Early on the morning of 1 December a German motorcycle patrol drove all the way to the train station of Khimki, only 11 miles from the Russian capital. A gap had opened in Moscow's defences, and for a few brief hours this route to the city lay open to the Germans. But there were no longer troops in place to exploit this opportunity.

Now that he was committed to Operation Typhoon, Hitler was struck by the fact that Stalin had held the traditional 7 November parade on Red Square, and had used it as a rallying point against the German invader. With this in mind, in a speech to the Nazi Party faithful at Munich a day later, on 8 November, Hitler had spoken of the enormous value of a rapid capture of Moscow. He believed it would reassure German public opinion and demonstrate once again the might of the Wehrmacht. The Führer even speculated that the news might induce Britain to negotiate for peace, ending the war on two fronts. He therefore became increasingly attracted to the propaganda value of a victory parade in the Russian capital.

On 30 November, Field Marshal von Bock made his preparations for a last-ditch assault on Moscow. His forces were growing weaker every day, his supply lines were overextended and the Red Army was fighting with fierce determination, but Hitler now ordered the Russian capital seized as quickly as possible. As Bock moved up to General Reinhardt's forward units to supervise the offensive, he received a call from Field Marshal Walther von Brauchitsch, head of the German Army. It was a difficult conversation. Brauchitsch said that Hitler wished to know when the capture of Moscow could be announced to the German public. Bock, taken aback by this, retorted that his forces were at full stretch and the enemy was bringing up fresh reinforcements. The attack was going ahead, but he was unable to guarantee the outcome. It was a supreme irony that as the power of the German offensive waned, Hitler's determination to capture Moscow waxed ever stronger.

Brauchitsch mistakenly thought that some German troops were already in Moscow. This was news to Bock. 'There have been some local breakthroughs,' he responded testily, 'but nothing on a large scale.' Undismayed, Brauchitsch then announced: 'The Führer is convinced that the Russians are on the verge of collapse. He needs a commitment from you as to when this collapse will become a reality.' Bock's protestations were brushed aside, as Brauchitsch repeated: 'The Führer wants to know when Moscow will fall.'

Bock was struggling with his own inner demons. In moments of reflection, he increasingly doubted whether he could force the issue. 'I am attempting to continue the offensive, in the face of fresh dangers and with totally exhausted troops,' he wrote. 'From a tactical point of view, only a frontal assault is possible . . . It will gain some ground, but at bloody cost. It will destroy some of the enemy but it will not be decisive.' 'Despite the difficult situation,' he concluded, 'I have not given up hope. There remains a possibility of capturing the city of Moscow. The last battalion will decide the issue!'

Conflicts now openly erupted between German generals conducting the attack. Colonel General Hoepner was impatient for Field Marshal von Kluge's Fourth Army to join the offensive, to take pressure off his own advancing Panzers, but Kluge was cautious about committing his forces. Hoepner found Kluge's response arrogant and dismissive. 'It is a matter of principle with him,' he wrote bluntly, 'that he has to tell you how to do everything.' Personal differences had been put aside in the days of the German advance; they inevitably resurfaced when the campaign reached its climax. 'I am having daily telephone conversations with Kluge,' Hoepner wrote at the end of November, 'and am trying to encourage him to start his own attack. My Panzer forces are left on their own here.' Kluge's offensive finally began on the morning of 1 December. Hoepner felt it should have started sooner, and with more troops. 'It was vital,' he continued, 'that after I pushed forward, Kluge attacked immediately, diverting Russian divisions that were blocking my path. But he has only just launched his offensive, and with a strength inadequate for the task.' Kluge, however, had scraped together everything that he had.

'We have launched this attack largely with infantry regiments,' Hellmuth Stieff wrote, 'and can give them little tank protection':

> Our high command has urged us forward with an almost unreal sense of optimism. I instinctively feel this cannot work. We have assembled everyone we can find, even bringing up security detachments and putting them in the front line. These men are unused to intense combat, and when their commanders were killed in the first hour of the offensive, the rest refused to continue. They have been driven forward only because our artillery units threatened to open fire on them.

The day before the offensive, volunteer reinforcements arrived from France – Nazi sympathisers, formed into a unit known as the French Legion. Kluge addressed these men on the field of Borodino, recalling how French and German soldiers had fought side by side in Napoleon's *Grande Armée*. Unsurprisingly, it was not a happy invocation. The French volunteer unit disintegrated in the fighting of 1 December and had to be withdrawn from combat.

Only one of Kluge's divisions achieved a breakthrough that day; some of the soldiers of the 258th Division fought their way through Russian defences and reached the motor highway to Moscow. Again, there were hopes that this might provoke a Russian collapse. 'Kluge has won a substantial success and is now moving towards the capital,' General Heinrici wrote. But there were so few German troops left. On receiving news of Kluge's breakthrough, placards sprang up in German-occupied Kalinin, declaring: 'Our flags are unfurled in victory! Moscow – the headquarters of the Bolsheviks' worldwide criminal regime – has been captured. To celebrate this, a firework display will be held in the open space by the railway station. It begins at 7.00 p.m.' No festivities took place.

Kluge had begun his assault on the Russian capital with Armand de Caulaincourt's history of the 1812 campaign by his side. 'General de Caulaincourt's memoirs could always be found on Field Marshal von Kluge's desk,' his chief of staff Günther Blumentritt recalled. 'It had become our bible. We constantly thought of Napoleon's fate. The ghosts of the *Grande Armée* began to haunt our dreams.' Meanwhile Colonel General Hoepner wrote, 'Napoleon's plight is foremost in our minds. Once again, I am reading Caulaincourt's book. We think of him often.'

On the road to Smolensk, Red Army prisoner Nikolai Obryn'ba stumbled across rather different reading matter. 'Suddenly, lying in the slush, I saw books,' Obryn'ba recalled. 'We were trudging past a village library that had been torched. There was a book by Stendhal, with a gilded cover, and then a copy of *War and Peace*, lying in the snow. It was my dream, before the war, to buy *War and Peace* and now here was a copy, in its leather binding, lying in the road. Every gram in my backpack felt like a kilogram, and I had been ditching everything I could – but I could not step over this book. I picked it up, and quickly stuffed it into my pack.' But Nikolai Obryn'ba did not get the chance to read Tolstoy's master-piece. As the column of prisoners halted in the snow on a bitterly cold night, Obryn'ba and three other shivering Russians burnt the book, page by page. The small amount of heat generated by their makeshift fire helped to keep the men alive.

Remarkably, in the midst of such conflagration, other works by the great Russian novelist were preserved. On the southern flank of the German advance, Colonel General Guderian had set up a command post in Tolstoy's house in Yasnaya Polyana, four miles south of Tula. Tolstoy's books and manuscripts were gathered together and locked in a room for protection. Guderian visited Tolstoy's grave, in the grounds of the estate, and the Panzer gen-eral then sent a memorandum to Hitler, asking that the property be preserved intact. The Führer unexpectedly agreed. Although he had shown no previous interest in Russia's cultural heritage, and had presided over the destruction of much of the country, he made an exception for the writer who had brought Napoleon's 1812 campaign so vividly to life. Hitler decreed that the Tolstoy estate should be kept as a 'national treasure'.

As the Germans made one last effort, the Soviet regime was feeling the strain. On 30 November Stalin complained to General Zhukov that Hoepner's Panzer Group had taken the town of Dedovsk, 20 miles north-west of Moscow, and demanded it be recaptured immediately. A puzzled Zhukov found that Dedovsk remained in Russian hands; the Soviet leader had apparently confused it with the tiny village of Dedovo. When informed of this mistake, Stalin exploded. 'Get the place back, wherever it is!' he demanded. Zhukov was instructed to bring with him Major General Konstantin Rokossovsky, commander of the Soviet Sixteenth Army, and General Leonid Govorov, commander of the Fifth Army. At a crucial moment in the battle for Moscow, this high-powered delegation turned up at Dedovo – an insignificant country hamlet. A bemused Russian divisional commander was summoned. He reported that the Germans had captured two houses on the far side of a ravine, but there seemed little tactical point in driving them out again. Zhukov accepted this, then declared that an attack had to be mounted on the express orders of Stalin. A rifle company and two tanks were duly despatched to wrest the houses back from the enemy, after which the Soviet generals returned to more important duties.

A day later, after the Germans had captured Krasnaya Polyana, a furious and abusive Zhukov rounded on Major General Rokossovsky and threatened to have him shot for allowing his soldiers to pull back. But Stalin, who had now gathered himself, was unflustered; he phoned the shaken Rokossovsky, offered his personal support and promised reinforcements. The same day Stalin released to Zhukov two reserve armies that had been held back, in case of an emergency. They would be used to plug the gaps in the front.

The Germans struggled on. Between Kluge's forces, pushing across the Nara river, less than 40 miles west of Moscow, and

Twenty-year-old radio operator Leopold Höglinger kept a diary and photographic record of the German advance to Moscow – and the terrible retreat that followed

Confident German troops march through a Russian village, summer 1941

The Wehrmacht rolls east

Victory at Smolensk: Field Marshal Günther von Kluge visits the
German 137th Infantry Division, 28 July 1941

Operation Typhoon commences: German troops occupy a Russian village,
early October 1941

Russian prisoners of war at the end of the Vyazma battle: hundreds of thousands
went into captivity, few survived the winter

Bewildered troops see the Wehrmacht's advance engulfed in mud

A German truck struggles through sludge, late October 1941

The advance on Moscow resumes in mud and snow – November 1941

The retreat begins – in winter snowstorms at minus 35 degrees Celsius

A day in hell: Höglinger's diary entry for 13 December: 'It is insanely cold . . . We begin to drive, lose our way, get stuck in the snow . . . We stand by our radio truck, freezing to death'

The radio truck is destroyed: Höglinger and his comrades watch forlornly

The replacement – a sledge convoy

The Wehrmacht becomes a 'Napoleonic Army'

A return to the horse-drawn era

Desperate Germans plunder boots from dead Russian soldiers

The mounting cost: Wehrmacht troops bury a comrade
in the frozen ground

'Scorched earth': German troops burn down a Russian village.
A civilian stands by with a few hastily recovered possessions

Reinhardt's, closing on the capital's northern suburbs, Hoepner's Fourth Panzer Group wearily fought for a succession of fortified villages. 'An icy east wind swept through the valley and over the hills,' recalled Lieutenant Ernst Streng, platoon leader in the SS *Das Reich* Division. 'Visibility was poor. Wooden poles marked the snow-covered route. Our columns spread out, motorcycle riders continually getting stuck in the heaped snowdrifts. An icy wind drifted over the tracks where we had passed only moments before. Men were wrapped in blankets, tarpaulins and whatever else was at hand.'

Streng noticed how much his soldiers had changed over the last month: 'They are emaciated by the constant strain, the physical and emotional exhaustion. Their faces are gaunt, unshaven for weeks, with dark shadows under the eyes and with a bitter turn to the mouth.' Their advance was being contested by the Siberian 78th Rifle Division. 'The resistance of these Soviet soldiers shows a stubbornness and fanaticism we have rarely experienced before,' Streng said. 'They dig themselves into circular foxholes that we can only work round with heavy losses. They throw their hand grenades, fire from holes in the ground and then duck back beneath their earthen shelters.' The war diary of Streng's Panzer Corps recorded: 'The Siberian 78th Rifle Division is the toughest opponent we have yet met in the eastern campaign. It is well-armed and equipped – and every man is fighting to the death.'

One particularly disturbing incident lodged in Streng's mind. His unit had unsuccessfully attacked a Russian position, and were regrouping for a fresh assault. One of the German wounded began crawling back towards his fellows, through the snow. Then he became disorientated, and veered off towards the Russians. Streng and his comrades watched his progress helplessly: 'He was now creeping directly towards the enemy,' Streng recalled, 'leaving a long trail of blood behind him. Metre by metre he laboriously struggled onwards, using his elbows for leverage and dragging his limp body behind him. I jumped up and down, waved to him, tried to divert him. He heard me shout, lifted his head up and I could clearly see through my binoculars how his face lit up. But he failed to understand my warning. Instead, with renewed will-power, he crawled on towards the Russian trenches.'

All the Germans were staring at the wounded man, transfixed. 'More and more of us leapt up, regardless of the danger of being shot at,' Streng continued. 'But the more we yelled and waved, the faster he crawled in the wrong direction. He was only 15 metres from the Russians, then 10 – and then we heard a shot ring out. His elbows buckled, and he slowly sank into the snow.'

On SS *Das Reich* Division's flank, the forward units of the 10th Panzer Division were pushing ahead. 'At the beginning of December, with our strength alarmingly depleted, we found our-selves on our own,' Wilhelm Schröder recalled. 'We no longer had any support to the left or right of us.' Schröder remembered an encounter that strangely mirrored Streng's experience:

I was moving along a forest track when I came across a wounded Russian soldier – a Siberian by the look of him – crawling with agonising slowness along the snow-covered path, on all fours. With horror I realised that the top part of his cranium was entirely miss-ing – a fragment from an exploding shell must have torn it off. His condition was hopeless, and yet he was still determinedly trying to reach his comrades. As I watched his laborious progress, I was struck by the incredible way Russians are able to endure suffering, and what strong will can achieve. On the approaches to Moscow, this was what confronted us.

North-east of Hoepner's struggling forces, Reinhardt's Third Panzer Group was also running out of strength. On the after-noon of 1 December Georgi Osadchinsky's 35th Rifle Brigade waited for the advancing Germans at Lobnya. 'Just after midday heavy artillery and mortar fire rained down on our position,' Osadchinsky recalled. 'Then the enemy appeared. German tanks and armoured support vehicles rumbled towards us, followed by their infantry. But there were not very many of them. They were shooting, pausing, and then shooting again. Then our own mor-tars opened up. We hit one armoured car, putting it out of action – the others kept advancing.'

Osadchinsky and his fellow infantrymen waited for the order to fire. The enemy grew closer. 'I had a German soldier in my sights, and my index finger was flexing and relaxing on the trigger. I took some deep breaths to calm myself, clouds of frost air rising out of my mouth. Then, with the enemy about 100 metres away, the command was given. We opened up with small arms fire, targeting the infantry.' The German tanks began to fire back, but there was little room for them to manoeuvre. Unable to get around the railway embankment, their vehicles were caught in an intense bombardment. More were hit and others started reversing away from the Russian defences. Osadchinsky saw a German soldier on all fours, floundering in the snow, and others crawling away. And then the enemy was gone, leaving his dead and wounded behind him. 'Relief and happiness swept through our ranks,' Osadchinsky said. 'The Germans did not seem so terrible now – they could be beaten.'

That night Osadchinsky and several companions secretly made their way to Krasnaya Polyana to observe the German positions. 'The enemy were burning fires and letting off flares – and periodically raking the approaches with machine-gun fire.' Osadchinsky and his comrades saw German tanks, armoured cars and motor vehicles. Six large guns, installed in the gardens of some of the outlying houses, were firing in the direction of Moscow. 'The Germans are gathering everything they can find,' Osadchinsky concluded. 'They still want to resume their offensive.'

The Germans were indeed pushing up every available unit. 'More strenuous marching in the direction of the front,' Horst Lange wrote on 2 December. 'In the distance, flak is going off. We can see the signs of recent fighting – dead Russian soldiers, lying where they fell. The blood appears to be fresh. We have reached the Moscow-Leningrad highway and see that Russian planes have shot up many of our vehicles.' Most Russians were now fighting strongly, but a few still believed the Germans would capture Moscow, and saw their cause as hopeless. Lange recorded an extraordinary interlude. On the afternoon of 2 December, with the fate of Moscow still in the balance, his unit captured some Red Army soldiers, who were hiding in a worker's house. They had deserted from their units. That evening the men were quartered in a glass factory, in the suburbs of Solnechnogorsk. It was freezing cold.

As the German soldiers huddled together, trying to get warm, they put their Russian prisoners under light guard and allowed them into the same room, where there was a little heat. From this small gesture of kindness an astonishing camaraderie developed. 'A Russian lieutenant is singing and playing a balalaika,' Lange recorded. 'Others are bringing out their pocket books – and showing us extracts from Russian novels and poetry. We are chatting through our interpreter.' Suddenly, Lange found himself casting old prejudices aside. 'To my surprise, I keenly felt their love of literature, of culture,' he said. 'Previously, I had given the Bolsheviks little credit for this, judging that they had renounced the treasures of their past. But now we read Pushkin together, and as I quoted from memory passages in German, they responded in the Russian. A wonderful sense of connection developed. We shared perceptions about life and love. I told them that I was a writer, and had written books. They asked me my name. And then one of them looked at me, his face suddenly serious. "What will you write about this war?" he asked.'

On the evening of 2 December the balance finally tipped away from the Germans. Moscow's northern defences had been stabilised, and fresh Red Army reinforcements now opposed the Wehrmacht's advance. 'Suddenly thousands of new troops arrived,' recalled Soviet soldier Dmitry Vonlyarsky of the 71st Marine Brigade, 'along with plentiful supplies and winter equipment. Our strength was totally replenished.'

The Germans were exhausted. Colonel Adolf Raegener's 9th Infantry Regiment (part of the 23rd Division) had come to a halt at the village of Spas-Kamenka, just west of the Moscow-Dmitrov highway. The Russian capital was only 20 miles away. They had won the position after a day of non-stop fighting, but there was no longer the strength or the will to continue. 'Two of my battalions have refused to advance any further,' Raegener wrote. 'The losses in officers and men have simply become too high – and there is hardly any ammunition left.'

As the day progressed, German artilleryman Gerhard Bopp noticed a dramatic increase in enemy air activity: 'A Russian fighter swooped low over our position, firing wildly. Others followed. We ran for cover.' Gustav Schrodek's Panzer tank also had a narrow escape: 'Our driver saw an emerging Russian T-34 just in time,' he said. 'He quickly reversed, and the shell whistled past us. But to the right of us there was an explosion. Another of our tanks received a direct hit in front of the turret. I saw the commander and driver struggling out of the vehicle. We are losing more and more of our soldiers.' Schrodek was increasingly depressed by the difficulties he faced burying dead comrades: 'The ground is frozen as hard as stone, and pickaxes and spades make no impression on it. Only by using hand grenades and explosives can we create a small, flat hollow for a grave.'

Late on 2 December, Schrodek and his unit from the 11th Panzer Division suddenly lost heart: 'We feel unable to advance one kilometre further,' he confessed. 'Russian resistance has become too much for us. The combination of bomber and fighter attacks, artillery and rocket fire and tank assaults has become intolerable. We never expected the Russians to defend their capital with such determination. They have fought us to a standstill.' Reinhardt's push on Moscow had run out of strength.

Things were little better with Hoepner's forces. 'We are only drawing near our final objective one small step at a time,' Ernst Streng noted. 'Our supply problems are growing worse and worse. Our soldiers, wearing plundered Russian coats and fur caps, are scarcely recognisable as the German Wehrmacht. Everyone is infested with lice.' That night Streng stood outside his quarters. Perhaps, in such extremes, the human need for beauty and meaning asserts itself, for he reflected: 'Above the suburbs of Moscow, rocket flares hang like constellations of stars. Searchlight beams are criss-crossing the sky. Between them are flashes from the Russian anti-aircraft guns. For a moment, I imagine these are strings of pearls. And the bursts of orange-red tracer fire have a strange, captivating power.'

Streng was quartered in a house belonging to two Russian women. One spoke good German. She worked in Moscow every day, and commuted back home by train. She told Streng how, only a week earlier, workers' brigades had been recruited from factories and women and children sent out to dig defence lines. Prisons had been opened up, and liberated convicts armed and sent to the front. But now more and more fresh Siberian troops were arriving and Red Army soldiers thronged the streets of Moscow.

On Army Group Centre's southern flank, a German soldier from the 134th Infantry Division – stationed near Yelets, 200 miles south of Moscow – wrote on the evening of 2 December: 'Snowstorms are blowing up all around us. We try to warm ourselves in a stable where we have set up quarters. There is nothing to eat. We will be sleeping on a cold floor, on frozen straw, amidst crying children, donkeys, pigs, chickens, innumerable cockroaches and lice – and large piles of animal excrement. What a beautiful night!'

At noon on 3 December, Field Marshal von Bock received a telegram from Hitler wishing him a happy birthday. Shortly after midday Field Marshal von Kluge's advanced formations were halted on Moscow's outskirts. A German soldier of the 258th Division wrote:

> Our attack went in two days ago, in the most unfavourable circumstances. It was bitterly cold, and we were faced by battle-hardened Siberian troops, in strong defensive positions, protected by extensive minefields and fortifications. As we moved forward, an icy blizzard swept across the snow-covered landscape, limiting visibility and preventing the Luftwaffe from assisting us. The ground was so slippery that our horses had difficulty keeping upright. Our machine guns did not work in the cold. Despite all these disadvantages, the spearhead of our attack broke through, and showing extraordinary courage, our leading units came within 30 kilometres of Moscow. But our losses were too high, and fresh Russian forces blocked our advance. So now we are back where we started. Only a tiny remnant of my company is left.

'This is where our retreat has ended,' said Boris Baromykin of the Siberian 32nd Rifle Brigade. 'The enemy was desperately trying to break our last defences, but we lured them into a trap. We constructed a line of brushwood, and doused it with inflammables. We let the German tanks across, and then set it alight. Their infantry was confronted by a wall of fire and drew back. The enemy tanks were now cut off – and caught in a narrow area in front of our camouflaged positions. Our artillery opened up on them – it was carnage.' 'The attack has failed!' wrote Hellmuth Stieff, staff officer with the German Fourth Army. 'We have suffered terrible losses.'

On the afternoon of 3 December the German SS *Das Reich* Division was fighting for the small town of Lenino, 23 miles northwest of Moscow. As the weather cleared, the city's suburbs were clearly visible to the naked eye. But the attack was called off with half the town still in Russian hands. At 5.30 p.m. Colonel General Hoepner announced: 'The offensive power of my Panzer Group has run out. The reasons are the physical and mental exhaustion of our troops, unsustainable losses and inadequate winter equipment.' The following day Hoepner wrote: 'I was so very close, but the final goal has eluded me. The troops have given their utmost. But my forces are insufficient . . . and the Russians grow stronger all the time. This is such a bitter pill to swallow.'

Shortly after noon that day, Private Gerhard vom Bruch's unit in the 6th Panzer Division received an unpleasant surprise. 'About fifteen enemy tanks burst out of the forest,' Bruch recorded, 'and headed straight for the village where we were quartered. We had to run for our lives. All our vehicles, artillery and supplies fell into the hands of the Russians. About thirty of our men are still missing, including the battalion commander, who was unable to get out in time.'

Horst Lange's 56th Infantry Division was closing on Krasnaya Polyana and the Moscow-Volga Canal. The men had been expecting to go into an attack, but something was terribly wrong: 'Enemy planes are in the sky above us,' Lange wrote, 'and more and more of their tanks are appearing. The woods on either side of us are full of Russians. Our assault has been called off. Instead, we are laying mines and trying to dig trenches – in the middle of a snowstorm.'

Close to Lange's position, Georgi Osadchinsky's 35th Rifle Brigade was on a reconnaissance mission: 'We found wrecked German tanks and the corpses of their soldiers, covered in snow,' Osadchinsky recalled. 'They had been caught in one of our air attacks. The enemy have gone onto the defensive, holding villages as strong-points, and patrolling the roads in their armoured vehicles.' On the body of one German, Osadchinsky found a leaflet, carrying a personal message from Hitler to his front-line troops. The Red Army fighters gathered round, and one translated it: 'Soldiers of Germany – forward to Moscow! Kill as many Russians as possible. They are a lazy, eternally drunk and corrupt people – incapable of managing the riches that God has given them. This wealth rightfully belongs to the German people. Forward to Moscow – victory and glory await you!'

Osadchinsky and his comrades looked at the dead Germans lying in the field. None had proper winter clothing, and under their helmets, their heads were swathed in Russian women's shawls. There was a moment of silence. Then a Red Army soldier said: 'How they despise us. They call us "cursed Russian pigs". They believe that we are perpetually drunk. Yet they have become drunk themselves – drunk on the myth of their own invincibility.'

'The snow blows almost horizontally, in blizzards that sometimes last all day long,' Lieutenant Siegfried Knappe of the German 87th Infantry Division wrote on 4 December. 'It brings earth and sky together, swirling over the level ground and forming strange, surreal patterns. We are in a village only 25 kilometres from the outskirts of Moscow – but our unit is exhausted, and can go no further. Our world has become a huge, frozen abyss, in which the white snow glitters with the flashes of gunfire and turns pink or green in the light of signal flares.'

On 4 December Luftwaffe commander Wolfram von Richthofen penned a long entry in his diary: 'Kluge's Fourth Army suffered a serious setback yesterday,' he began. 'Its tanks were cut off from its infantry – the Russians let them roll over their positions, and then emerged behind them. Our advanced forces were surrounded, and Kluge was forced to pull everyone back. What a grim day! Our efforts to drive home the offensive on Moscow have failed. Further attacks from the north or north-west of the city are now pointless. The troops are utterly exhausted, and there is no likelihood of any reinforcements arriving in the near future.' Richthofen declared sadly: 'We have suffered our first major failure. We have always been an attacking army. Now we must try to adjust – in highly unfavourable circumstances – to winter defence. The only hope – from a propaganda point of view – lies with Guderian's Panzers, around Tula. Everything else has gone badly for us.'

But Colonel General Guderian's Second Panzer Army was also utterly spent. On 4 December General Gotthard Heinrici, whose armoured corps was fighting with Guderian, complained:

> Our position in the forest might be idyllic in summer weather; in the winter it is utterly dreadful. We lack any kind of decent shelter. In nearby villages our infantry, artillery and supply vehicles are all cluttered together; everything is so overcrowded that a unit of 30 men is overjoyed if it can find a space of its own. It is impossible to lie down and spread out; men huddle together for hours simply to try to get warm. Washing oneself is impossible. Everything is infested with lice – men are continuously itching and scratching themselves, and many have festering wounds, severe blistering or intestinal illnesses from lying on the frozen ground.

Heinrici declared despairingly: 'If one has to invade Russia at all, hopefully one will never have to advance far into this vast country. This war has thrown all rules of strategy and tactics onto the rubbish heap. We deal in distances that seem almost incomprehensible. We hold lines of several kilometres with companies reduced to 40 men. Everyone struggles to cope in such conditions and the nervous tension is taking its toll . . .' The general then asked the question that was sweeping the entire German army: 'Why have we been sent into a winter battle so poorly equipped? Does no one realise what it is like here?'

Heinrici had just visited an outlying regiment: 'Artillery fire was rolling over its position,' he recalled, 'with salvoes constantly being fired, guns cracking, and one Russian counter-attack following after another. The regimental commander greeted me with tears in his eyes.' Things were happening that Heinrici scarcely thought possible. 'Some men are dropping their weapons and running away; others break down and weep, saying "We can do no more".' Heinrici commented: 'I am seeing the strength of my regiments bleeding away, with nothing left to replace the losses. When company strength is reduced to 19 or 20 men, how is it possible to hold the line, let alone push forward? And the Russians are constantly throwing new men into the fight. The plea for decent food, winter clothing and reinforcements is heard again and again from our demoralised troops.' Colonel Dreschner, the regimental commander Heinrici visited, did not mince his words: 'Our soldiers are in such a state,' he confided, 'that some, through sheer desperation, may turn their guns on their own officers. They are going out of their minds.' Three men had deliberately wounded themselves in the last two days – men regarded as well-balanced, and good soldiers.

Yet the Germans had to summon the will for one last offensive. Shortly after midday on 4 December, Colonel General Guderian arrived at Heinrici's command post. The two men lunched together, and discussed the military situation. They had long since abandoned plans for a further advance on Moscow, but their forces were close to encircling the industrial city of Tula. Guderian and Heinrici debated whether they had the strength to push through the attack. Guderian gave a brief outline of troop dispositions. A battle group under Colonel Heinrich Eberbach was now astride the motor highway north of Tula, 100 miles south of Moscow. If Heinrici's men could break through and join him, Tula would be surrounded. There was a slender chance of achieving this military success before winter brought operations to a halt. 'We must bring the attack forward to the early hours of tomorrow morning,' Guderian concluded.

Soviet Lieutenant General Ivan Boldin was organising the

defence of Tula. He acknowledged that the Germans were close to encircling the city, but then he added: 'We pulled back our troops, regrouped and created strike forces of mobile artillery and tanks. We knew that the enemy was dangerously overextended, and his fuel and ammunition were running low. On the evening of 4 December we received substantial reinforcements from the Army's Strategic Reserve.'

That night temperatures dropped to below −30 degrees Celsius. General Heinrici drove out to speak to some of the soldiers who would be making the assault:

> I found a battalion huddled together in a small ravine at the edge of the forest. The men are in a miserable condition. They cluster round small fires, and jump up and down, trying to get warm. The cold is so intense that it is painful even to inhale the air. I go from fire to fire, chatting to them, hearing their complaints and acknowledging how truly awful the situation is. In the last twenty-four hours they have eaten nothing except a little bread, and the coffee in their flasks is frozen solid. If the Russians see the state our soldiers are in they will no longer fear them − they look so pitiful. But I try and encourage these frozen, unwashed, hungry men to make one last effort. They all know what is at stake. Only a few kilometres separate us from the German tank force that is now astride the motor highway, and if we reach them Tula will be surrounded. It will be a major success.

At 11.00 p.m. Heinrici reached Guderian on the field telephone. He was candid about the state his men were in, but added that despite everything, resolve could be found for one last push. They discussed logistical problems, the crippling lack of fuel and supplies and the growing strength of the Russian forces. They were alarmed by the steadily dropping temperature, and the impact this might have on the attack. Then Heinrici said: 'The die is cast.'

On the motor highway, Lieutenant Hermann Hoss was nervously assessing the situation. The German battle group, led by Colonel Eberbach, one of Guderian's best commanders, now had fewer than thirty operable tanks, and these were spread over a wide area. To dislodge the group, the Russians had brought up a fresh armoured brigade, which included more than seventy T-34s. They were only a mile away and Hoss could hear their engines revving: 'Our line is dangerously thin,' he wrote. 'If they attack en masse they will simply roll over us.' Hoss felt the utter precariousness of the position. 'It is five minutes to midnight for the German Army,' he said. 'There is still a chance to surround Tula and capture the city. But our forces are dwindling away. Many of our tanks have broken down – and there is not enough fuel or ammunition for the remainder. We are freezing in our thin uniforms – more and more of our soldiers are getting frostbite. Fresh Siberian troops are being thrown into battle against us. They are well trained – and their equipment is excellent.' The Germans somehow clung to their positions. 'We know that Heinrici's forces are trying to join us,' Hoss stated. 'We have to hold on here. At least it will give our war diary some more exciting content.'

Heinrici's attack was spearheaded by Regiment 17 of the 31st Infantry Division. At 11.40 p.m. on 4 December the men gathered in the assembly area. Knowing casualties would be exceptionally high, they asked the divisional chaplain, Heinrich Link, to accompany them to the front-line positions, and pray with them. 'We moved forward in the most bitter cold imaginable,' Link wrote. 'The condition of the men was catastrophic. Each man possessed only a thin greatcoat, helmet and thin gloves. The temperature had now dropped to below −35 degrees Celsius. The food ration – about 30 grams of fats and a little bread – was utterly inadequate. The soldiers lined up for the assault and waited, without any shelter from the freezing wind. The night was lit by a bright moon. At 1.00 a.m. the attack order came through.'

The first German battalion advanced into the Russian-held village of Ketri, and was immediately surrounded by strong enemy forces. The second tried to relieve them, but was beaten back. Because of the extreme cold, supporting artillery fire was sporadic and largely inaccurate, machine guns failed to work and the men even struggled to reload their rifles. The Germans in the village were wiped out, and their comrades forced to spend the remainder of the night in the open, around the village, prostrate on the freezing snow. The number of wounded and frostbite cases rose steadily. Next morning the attack was called off. 'Seeing the state of the few remaining soldiers was a heartbreaking experience,' Link said. 'Nearly all of them had severe frostbite, and most would not even survive the journey to the military hospital.'

On the northern flank of the German advance, thousands of Red Army soldiers were also on the move. Heinz Otto Fausten was with the 1st Panzer Division. On 5 December he wrote: 'The Moscow-Volga Canal lay before us, and on the other side, masses of Russians were suddenly appearing. The sheer number of them left us speechless. There were endless marching columns, soldiers on skis, in white winter coats. And then there were tanks, artillery units and countless motor vehicles. Where had they all come from?'

Lieutenant Kurt Grumann of the German 87th Infantry Division was counting his unit's rising casualties: 'Today we lost another 11 killed and 39 wounded — and 19 more are badly frostbitten,' he noted. 'Russian heavy tanks launched a surprise attack on our village. We are helpless against these juggernauts — it's enough to drive anybody to despair. The snow is cutting into our faces and our breath forms into an icy crust around our helmet strapping. We watch each other constantly for symptoms of frostbite.' On the evening of 5 December Russian long-range guns opened up on the German position. Grumann was worried; instinct told him an enemy attack was imminent.

That night the attack on Tula was also abandoned. Lieutenant Hoss was with Colonel Eberbach when the telephone shrilled. He heard the entire conversation that followed: 'The Russians have started to counter-attack all along the front,' Eberbach was told. 'Your battle group is in a particularly exposed position. You must pull back — and anything that cannot be moved must be destroyed immediately. Our overriding concern is now self-preservation.'

Colonel Heinrich Eberbach was an aggressive tank commander, always in the forefront of the advance. But the Germans were no longer advancing. Eberbach put down the phone and turned to

Hoss, with an expression on his face the Panzer lieutenant had never seen before. 'It is an order,' he said, unusually slowly, and in a flat tone of voice. 'We haven't managed to pull it off. Our army has to retreat.'

5

Ten Days in December

GERMAN ARTILLERYMAN Josef Deck never forgot the first day of the Soviet counteroffensive on 6 December 1941. Colonel General Heinz Guderian's attempts to capture the city of Tula and to push on to Moscow from the south had been abandoned, and in blinding snowstorms the German forces pulled back over frozen roads and past burning villages. 'The Russian commander most quoted by my comrades,' Deck remarked, 'was "General Winter", and he had triumphed over our modern, professional army.' Lieutenant Hans-Erdmann Schönbeck added: 'The fact that we hadn't taken Moscow was a colossal disappointment. We were ambitious and highly motivated, and our motto had always been "We can do it!" But at Moscow we didn't do it – and that had never happened to a Panzer division before.'

For most German soldiers, it was more palatable to blame the weather than to pay tribute to the resurgence of the Red Army. But the winter cold was a formidable adversary in itself. The devastated Russian countryside – once dotted with well-equipped collective farms – now resembled a gigantic ice rink, upon which humans, animals and vehicles skidded around helplessly. 'The ghost of the Napoleonic *Grande Armée*,' said Deck, 'hovers ever more strongly above us like a malignant spirit.'

On 6 December, the day on which the Soviet Union began its main counteroffensive, the temperature in some parts of the front sank to −40 degrees Celsius. Innumerable German tanks and support vehicles – in some cases frozen solid to the ground – had to be blown up. 'The Germans were surprised by the ferocity of our attack,' said Dmitry Vonlyarsky of the 71st Marine Brigade, as the First Shock Army of Colonel General Fyodor Kuznetsov rolled on to the offensive, 'and they did not expect us to launch it in temperatures below −35 degrees Celsius. The force of our artillery barrage knocked out many of their firing points, and then we charged forward in a massed infantry attack. The men around me were screaming and howling as we jumped into the enemy's trenches. We finished off the remaining defenders with grenades, bayonets and knives.' Just over two months earlier, Operation Typhoon had begun with brutal fury. Now, that fury had been matched.

The Russian high command struck the Germans at the moment when Operation Typhoon had run its course, but before they had prepared proper winter positions. Timing was crucial. Army Group Centre's chief of staff, Major General Hans von Greiffenberg, paid tribute to Soviet General Georgi Zhukov for not losing his nerve at the vital moment: 'He kept back his reserves until they could be massed at the right place, and waited until our own attack had completely collapsed before he committed them.' Greiffenberg recalled that 6 December began with an intensive Russian artillery barrage, followed by waves of successive infantry attacks, which were difficult to counter: 'When the enemy troops advanced, they did not find a coherent defence line − we had not time to make one − but only a loosely connected series of strongpoints, without anti-tank ditches or effective obstacles. The sheer number of Russians thrown into the attack had a depressing and discouraging effect on our exhausted soldiers. Our line was penetrated in many places.' Major Alexander Conrady of the German 36th Motorised Infantry Division added: 'Visibility that day was extremely poor. Temperatures had sunk to approximately −35 degrees Celsius, and an icy wind swept over the flat landscape from the east. Salvoes of enemy artillery fire rolled along our lines, growing in intensity. And then the Russian infantry attacked en masse. They quickly penetrated our positions.'

Zhukov had launched three Soviet armies − the First, Twenty-Ninth and Thirtieth − against the German forces north-east of Klin, on Army Group Centre's northern flank. 'The delirious dream of the conquest of Moscow,' a Russian radio broadcaster announced, 'has turned into a nightmare for the German Fascists.' 'We had been used to small setbacks,' said Fritz Hübner, but were in no way prepared for this dramatic transition from attack to defence. We were physically exhausted, and now faced a new problem. Our military equipment was not functioning properly, because our vehicles, planes and weapons did not have the proper lubricants to withstand the extreme cold.'

This possibility had already been anticipated by the Russians. They knew that the great strength of the German Army was its mechanised troops, who had done so much damage to the Red Army in the summer and autumn of 1941. But the Germans had not been supplied with the necessary materials – cold-resistant oils and glycerine lubricants – to maintain their engines in weather well below freezing. General Zhukov wrote: 'The Germans were vulnerable in winter fighting because in extreme cold – at temperatures below −30 degrees Celsius – the engines of their tanks and motorised artillery would be rendered useless. And this would break the backbone of their army.'

On the morning of 6 December, Lieutenant Ludwig Freiherr von Heyl of the 36th Motorised Infantry Division wrote in his diary:

> The heavy-machine-gun truck will not start. The artillery support vehicle's steering does not work. The engine of the radio lorry only stutters. I try three different connecting wires, but it makes no difference. My commander comes over and tells me to get a move on: an enemy attack is imminent. I drive off slowly in our sole functioning vehicle – hopefully the others will follow shortly. The order to hold our positions seems unduly optimistic to me.

Fritz Hübner described this scenario:

> Our planes – on forward airfields, with little protection from the elements, were no longer able to start their engines – and at a stroke we were deprived of all protection from the air. With the tank engines it was exactly the same – the tanks were no longer able to move, and stood there motionless – so they were no use to us either. The firing mechanisms on our artillery also failed to work, depriving us of

supporting fire from our big guns. The heavy machine guns would constantly jam – in short, it was a total disaster.

Hübner and his men were forced to pull back. 'Our engineering units were particularly badly hit,' he continued, 'because we were always left with the orders to destroy everything – weapons and vehicles which had been hurriedly abandoned by our soldiers.' In the first days of the retreat, the Germans had no idea why their vehicles were not moving, being completely unaware that the engine grease and oil had frozen solid. In the beginning they tried to make them start by towing them, damaging their engines even further. The breechblocks of their artillery had also become absolutely rigid. If the blocks were heated carefully, they would briefly become fit for firing, then – in the icy cold – revert to their former state again. So, most of the equipment was jettisoned. 'Artillery was usually put out of action by pushing a hand grenade down the barrel,' Hübner continued, 'and the tanks had a three-kilogram explosive charge fixed to the hatch, so that the whole of the interior was destroyed. With the trucks and other motor vehicles we drilled a hole in the engine, and again inserted a hand grenade. It was heartbreaking work.'

As they retreated, most German soldiers had nothing to protect themselves from the inexorable cold except their regular army uniforms and greatcoats. They saw well-equipped Siberian troops attacking their positions, clad in quilted, waterproof garments, fur caps, gloves and felt boots. Their own clothing was totally inadequate for such low temperatures. The consequences were horrific. 'A child-care centre has been turned into a field dressing-station,' Lieutenant Kurt Grumann wrote at the beginning of the Soviet counteroffensive. 'Eighty men were brought in here today, half of whom have second or third degree frostbite. Their swollen legs are covered in blisters, and they no longer resemble limbs but rather some formless mass. In some cases gangrene has already set in. What is it all for?' Grumann concluded despairingly.

Medical orderly Anton Gründer recalled trying to tend the wounded amidst the chaos of the retreat: 'I had woken up at about

6.00 a.m. on 6 December,' he remembered, 'and was just getting something to eat when all hell broke loose outside. Everyone was pulling out. There were no orders any more. Seeing some fleeing, others panicked. Many vehicles would not start in the extreme cold. We succeeded in getting most of our medical equipment out, and tried to keep up with the remnants of our company – but whoever fell behind was lost.' Even in conditions of total disorder, Gründer and his comrades still tried to take care of the wounded. 'We saw the most terrible things. Many presented themselves for treatment with emergency bandages that had been applied more than a week before. One soldier had an exit wound in his upper arm. The whole arm was now black, and puss was running from his back down to his boots. We had to amputate it at the joint. Three of my helpers smoked cigars during the operation because the stench was so great.'

For an army which prided itself on its order, discipline and cohesion to succumb to such mass panic was a shocking and bewildering experience. German infantryman Albrecht Linsen never forgot that day:

Out of the snowstorm soldiers were running back, scattering in all directions like a panic-stricken herd of animals. Some hesitated, others fled in a blind stampede. One lone officer stood against this desperate mass; he gesticulated, tried to pull out his pistol and then simply let it pass. Our platoon leader made no attempt to stop people at all. I paused, wondering what to do and then there was an explosion right next to me and I felt a searing pain in my right thigh. Within seconds I realised that my leg would no longer support me. I thought: 'I am going to die here, 21 years old, in the snow before Moscow.'

Linsen turned and shot his remaining bullets in the direction of the enemy. He was already feeling light-headed, as if in a trance. Then he limped over to an officer and reported that he was wounded. His trousers – frozen solid – had become as rigid as sheet metal but underneath, the pain was growing. Somehow Linsen was able to start moving, supporting himself on his rifle: 'In the distance, between flurries of snow, I could still see my fleeing comrades. I came across one of our wagons smashed against the roadside, evidence of a panic-stricken driver bungling his escape. Three or four wounded had been left on it, clutching the air helplessly. Another wounded man was crawling forward slowly, holding a pistol.'

Linsen struggled along the frozen road as darkness was beginning to fall: 'I passed abandoned vehicles, heard the desperate revving of engines and saw shadowy groups of men disappearing into the dusk. There was a sudden loud cracking sound. A Russian soldier had ridden by, firing indiscriminately from his horse. The pain in my leg was becoming unbearable but I fought against the urge to lie down in the snow, knowing that I would not get up again.' And then Linsen saw the lantern-lit windows of a nearby village. German soldiers were stationed here, and it was a unit that had not succumbed to the prevailing panic. 'I was helped into a farmer's room and carried to a makeshift operating table. My trousers were cut away, the wound tended and dressed, and I·got a tetanus injection. Then I received a form stating I was wounded. What a wonderful piece of paper! After the hell I had gone through, I felt as if I had received an absolution.'

Soviet Marshal Semyon Timoshenko now attacked Army Group Centre's southern flank with two more armies, the Third and the Thirteenth. Willy Reese's German 95th Division – near Volovo, 150 miles south of Moscow – was directly in the path of the Soviet Third Army. Late on the evening of 6 December Reese and his comrades were suddenly attacked by Cossack cavalry, who managed to infiltrate their positions from a nearby gully. Some of the German troops panicked. 'Half-dressed soldiers, men in their shirts, in socks, barefoot, rushed past us in terror,' Reese recalled:

A full moon lit their frantic, mindless flight. A score of us formed up – armed with rifles, pistols and a bazooka. Horsemen swirled around us, hand grenades were thrown into our midst . . . Our assailants were so close that we fought some of them with rifle butts . . . Then they melted away – the ordeal was over. All through the night, fugitives kept returning. Men who had hidden somewhere, or kept running – at their wits' end – now came back without knowing whether the Russians had taken the village or not. Most of them had frostbite.

For other units the retreat was more orderly, but for all it was a difficult experience. Lieutenant Hermann Hoss of the 4th Panzer Division – stationed north-east of Tula with Guderian's Second Panzer Army – remembered 6 December as a day of constant motion. 'We didn't have much time to think, our concern was to take what we needed and destroy the rest. Everything that could drive was prepared for our departure; everything that couldn't was destroyed on the spot.' Inevitably there were mishaps. The flak crew attempted to pull their gun over a ravine with a rope hoist, but in the exceptional cold the rope ripped apart like shreds of paper. The brakes on motor vehicles froze, so they had to be tipped over the side of the road and set alight. That evening Hoss and his comrades found the Russians already in the village they wanted to occupy, and had to deploy their last operable tanks to chase them out. It was a sad finale for a division that had spearheaded Guderian's advance on Moscow. Hoss recalled the day's end:

> We formed a ghostly, struggling line, a long worm winding westwards, crawling as fast as the light and the conditions of the roads would permit. A full moon hung over the winter landscape, making everything colder. I thought of a picture, a Russian winter picture that I saw once – in warm southern France. And I saw the pole star. It had marked out our direction when we sped eastwards. Back then we drove at high speed, and covered huge distances.

Everything had changed, and the sense of German superiority – so prevalent in the opening stages of the Russian campaign – was now dissolving. 'Men are in a state of shock,' observed Colonel Adolf Raegener of the Wehrmacht's 23rd Infantry Division. 'The sudden collapse of the offensive, followed by a disorderly retreat westwards, is difficult for our soldiers to understand. Everyone is thinking about the fate of Napoleon in 1812 – and some even say that our army has been cursed.'

'We are losing our confidence and self-belief,' Horst Lange wrote on 6 December. 'It is eroding rapidly, even among our officers. The Russians have firmly grasped the battle initiative as

our troops move back. We have received an order to burn everything before we leave, and buildings are starting to go up in flames.
One house is full of refugees – women and crying children, and
they are all absolutely terrified.'

Lange and his comrades from the 56th Infantry Division – close
to the small town of Krasnaya Polyana – were in the path of two
more Soviet armies, the Sixteenth under Major General Konstantin
Rokossovsky and the Twentieth under Lieutenant General Andrei
Vlasov. General Zhukov was deploying no fewer than five armies
on this section of the front. Lange reflected on the dramatic change
in fortunes: 'The triumphalism with which we began our advance
on Moscow has completely evaporated,' he declared. 'Instead, we
are conscious of a growing fear of the Russians. And it is more than
fear, it is verging on hysteria. We thought that we could overcome
the forces of nature and disregard the approaching winter. And
now, in this crisis, many of our divisions have less than 2,000 fighting men available and some companies have dwindled to less than
twenty.' Lange concluded starkly: 'The war has simply become too
big to grasp.'

Hitler refused to accept this new situation. On 6 December
he was briefed on the sudden reversal of fortune at Moscow, the
depletion of the German units and the new forces the Russians
had brought into battle. The assessment was incomplete, because
the Germans had failed to identify all of the Soviet armies assembling for the counteroffensive. But even as the briefing stood, the
Führer was unable to comprehend how the Russians had made
such a recovery.

There had been an utter failure in the Wehrmacht's military
intelligence. Only a day earlier, Army Group Centre had confidently declared: 'The combat power of Red Army forces opposing
us is insufficient to launch a major counteroffensive.' Remarkably,
the Wehrmacht's operational maps of 6 December did not show
three of the Soviet armies (the First, Tenth and Twentieth) deploying against them. The Tenth Army went straight into combat after
a series of night marches, relying on its fast movement and the bad
weather to produce a degree of surprise. But the Soviet First and

TEN DAYS IN DECEMBER

Twentieth Armies had been substantially reinforced and prepared for the offensive in close proximity to the enemy. Astonishingly, their entry into battle took the Germans completely by surprise.

Luftwaffe commander Wolfram von Richthofen captured the mood at Hitler's headquarters: 'The Führer wants to go to the front,' he noted on 6 December, 'to get a personal impression of the condition the troops are in. His preliminary decision, which was to halt, has been pre-empted by the actual course of events: the plight of our armies and the activity of the enemy.' A terrible indecision prevailed. Richthofen added:

> We have found out that our army has less than a quarter of its winter supplies, for necessary stores only began to be assembled at Smolensk towards the end of October, and nothing was located near to the front. Now there is a chronic shortage of materials to construct a defence line, and this vital work is proceeding slowly, in the short daylight hours and with the soil frozen solid.
>
> Everyone here is quite overwhelmed. What shall we do now? There is a terrible sense of anxiety. If the front-line soldiers are not able to hold their lines everything will go to the dogs, for in a fluid situation of retreat, resupply will be virtually impossible. We can do little to mitigate the effects of the Russian climate. If one looks at the bigger picture, it is clear we are facing an imminent catastrophe.

Major General Hans von Greiffenberg, Army Group Centre's chief of staff, believed that Hitler had become a victim of his own propaganda:

> The Führer and the members of his entourage – unfamiliar with conditions on the front – did not want to acknowledge this reversal in fortunes. They had always portrayed the Russians as 'subhumans', whose 'primitive' combat methods stood no chance against the modern Wehrmacht, and whose resources in manpower and material were almost completely exhausted. Hitler's own press ministry had, after all, already announced that 'the campaign in the east has been decided'. For several days the Führer clung to the belief that Russia's final collapse was still imminent, even after we had been thrown onto the defensive.

Hitler, unable to acknowledge his own part in this abrupt reversal of fortunes, sought instead to blame others. 'Scapegoats are being sought for the failure of the attack on Moscow,' wrote the Führer's adjutant, Major Gerhard Engel. The first was Field Marshal Walther von Brauchitsch, commander-in-chief of the German Army. 'Relations between Hitler and Brauchitsch can no longer be patched up,' Engel added on 6 December. 'Every situation conference is unpleasant.' Underneath these angry exchanges, Engel was struck by the fact that Hitler was at an utter loss: 'His perplexity is self-evident,' he concluded.

The Soviet counteroffensive had begun with the intention of making Moscow safe, and for its commander, General Georgi Zhukov, the immediate objectives were limited: to hold the Germans in the centre and push them back on the flanks, to the north and south of the Russian capital, thereby gaining greater space for manoeuvre. He had amassed five armies, reinforced by six new Siberian divisions, for an attack on the Third Panzer Group; a further three armies had been thrown into battle against Guderian's Second Panzer Army. But over the next few days both Zhukov and Stalin were surprised and delighted by the extent to which the Germans were falling back, surrendering the military initiative to the Red Army.

'A kind of paralysis fell over us,' said German artilleryman Josef Deck of the 17th Panzer Division. 'Its cause was not only the exceptional cold of those December days, and the understandable disappointment that our offensive had failed. It was also the heartfelt and bitter realisation that our army was no longer proudly marching into Russia, towards a glorious future but – lost and bewildered in this vast country – now reduced to desperately crawling about on its hands and knees.'

On 7 December Lieutenant Ludwig von Heyl's 36th Motorised Division could no longer contain the enemy. Heyl noted how everyone had been drafted into the front line: engineering units, rear-area security detachments and even clerks from the company HQ. It was not enough. 'The situation looks really bad,' he wrote. 'We have lost radio contact with our neighbours. Our guns are not working properly – and the houses around us are in flames from Russian artillery fire. A group of engineers is trying to get a solitary heavy machine gun into position. I send a message to HQ in our last functioning vehicle, but it does not get very far: the lorry skids helplessly – the clutch keeps slipping. The enemy is now approaching the outskirts of the village.'

Early on the morning of 7 December, Horst Lange watched lines of German troops retreating westwards. The forward units of General Reinhardt's Third Panzer Group had only been 20 miles from the outskirts of Moscow, but they would never see the city. The attack across the Moscow-Volga Canal had been called off and the Red Army was now dictating affairs: 'Our infantry continues to pull back,' Lange wrote, 'the men irritable and quarrelsome, insults flying between them . . . We have orders to occupy a new village, which is already under Russian artillery attack, and build shelters and set up defence positions. This task is to be undertaken in temperatures of −35 degrees Celsius, with the earth frozen to a depth of several feet. We are approaching our new quarters in the cold, blue-grey light of morning, over the brow of a wooded hill.'

In the village below, several houses were already burning and the remainder were crammed with German troops. Lange's unit began to set up its artillery. But in the intense cold the guns would no longer fire properly. The Russian artillery – effectively insulated against the extreme weather – continued to shoot unhindered, and noticing little defensive fire in response, its salvoes became more and more frequent. The sky was clear, its features etched sharply in the morning light, criss-crossed with vapour trails. Then suddenly Russian planes were directly overhead. Everyone pushed inside one of the houses.

'The Red Air Force is swooping down on us, their fighters raking the village with their machine guns,' Lange recorded grimly. 'The bombers will soon follow. No German aircraft are to be seen, and apparently our flak guns have seized up. We are crowded together in a small room, where a glowing iron stove is generating a little heat, on chairs and bunks, exhausted and in a state of collapse. In the corner there is a tiny St Nicholas figure, made with cotton wool and glitter. The men find a toy metal car, its paint peeling, and run it backwards and forwards across the table.'

Lange was dozing fitfully when a sudden crescendo of sound announced another air attack. The platoon leader, Max Surkowski, rushed back inside the house, completely out of breath and covered in snow. 'One plane was flying so low it almost knocked my head off!' he exclaimed. Lange shuddered: 'Our cold indifference – our numbness – was replaced by a brief surge of fear. But a stubborn determination replaced it. We are caught like mice in a trap – so what is the point of worrying? We cannot expect much help from others. The Russian mortars have now opened up and our own heavy weapons remain silent.' Lange began to doze again, when there was a loud crash outside, a roar of engines and a staccato burst of machine-gun fire. Everyone threw themselves onto the ground.

'I fell off my chair in shock,' Lange said, 'and in the moment of falling saw the bright, pin-point light of tracer fire smash through our window. My hand and sleeve were covered in blood and I tried to bind it up, but there was no pain. Then I realised – the blood was not mine. Others were lifting themselves up, calling out "They got Max!" There was the sweet smell of blood, oozing and sticky – and Surkowski lying on the floor, quite still. He had been shot in the head.'

They heard the plane coming back. For several minutes Lange crouched on the floor, next to his dead commander, as machine-gun bullets whizzed overhead. 'Another senseless death,' Lange exclaimed, 'and this one has really shaken me. We are imprisoned in this house, unable to move, and next to me is a human being who suddenly has no future, who has not been able to grow old, to strive after things in life. Everything about this man that was precious, that made him different from others, has ended.' Lange felt a swirl of emotions – anger, pain and bewilderment – as if a dark arena was opening before him, previously glimpsed out of the corner of an eye but now coming fully into view. 'Why did a random bullet take this man, not someone else?' Lange wondered. 'He has baptised me with his blood, in the most terrible sense of the word.'

The Russian aircraft left. Around noon the German troops received the order to pull back to another village, Nikolskoye, 28 miles north of Moscow. The men were nervous and jumpy. Lange continued:

> We are marching along a road covered with dead horses. The poor animals were caught in the last air attack. Russian mortars are shooting constantly. We move quickly, all the time looking up at the sky, looking for places to take cover. Along with Surkowski, we lost four other men in the last attack, and two more are heavily wounded. When we get to Nikolskoye it is jammed full of abandoned vehicles – tanks, cars and lorries – none of which can function in this extreme cold. When one sees such chaos, the cause of our present military difficulties is not too difficult to grasp.

Heavy flak guns stood at the entrance to the village, pointed vertically to fend off Russian ground attacks. Lange and his comrades marched through it to a rendezvous point on the forest edge. Then Russian planes appeared. The men were caught in an open field and Lange flung himself onto the snow: 'I saw the muzzle flashes of their machine guns. There are only 100 metres to the shelter of the forest, but now bombers are coming. Our men are hiding under bushes and beneath a small timber bridge. Then, as one, we all dash forward.' The troops reassembled under the trees and debated what to do next. 'The psychological effect of these air attacks,' Lange noted grimly, 'is considerable. They take us by surprise, in a state of utter helplessness. We move slowly and ponderously, are easily visible and almost inviting attack. The enemy's planes seem to move around at will.'

The Russians began to bomb a nearby village, their aircraft operating in relays. There was little hope for those German soldiers trapped inside. When Lange and his comrades emerged from the forest they saw – about a mile away – the results of the attack: fire, smoke and tangled wrecks of burning vehicles. Everything was strangely quiet: 'The sky is empty,' Lange wrote. 'It is green, golden and expressionless – yet watching us coldly. It lets this day glide away, and opens the door to other worlds.'

As the German position worsened, Hitler continued to vent his fury on the hapless Brauchitsch. The chief of staff of the German Army, Colonel General Franz Halder, noted on 7 December: 'What has happened today has been heartbreaking and humiliating. Brauchitsch is now no more than a messenger boy, if that. The Führer bypasses the army high command . . . but does not understand the condition the troops are in, and indulges in ineffectual patchwork when only big decisions can help.'

On the evening of 7 December Georgi Osadchinsky's Soviet 35th Rifle Brigade was outflanking the German position at Krasnaya Polyana, and striking out to the north-west of Reinhardt's Third Panzer Group. About a mile from the village of Ozeretskoye, Osadchinsky stopped short, his knees buckling involuntarily: 'A black crater gaped in the road; the snow all around had been turned black. In the snow lay the disfigured corpses of a woman and child, broken toboggans and scattered potatoes. The Germans had mined the opening to the village. Desperate hunger must have forced this woman, with her young child, to try and bring provisions through the battlefield to feed the rest of her family.' As Osadchinsky reflected on this, the horror, which had paralysed him at first, gave way to a fierce hatred of the enemy: 'I vowed to kill as many of them as possible,' he concluded grimly.

The Eastern Front was going up in flames. Artilleryman Gerhard Bopp's radio unit had received a stark message on the evening of 7 December: 'A critical situation has arisen – the whole front is pulling back. Everything is to be destroyed until we reach a new combat line. Burn it down, or blow it up.' The following morning Bopp's radio team pulled out. Houses were burning all around them. They still had their truck, but as they drove carefully along the road they passed column after column of riders and horse-drawn wagons. It seemed to Bopp that his 35th Infantry Division had just stepped back into the nineteenth century. 'We are now a cavalry force, just like Prince Wittgenstein [who protected the

Russian retreat in 1812] – following a route marked out by burning buildings.'

The trail of destruction had particular significance for Red Army artilleryman Pavel Ossipov:

As the counteroffensive began our young soldiers – from Siberia and the Far East – saw the real horror of this war. We were attacking the Germans in temperatures below −30 degrees Celsius, and anyone wounded and left in the deep snow would quickly die. And there were many wounded, particularly among our machine-gun crews, who had to pull their weapons behind them. Because we had to keep moving forward there was no one to help them. We despatched one of our men to administer basic first aid, and to report their whereabouts to our rear area service personnel, so that the motorised units following behind could pick them up.

We also saw a lot of dead civilians, mostly women and children. They were not expecting the offensive, and many of them – panic-stricken – had run, virtually naked, out into the open during the fighting.

When Ossipov reached his own village, near Volokolamsk, some 60 miles west of Moscow, he found his own house burnt to the ground and was told that his family had fled. He had no idea where they had gone.

The abrupt drop in temperature and the unexpected Russian counteroffensive had plunged Heinz Otto Fausten's 1st Panzer Division into chaos. On 7 December, colliding with enemy forces and unable to plug the widening gap in the front, its discipline began to collapse. Fausten and a comrade were now on foot – their armoured vehicle had already broken down – and heading towards the town of Klin, 50 miles north-west of Moscow: 'We followed the road along the edge of the forest,' Fausten recalled, 'over an open, snow-covered plain and then up towards the crest of a hill.' When the two men reached the top they saw a terrible sight. 'Ahead of us, burning, abandoned vehicles lay scattered on both sides of the road. Some of our troops were desperately trying to right their trucks and lorries, which were skidding all over the motor highway. The road was as slippery as an ice rink. Russian planes flew overhead, bombing at will. Each successive attack left more and more wounded strewn over the snow, but no one made any effort to help them.'

By the side of the roadway Fausten and his friend found the corpse of a German soldier. He had been run over, and then pressed flat into the snow by successive vehicles. A sheet of ice had formed over him, preserving his agonised features: 'We stared at him, and then we turned and looked at each other,' Fausten remembered. 'In that moment, the exhaustion, the chaos, the cold and hunger completely overwhelmed us. We took the ammunition box, which we had laboriously carried up the hill, and flung it into the snow. Then we smashed up the heavy machine gun, which we had been carrying on a sledge, and threw it down the slope. Our other equipment followed.' That night the two men stole food from a group of trucks parked by the roadside.

The difference between a retreat and a rout rested on whether order and cohesion could be maintained in the German Army in such exceptionally difficult circumstances. Field Marshal von Kluge, the commander of the Fourth Army, had read and reread Armand de Caulaincourt's history of Napoleon's 1812 campaign. For Kluge, the crucial moment came – during the retreat from Moscow – when the *Grande Armée* lost its army discipline. He stated to his staff: 'Do not doubt – the upholding of military order will be the crucial factor. Napoleon's army perished because it degenerated into disorderly plundering. The watchword for our army must be a strict maintenance of discipline.'

But German soldiers were now finding the mechanisms of their rifles and machine guns were freezing solid. The troops made a series of frantic experiments, eventually discovering that kerosene, used in Russian villages for lighting lamps, was cold-resistant and could be used as a lubricant. It had no lasting properties, and thus had to be renewed frequently. And no one knew whether it would corrode the metal. But at least their weapons were functioning again.

On 8 December a hesitant Hitler belatedly recognised that the attack on Moscow had ended, calling off the offensive because of 'the unusually early severe winter weather'. The winter weather was neither 'unusually early' nor more 'severe' than normal. These were simply face-saving excuses, as a Soviet military communiqué quickly made clear: 'The Germans complain that it was the winter that prevented them from taking Moscow. Yet they had not bothered to equip their army with warm clothing – and the reason for that was they hoped to finish the war before winter began. That was a most serious and dangerous miscalculation . . . It is not the winter that is to blame, but an intrinsic defect in the way the German high command planned for the war.'

Hitler was still reluctant to believe reports of the new Russian forces outside Moscow. 'He considers it all a bluff,' Major Gerhard Engel noted, 'and embarked – as so often – on an endless monologue . . . But from it all, one sees how unsettled and uncertain he is.'

The Third Panzer Group was now in headlong flight, and its operations officer, Carl Wagener, was scathing about the Führer's indecision: 'On 8 December Hitler finally permitted a transition to defence. The majority of our armies had, on their own initiative, already done this – three days earlier. With the enemy attacking in such force clear, overriding instructions were essential. But for three days Hitler and our high command made no decision whatsoever. From Hitler himself, there came only a succession of inquiries. He criticised little things, and offered us tactical advice – hardly necessary for troops with extensive combat experience in the east.'

At 5.00 a.m. on 8 December Horst Lange's company was on the march again. As they retreated westwards the grey light of dawn was masked by the flurries of snow. Along their route from the village wooden barricades had been set up, marking sections for demolition: all roads were to be blown up behind them. They passed groups of stragglers, all from different units, and found six infantrymen – all with badly frostbitten feet – just standing by the roadside, apathetic, no longer caring what might happen to them. After a lot of cajoling, swearing and shoving, Lange and his fellows eventually got them moving again. Behind Lange's column

Russian artillery was firing constantly. There were rumours that enemy tanks were approaching. Lange felt so very tired, a mixture of combat fatigue, nervous strain and sheer physical exhaustion. 'I'm at the end of my tether,' he wrote. 'The division to the left of us has pulled back without permission, leaving a gap in our line. The Russians to the south will soon overtake us. We shall be encircled.' Lange felt a sense of utter hopelessness. 'I don't think I will survive this retreat – my will to live is fading.'

That evening they reached a hamlet between two villages, Pokrov and Kotchugino. It was held by a solitary infantry company, all of whose men were exhausted. Lange's unit learnt that the Russians had taken Pokrov and were in the woods just 300 metres away. Nearby settlements were in flames, and the enemy artillery opened up, but there was no infantry attack. At dawn the men moved off again. They had been promised a convoy of motorised transport; if it did not reach them, they would be overwhelmed by the Russians.

On the evening of 8 December Georgi Osadchinsky's Red Army 35th Rifle Brigade stormed the village of Ozeretskoye. The Germans resisted fiercely but the combined strength of the Soviet forces – attacking with T-34 tanks and strong artillery support – was too much for them. Osadchinsky jumped into the defence trench. A dead German, with a light machine gun by his side, lay on the parapet. Another was still alive. Badly bloodstained, with his hands clutching his stomach, he looked up and started to say something. The man wanted to surrender. But Osadchinsky felt only hatred for him: 'I recalled the mangled corpses of the woman and child, blown up in the German minefield. Then I walked right up to the injured man, and shot him in the head.'

The Russian tank, the T-34, was a relatively new weapon, and it was now appearing in increasing numbers and causing the Germans real problems. 'These tanks were heavily armoured,' Major General Hans von Greiffenberg noted:

and were more mobile than our own vehicles, particularly in snow-covered terrain, because of their wide caterpillar tracks. The only

weapons of ours that could deal with them were the guns on our
Panzer Mark IVs, and our 88mm flak guns. However we only had
limited numbers of these. So the Russians exploited this superiority
in the battles for strongholds. They drove their T-34 tanks into the
villages we were holding, and fired upon the houses until they went
up in flames. Their infantry followed up behind, and shot down the
German troops 'smoked out' of their defences.

An officer in the German 35th Infantry Division – part of
Reinhardt's Third Panzer Group – noted in his diary: 'At 7.10 a.m.
the Russians attacked. Two heavy tanks with an infantry company
in support advanced over the brow of the hill and broke into the
village. The tanks went straight across our minefields – our mines
were totally ineffective against them. Then they crushed our artillery and machine-gun posts with their tracks. We were forced to
withdraw to the edge of the village.' Lieutenant Ludwig von Heyl
of the 36th Motorised Infantry Division added: 'On 8 December
the enemy made a sudden attack on a neighbouring village. They
pushed in three T-34s and simply rolled over the defenders. We
found a handful of survivors sheltering under a railway bridge.'

Soviet tank gunner Alexander Bodnar said: 'A tank brigade
during the battle for Moscow would have perhaps six or seven
KV tanks and between ten and twenty T-34s – the rest would be
lighter models. The Germans could not easily hit our heavy tanks
from the front [only 75mm rounds could penetrate the T-34's
strong, sloping armour] – so they led our attacks, shielding the
infantry.' The growing number of T-34 tanks left German troops
angry and dismayed. Hitler had, after all, proclaimed that Russia
was on the verge of collapse and had largely lost its industrial
capacity. This now seemed an idle boast. 'A gap had opened up
between our troops' view of the enemy's capabilities, and those of
our high command,' Hans von Greiffenberg observed, 'who continually overestimated our own strength and underestimated that
of the Russians. And this in turn undermined our soldiers' trust.
Morale began to plummet.'

Soviet Major General Konstantin Rokossovsky felt German

resistance weakening at the end of the third day of the counter-offensive, noting how more and more of their troops were flee-ing westwards, abandoning much of their military equipment. At Kamenka he captured two German heavy guns that had been brought up to shell Moscow.

On 8 December the commander of Army Group Centre, Field Marshal von Bock, surveyed the ruins of his offensive. He wrote a long, anguished entry in his diary, bemoaning lost opportunities, the October mud and the difficulties in supply when his troops were rolling forward. Then he acknowledged frankly: 'We under-estimated the strength of the enemy, and his ability to recover after suffering losses that would have toppled almost any other nation . . . My soldiers have given all they have; they can do no more.'

In the midst of this military crisis, Army Group Centre was becoming increasingly concerned about the Russian prisoner-of-war situation. Its chief of staff, Hans von Greiffenberg, wrote to the army quartermaster about the fate of the hundreds of thousands of Red Army soldiers accumulated after Operation Typhoon, emphasising: 'The extreme cold is having a devastating effect on the health of already weakened prisoners, who are now dying in large numbers.' He then stated: 'This situation has cre-ated a lack of compassion towards the condition of these men – an attitude which ignores the basic value of a human life and, in stark contrast, encourages a belief that against these defenceless ones any kind of mistreatment is permissible. Such behaviour – alien to the vast majority of German soldiers – must be fought by all means possible.' General Rudolf Schmidt, the new commander of the German Second Army, commented bluntly: 'These POW camps are now openly called "starvation camps", and it brings shame upon the German armed forces if, right under our noses, prisoners die like flies.'

During the heady days of the advance, the majority of German soldiers – deluged with race-hate propaganda about the inferiority of the Slavs – had shown little concern about the fate of Red Army soldiers, or the treatment of the Russian civilian population. They had concentrated on the military objectives ahead of them, and the goal of winning the war as quickly as possible. But with their army flung into retreat, and the scale of the human catastrophe growing, some were beginning to feel genuinely worried about what was happening.

Major Hans Reimann remembered the way prisoners were transported to the camps. He had boarded one of the prison trains: 'It was really gruesome. They were driven like cattle from the trucks to the drinking troughs, and bludgeoned to keep their ranks . . . There were sixty or seventy men in each cattle truck, and each time the train halted ten or more of them were taken out dead.' Cavalry regiment commander Friedrich von Broich recalled: 'Everything was such a mess at this time. We marched past a camp where there were 20,000 POWs. They were howling like wild beasts – they hadn't got anything to eat . . . Further along the road a column of about 6,000 tottering figures went past, completely emaciated, helping each other along. Every 100 metres or so two or three of them collapsed. Our soldiers rode along on bicycles, and everyone who had collapsed was shot and thrown into the ditch. That happened at regular intervals.'

Yet others felt – in an increasingly difficult military situation – that such cruelty was entirely justified. On 7 December Wilhelm Prüller wrote: 'Villages lying in front of us are burning down . . . The population really isn't to be envied. But all softer emotions must be sacrificed for tactical necessity.'

'The war is asking too much of us, and of the whole German people,' General Heinrici wrote to his wife on 8 December. 'Our men have been fighting the enemy in the freezing cold for weeks, with thirty or more of them crammed together at night in a filthy peasant hut, without even any soap, with wounds that are festering and not properly bandaged up, tormented by constant itching of lice that infest their dirty uniforms.' Heinrici was finding that some German soldiers were deliberately wounding themselves in an attempt to escape the front, and certain units – utterly demoralised and exhausted – refusing to fight altogether. 'Belatedly, I have read Stalin's speech on the anniversary of the October Revolution,' he continued. 'Russian planes kindly dropped copies of the text on our lines, printed in German. Stalin hopes that our army – grievously damaged by the winter weather, supply difficulties and the impact of fresh Siberian divisions – will disintegrate. It is our task to defy this prophecy, and therefore all vacation leave has been cancelled.'

'Such bitter cold!' wrote a German private, Reinhold Pabel, 'and yet the mornings begin with a magical light that could have come straight out of a fairy tale. The golden rays of the sun are shining on the straw roofs of the peasant huts where we are quartered. The air is crystal clear and the cold cuts into us like a knife. The snow crunches underfoot with a spitting sound. And our hard leather boots, with no room for padding, hurt our toes unbearably . . . One cannot risk taking one's gloves off, even for a moment, for within seconds the fingers begin to whiten with the first signs of frostbite.' Pabel's unit reached the next village after a couple of hours' marching. The cold was unyielding. 'The accommodation looks primitive,' he noted, 'we will certainly not be bedded on roses here. We are hearing worrying rumours about the Russian counteroffensive. During the night – in the distance – we hear the rattle of heavy machine guns and flares light up the sky.'

The night was not only lit by flares, but by countless burning towns and villages. To the south of Moscow, Colonel General Heinz Guderian's Panzers were in full retreat. 'I would never have believed that such a brilliant military position could be completely ruined in two months,' he wrote in frustration. 'Our supreme command has completely overreached itself. The Russians are now pursuing us closely.' His soldiers continued to retreat westwards. On 8 December Josef Deck wrote: 'Today, as we pulled back, we saw below us the small town of Bogoroditsk, with its mining industries, its agricultural and medical schools going up in bright flames. We passed through some outlying suburbs, and a woman with a baby – which looked in its wrappings like the pupa of a butterfly – pleaded with us that they might be allowed to stay alive. Her distress was clearly a "tribute" to the work of our German demolition squads,' Deck continued with bitter irony. 'I found a temporary place for her to stay in the barracks. But as we moved along the road, and in a haze of heavy, leaden exhaustion entered another house, we saw even more clearly the horror of our retreat for the civilian population caught in the midst of it.'

In a corner of the room a young woman was kneeling and praying, with her two young sons by her side. 'When she turned towards us and recognised our uniforms she was terrified, and pressed her children closely to her,' Deck related:

Fearfully she asked whether they would be allowed to leave, and whether the house was going to be set alight.

When we said that the house could stand she brought out little disks of black bread, and gave one to each of us with salt. But then we learnt that a German engineering team was in the vicinity, and that they had been ordered to burn everything in their path, creating an 80-kilometre-wide 'dead zone'. So we stayed in her house until the engineers had moved on. As we departed she made a three-way sign of the cross over each one of us.

We went outside into the night and I saw a sight which I can never forget. All along the horizon rose flames from burning towns and villages. And these flames began to mingle, in my thoughts, with the image of golden candles lighting up religious icons. But for the suffering Russians, no holy pictures are reflected in our own dark work.

Bogoroditsk was 140 miles south-east of the Russian capital. Georgi Osadchinsky's Red Army 35th Rifle Brigade was approaching the village of Rozhdestveno, 30 miles north-west of Moscow. The snow was falling, and the men were advancing cautiously. Suddenly, Osadchinsky saw a flash of red: 'A house on the outskirts of the village flared up, followed by several more. We were still about 100 metres away, and illuminated in the glow we saw German soldiers, torches in their hands, setting straw roofs alight. We rushed forward, but it was already too late. High-powered engines roared behind the burning buildings, and the Germans drove off in a convoy of armoured vehicles. There were no inhabitants left – they had already fled.'

On Army Group Centre's northern flank, Colonel General

Erich Hoepner had no qualms about burning villages. He had always advocated the harshest measures against the Russian civilian population. Now he felt the disappointment of the retreat as strongly as anyone. He wrote on 8 December: 'A day of unbearable tension. We are in an emergency situation and to keep my formations intact I have had to pull back again, after heavy fighting, abandoning some of our wounded and also much of our artillery. My northern neighbour, Reinhardt, faces the total disintegration of his forces. We have an absolute crisis here.' The two Panzer Groups were indeed in deadly danger.

And yet, there were respites from the horror. Hans Meier-Welcker's diary contained a remarkable entry for 8 December:

> Yesterday evening I attended the premiere of a 'village cultural event' in a large, disused cinema. The divisional quartermaster had devised the proceedings, assembling a pool of talent from the army and also the inhabitants of the village we are quartered in. We had regimental musicians, Russian farmers, girls and old men. The local people sang several songs. When one is able to experience Russian music, then one truly begins to love Russia. This country has an extraordinary capacity to endure suffering.
>
> The young girls danced delightfully and well. Our *Landsers* were entranced. And when we treat the Russians with real decency, their eyes light up with gratitude, which casts a warm glow over this dark existence we are living.

The retreat had many faces. A German lieutenant, Alexander Cohrs, had a sinister experience in a field hospital that he visited:

> I had already heard terrible rumours that wounded from our medical stations – men whose lives could still be saved – are suddenly disappearing, usually during the night. I believe that some of the medics are involved in this murderous practice. I had a staff map of our defence positions – which also showed the location of our wounded – and a medical orderly asked me to give it to him. I did not trust the man, and refused. When I returned to the hospital the following day I noticed that many of its own wounded were no longer there.

These men were being jettisoned in a desperate attempt to slow the Russian advance. They were abandoned with the deliberate intent that they would dig in, survive as long as they could and by doing so impede the Russians. It was an illicit operation, never formally approved. Most German officers would have found it deeply shocking and would not have permitted it. It had mysteriously taken root, nonetheless.

Red Army Lieutenant Ivan Savenko recalled an encounter with a German soldier left behind by his retreating division. He was highly disturbed by it:

> On 8 December, after we had switched over to the counter-attack, we discovered a German soldier, wounded but still alive, in a camouflaged position on the steep bank of a small river. We had come across a number of these hopeless 'desperado' holdouts over the last few days. I felt an uneasy chill. There was no doubt that it was a 'Fritz', and in his fear he was unleashing burst after burst of machine-gun fire, perhaps hoping for help from his comrades. But he was simply giving away his position to us.

Savenko and his men moved forward carefully, sometimes up to their waists in snow, and formed a ring around the lone German fighter. 'He had probably lost the self-control to wait for our approach,' Savenko continued, 'so we let him continue to fire off all his ammunition. Then we closed in on him, and as we got nearer the bursts of fire became more haphazard and uncertain – the long tracer flashes lifting high above us – and eventually they fell completely silent.' A Soviet sergeant looked at their quarry through his binoculars, then passed them to Savenko, saying: 'He seems to be dressed like one of our own women.' With a start Savenko saw through the field glasses a dishevelled lump, lying prostrate in the snow adorned with various items of Russian clothing. They were the kind that farming women wore in the countryside: 'This sorry-looking bundle was groaning loudly and only seemed semi-conscious,' Savenko recalled. 'He had dropped the sub-machine gun to the ground a couple of feet away. When we approached the poor devil we saw a trail of blood in the snow, and it was obvious that he had been left in this spot, already badly wounded. His breath came out in hacking bursts and he let out loud, incomprehensible curses and groans.'

'Shall I put him out of his misery, Comrade Second Lieutenant?' the sergeant said, taking his pistol out from its holder. Shooting lone German stragglers was a routine measure. But Savenko felt a sudden surge of pity. And on the spur of the moment he invented a justification for keeping the soldier alive, although it sounded pretty implausible when he relayed it to his comrades. 'No,' he answered. 'This man might be a high-ranking officer – if revived, he could tell us something important. Take his weapons and papers, and then carry him to the regimental medical station. Do this quickly, otherwise he will soon die.' The sergeant pulled an incredulous face, and then obeyed the order.

'My soldiers began to unwrap the "Fritz" from his various layers of clothing in order to find his papers,' Savenko continued. 'They were left speechless by what they saw. So this was the all-powerful conqueror, seeking *Lebensraum* for his master race. We untied a strange piece of female headgear and then, under his coat, found a skimpy woman's cardigan and a goatskin waistcoat. The "Fritz" had pulled large straw shoes over his boots. How one could fight in such an odd assortment of garments was difficult to imagine.'

Savenko thought of the invading German Army, abruptly thrown onto the defensive, its men in regular soldiers' coats, with inadequate headgear, gloves and boots, now having to fight out in the open or standing at night on sentry duty in temperatures dropping to −40 degrees Celsius: 'How could the Führer and his generals leave their soldiers in such a state during a Russian winter – with their men freezing in forward positions on snow-deep roads close to the suburbs of Moscow, suffering agonies, while our fresh Siberian divisions gathered for the counteroffensive?' It seemed inexplicable. The extent to which the German high command had underestimated the effect of the Russian winter was astonishing to Savenko. 'They had counted on a quick victory in a matter of weeks,' he said. 'I believe that in the first weeks of December 1941 the Germans suffered far more from frostbite and the extreme cold than from the impact of our troops. And as we attacked their positions in the deep snow, we were sweating in our warm winter clothing.'

Lieutenant Ludwig Freiherr von Heyl's 36th Motorised Infantry Division was trying to repulse Russian attacks on the village of Archangelskoye, north-east of Klin. At 11.00 a.m. on 9 December, Red Army soldiers broke into the village. Heyl mustered a relief force and threw them out again. He noted in his diary: '11.45 a.m. – crisis passed. About 150 Russians lie in heaps. Our soldiers immediately pull the boots and fur coats off the dead bodies.' Heyl was embarrassed to see his troops robbing corpses, but added: 'In such winter conditions, survival is our first priority.'

Amidst the horror, Hans Johann Kröhl remembered an extraordinary interlude. It was 9 December, and Kröhl, a military driver, was stationed at Istra, 30 miles north-west of Moscow:

I had received an order to drive to Mozhaisk, pick up a high-ranking officer – who had been wounded – and take him to the military hospital. After a few kilometres the officer accompanying me, seeing the state we were both in, said: 'We'd better go into one of those houses and give ourselves a proper wash.' With a wash bag under my arm I managed to find an intact house, a well and a still-functioning water pump. Afraid that there might be hidden partisans in the building I quickly explored it and stumbled across a small room, near the cooking and washing facilities, where many books were stored. They were all in German!

I forgot my original intentions, got out a cigarette and began to smoke. It was my first encounter with books since University, and what a place to find them – in the middle of this war! Then, as I was happily browsing, I heard a quiet rustling behind me. I reached for my pistol, and to my horror realised that, intent on having a quick wash, I had left it behind in the car! This breach of army regulations could easily have fatal consequences. Mortified, I turned around and looked straight into a pair of eyes even more scared than mine.

Out of the darkness a fifty-year-old woman had appeared. She spoke to me in fluent German, saying: 'Please may I offer you some of my books? In the next few days retreating German soldiers will burn down our house anyway.' I began a long conversation with the

woman, who, it emerged, was a Jewish professor and a high school
graduate in German. She was now in hiding from the Waffen SS, who
were occupying Istra.

After a quarter of an hour my NCO suddenly appeared and
reminded me to hurry up. Our conversation was brought to a sudden
end. The Russian woman gave me a small book of poems, some
Goethe and some Schiller, all with beautiful bindings. Touched by
her generosity, I naively asked her if she could put her address on
the cover. 'No,' came the laconic reply, 'that could get me into a lot
of trouble!' And catching sight of the NCO again, who, following
regulations, was washing with his pistol properly in its holster, I said
farewell and left the dark, book-laden room.

In the Second World War, the German Army had won its successes in summer campaigns, on the attack. It had not prepared
for winter warfare, nor for fighting a retreat. With an absence of
clear guidance from its high command, commanders in the field
weighed the merits of two rival, improvised strategies. The first,
favoured by Colonel General Guderian, was to disengage from the
enemy and pull back a substantial distance, thereby gaining time
and freedom of manoeuvre. The disadvantage of this plan was that
a vast amount of equipment would have to be abandoned in order
to make a rapid retreat. The second, favoured by the commander
of the Fourth Army, Field Marshal von Kluge, was to fight as close
to the front-line positions as possible, tying down the Red Army
in a battle of attrition until reinforcements and winter equipment
arrived. The danger here was that the German line was perilously
weak, and there were no reserves. If the Russians broke through,
the whole of Army Group Centre would be in peril.

In the event, a compromise evolved. The Germans constructed
a series of local strongholds, and defended them tenaciously while
the remainder of their troops pulled back westwards, buying time
for their forces to regroup. There was an obvious psychological
incentive to hold these defences, as Army Group Centre's chief
of staff, Hans von Greiffenberg, made clear: 'Our troops, inad-
equately protected from the winter weather, feared a withdrawal
to some "imaginary" defence line, where no construction work

had been done, and they would be forced to spend the nights out in the open. It was therefore understandable that they clung to these fortified villages, where they could find at least temporary protection from the cold. But the Russians quickly took advantage of this.'

Soviet commander General Georgi Zhukov trumped this strategy, ordering his armies to avoid wasteful frontal attacks on the enemy and instead outflank its positions. On 9 December he enjoined: 'Avoid trying to push the Germans back frontally – allowing them the chance to redeploy and reorganise. Instead, go around their positions and threaten to encircle them.' Zhukov's orders had an immediate effect. At the end of the same day, German Colonel Adolf Raegener of the 9th Infantry Regiment wrote: 'The Russians are employing new tactics – and they are highly effective. They push around the sides of our strongpoints, using heavy tanks and infantry on snowshoes, and then attack our positions from behind. We are suffering increasing losses as a result.'

Soviet Major General Dmitry Lelyushenko, a skilful tank commander who revelled in fast-moving warfare, now tore a substantial gap in Army Group Centre's northern flank. On 9 December, when his advance units seized the town of Rogachevo, 50 miles north of Moscow, he was already 15 miles ahead of many of the retreating German forces. 'After the loss of Rogachevo the position of our northern flank became critical,' Hans von Greiffenberg declared. 'We had no reserves left, and had to hastily arm and send out anyone we could find, including train crews and construction workers.'

General Zhukov now ordered Lelyushenko to advance on the town of Klin, 18 miles west of Rogachevo, as rapidly as possible. The Red Army was hoping to execute a pincer movement with Lelyushenko's Thirtieth Army and General Kuznetsov's First Shock Army. If it succeeded, many of the best formations of the Third Panzer Group – including four Panzer and two motorised infantry divisions – would be encircled.

Early on the morning of 9 December Horst Lange and his

comrades were retreating through a section of forest. The company had been dispersed by a Russian air attack and now there was only a small group left, twelve men and a lieutenant. Suddenly there was an explosion close by, and a large tree disintegrated. The men were directly in the path of an artillery bombardment. Trees began to topple all around them and clumps of earth blew up into the air. Men fell to the ground wounded and Lange's comrades ran off in terror, trying to hide.

Suddenly, Lange felt an agonising pain in his left eye. He sank to his knees. He felt blood all over his face – and he could no longer see. He called out for help. A medic pressed some gauze to his eye and two fellow soldiers picked him up. Miraculously, Lange was brought back to a small medical station at Kotchugino. He had regained his sight in his right eye; the left would have to be operated on. 'I have experienced so much, seen so much, lost so much,' wrote Lange, 'but somehow I have survived. This war has become so terrible.'

Faced with a struggle for survival, German soldiers resorted to hasty improvisation. Some organised sewing workrooms in nearby Russian towns, employing local inhabitants who produced earmuffs, waistcoats, footcloths and mittens from used blankets and old clothing. Some soldiers protected their heads and ears with rags and flannel waistbands. They heated the engines of their tanks and trucks overnight, often lighting fires underneath the vehicles, so that they would be able to start in the morning. When marching, the troops tried to orientate themselves in a landscape covered in deep snow by beating out paths and marking buried tracks and roadways with small flags. 'Travel becomes slow and exhausting in snow more than a metre deep,' wrote General Lothar Rendulic, commander of the German 52nd Infantry Division, struggling to master an entirely new form of warfare. 'In such conditions, it took my men more than nine hours to cover a distance of four kilometres. All were close to exhaustion when they reached their objective. Some sank into the snow, and had to be extricated with poles and ropes.'

When marching through lighter snow, soldiers would trample

out a path, packing it down tight for those following behind them. It was strenuous work, and the men worked in shifts. In contrast, Rendulic noticed that the Russians were able to use their T-34 tanks, with their wide tracks, to carve out a path for their infantry. The tanks were surprisingly mobile in the deep snow. The tracks of the German Panzers were too narrow for this purpose.

The Russians were far better equipped for such conditions, many having skis or snowshoes. Red Army platoon commander Georgi Osadchinsky recalled his reconnaissance missions: 'During the severe winter weather around Moscow,' Osadchinsky related, 'we had to cover considerable distances, on roads the Germans considered impassable because of the deep snow. Under such conditions my senses heightened and I gained an instinctive feeling for this kind of combat – which often came to my aid in moments of crisis. On the darkest nights I was able to see as if by twilight, and inhaling the wind rushing past my nose, could usually detect the smell of tobacco smoke, indicating if enemy soldiers were nearby. I could feel the proximity of danger.'

Under cover of a blizzard, Osadchinsky and his patrol located a German sentry post and put it under observation: 'The snowstorm strengthened. The howl and whistle of the wind muffled all sounds. And then I smelled something. Again, the tell-tale whiff of tobacco smoke. A little time passed, and from the haze of snow flurries five figures appeared. It was the relief detachment. The enemy soldier who had brought up the rear had been smoking into his sleeve, to mask the glow of the cigarette. But I had smelled it minutes earlier.' The Germans had no inkling that anyone was lying in wait, on the snow-covered ground. Osadchinsky and his reconnaissance scouts moved forward silently in their long, white snow coats, then rushed the post, finishing off its startled occupants with their knives.

The war had become unyielding in its brutality. The death rate of Russian prisoners was now astronomical. Lieutenant Paul Seyffardt said bluntly: 'They were killed in their thousands. 400,000 were said to have died on the march from Gzhatsk to Smolensk alone.' 'There were so many of them,' added company commander Ludwig Heilmann, 'and they were given so little food.'

Hans Jürgen Hartmann and his comrades, stationed south of Army Group Centre at Kharkov, were now realising the full scale of the disaster outside Moscow: 'We are hearing that things look really bad,' Hartmann wrote. 'Units are surrounded, tanks and vehicles unable to move, our forces are at the end of their tether. If all this is true, we are in real trouble.' Meanwhile the military situation worsened day by day. On 10 December Colonel General Guderian, in a candid acknowledgement of the *Siegseuphorie* that had swept over German commanders and soldiers alike in the early days of Typhoon, said: 'We have seriously underestimated the enemy, the size of his country and the vagaries of his climate – and now we are paying for it.'

On the same day an unknown German soldier wrote to his wife: 'Here, outside Moscow, the devil has been unloosed – the Russians are hitting us with everything. One of their planes flew over our column, forcing us face down in the snow, strafing and killing our horses. Then their tanks came, driving through our lines, scattering everyone. We are now huddled together in a village amidst scenes of chaos.'

Georgi Osadchinsky's Red Army unit had reached the Moscow-Leningrad highway near the town of Solnechnogorsk, 40 miles north-west of the capital. They saw German troops retreating along the road in two long columns, and moved in to attack:

We howled wildly and rushed towards the enemy. Hand-to-hand fighting began. A tracer round hissed past my left shoulder and before me arose a figure, emerging out of the flurries of snow. I shot at point-blank range. Another German swung at me with his rifle butt. I grabbed the rifle with both hands, and we struggled together in the deep snow among the fir trees. The German flung himself on top of me, and pushed his rifle against my throat. I started to lose consciousness, but by pure instinct pulled out my knife and stuck it into his side. I had only one thought: 'Stab above his belt!' I heard the German moan, and the pressure was suddenly released. I pulled out the knife from under him, and in wild fury stabbed him again and again in the chest.

Osadchinsky concluded: 'A ferocious hatred of the enemy over-rode all fear and reason. We did not take prisoners.'

On 10 December Private Gerhard vom Bruch's 6th Panzer Division was pulling back further north along the Moscow-Leningrad highway, towards the town of Klin. Enemy pressure was increasing. He wrote: 'The remnants of our company formed up in a long, silent column. We secured a small hillock, atop of which lay a ruined church. Before us was a bridge over a frozen river, which had been prepared for demolition as soon as our forces crossed it. At noon the enemy attacked first, striking against our left flank with a mortar bombardment and salvoes of rifle fire. Our unit extricated itself with difficulty – our losses are growing.'

When Georgi Osadchinsky and his fellow Red Army soldiers reached the village of Rekino-Kresty, three miles south-east of Solnechnogorsk, they found that the Germans had fled in haste, leaving wagons full of weapons, ammunition and uniforms. But Osadchinsky noticed something:

> I looked around, and in the snow saw traces of blood. Evidently, an injured soldier had been crawling, searching for shelter. I followed the trail, which led to a vegetable garden and a covered slit trench. I edged forward, and suddenly a shot thundered past me. The injured German had missed me. I let off a burst of machine-gun fire and jumped into the trench. He lay there dead.
>
> I searched him, but there were no documents. His machine gun lay by his side, its magazine empty. He had used his last cartridge to try and kill me. And then I saw the prize he had so desperately defended. His other hand was still clenched around a small can of condensed milk.

German Lieutenant Ludwig von Heyl feared for the future. His soldiers were holding a fragile defence line north-east of Klin: 'The Russians launched a night attack on our position,' he wrote on 10 December. 'The remnants of our company immediately ran off. I stood at the edge of the village – pistol drawn – with two other officers, restoring discipline among the fleeing troops.'

Luftwaffe commander Wolfram von Richthofen was becoming

increasingly despairing of the military situation, declaring on 11 December: 'Because of the weather, and the short winter days, we have been unable to make many flights, and as a result have had little effect on things. Our troops are unable to hold their ground and there are no more reserves. The Russians seem to be able to go anywhere they please. Luck and good fortune, and some kind of higher intervention are needed; all our measures, and all our skill, may not be enough to extricate ourselves.'

Alexander Cohrs was struggling against the innumerable lice: 'Once I counted more than 130 of them in my shirt,' he declared. 'Now I have simply given up estimating their numbers. One of my comrades – tormented by their itching – has rolled himself up into a ball, like a hedgehog.'

Red Army attacks were gaining momentum. On 11 December German Private Gerhard vom Bruch continued: 'The enemy realises how weak we are, and is pushing hard after us. Our vehicles are in a terrible state. We are driving slowly and carefully, hoping that in a couple of days we will be in Klin. The main roadway is being used by several German divisions and has become one huge car cemetery. It is a bleak picture: hundreds and hundreds of our vehicles lie abandoned on both sides of the road.'

Lieutenant Ludwig von Heyl's 36th Motorised Division was now astride the same highway: 'We have laid mines behind us,' Heyl wrote at 6.00 p.m. on 11 December. 'We have no vehicles left. We are to march the whole night. We ate a last meal from the field kitchen, and then, unable to carry it with us, blew it up.' Major Alexander Conrady added: 'We are called a "Motorised Division", but all our soldiers are now retreating on foot. We load the wounded onto carts.'

The remnants of these once-proud German divisions were now suffering terribly. On 12 December Bruch added: 'Since yesterday evening we have set up camp in a forest. We are out in the open, with a temperature around −30 degrees Celsius, trying to keep ourselves warm in the snow. There will clearly be no opportunity to get some sleep this night. We set up large fires, whose thick smoke smarts the eyes, which are then "refreshed" by the stinging cold.

The Russians are close by, and have already occupied villages to the left and right of our notional security line, which in real defensive terms has no significance whatsoever.' The following morning the Russians discovered Bruch's forest camp, and the exhausted German soldiers only narrowly escaped the clutches of the enemy.

Soviet Major General Dmitry Lelyushenko was coordinating the Red Army attack on Klin, 50 miles north-west of Moscow, with a strike force of three rifle divisions and two tank brigades. On 12 December he smashed the main German tank forces defending this important junction point and closed in on the town. Along the road he found the Germans now abandoning their wounded as well as their equipment. German officer Ekkehard Maurer was retreating with the 23rd Infantry Division: 'Another soldier and I were carrying a wounded man between us. We dragged him back through the snow. Then the man who was helping me – who also had been wounded in the leg – couldn't pull any more. Neither could I. So we left that man, lying there. We had to leave him behind. He kept calling out to me, calling out my name, his cries growing fainter and fainter.'

'Our regiment lost more than 1,000 men outside Moscow,' remembered Franz Peters, a soldier from the same division, 'and I use the word "lost" deliberately. For what happened to them? We couldn't bury anyone – the earth was frozen too deep. We piled them together and covered them with snow, so that they could no longer be seen.' This was the 9th (Potsdam) Infantry Regiment. Its commander, Colonel Adolf Raegener, added: 'The regiment no longer existed as an effective fighting force. Its bloody remnants lay along the Moscow-Klin motor highway, shot to pieces and frozen solid in the ice and snow.'

Even hardened Soviet security detachments were shocked by what they found. 'We had at the front the so-called "burial brigades", whose job was to gather the corpses,' said Lieutenant Vladimir Ogryzko of the 1st NKVD division. 'The snow was waist deep in the fields, and under its top layer we uncovered the bodies of thousands of German soldiers. Their limbs had twisted and contorted in the icy cold. Bodies, bodies – everywhere.'

On 12 December the Soviet Sixteenth Army captured Istra, north-west of Moscow. 'One only hears bad news,' Colonel General Hoepner wrote that day, 'it is frightening each time the telephone rings. Things are getting worse and worse. The mass of Russians is crushing us . . . Our men are so exhausted that they fall asleep standing up; so apathetic, they no longer throw themselves on the ground when shot at. Losses from frostbite are far more numerous than battle casualties. Our situation has an awful similarity to Napoleon in 1812.' The similarity was greater than Hoepner realised, for Zhukov now ordered Major General Lev Dovotar's Cossack cavalry force to ride around the German lines and disrupt vital communication and supply links. And so – in an uncanny echo of 1812 – Cossack cavalry were once more unleashed upon the invaders.

On the southern flank of Army Group Centre, General Gotthard Heinrici was also experiencing a return to the nine-teenth century for Germany's mechanised army: 'I have walked three kilometres to the next dirt village in our defence line,' he noted on 12 December. 'I am now arranging that horse relays will be put in place, so that in future we can travel like old Napoleon in our wooden "carriages".' Then he added: 'This country is extreme in everything – its size, its forests, its climate and its masses of people. A vast area has to be held with a small number of our troops – and the Russians are attacking along our whole front. They need only concentrate their forces at one particular point and we are immediately in trouble. In all my years as a soldier I have never been in such a difficult position. We feel that fortune has completely deserted us.'

Hitler bore ultimate responsibility for the suffering of his soldiers. But he was reluctant to accept this. Incredibly – while his armies were dying on the Eastern Front – after Japan had bombed the American fleet at Pearl Harbor on 7 December he also declared war on the United States four days later, enlarging the scope of the war even further. This was an astonishing decision, defying any understanding of reality. 'The Führer has given a speech declaring war on America,' Lieutenant Georg Kreuter wrote in bemusement on 12 December, 'while here we are struggling to hold on to our defences.' Medical officer Willi Lindenbach recalled: 'Like a thunderbolt from the sky came the news of Japan's declaration of war against Britain and America. And now we have declared war against America too. The plan clearly was for us to take Moscow, and then for Japan to engage the British and Americans. The news that the Japanese have sunk much of the American Pacific fleet is certainly very good. But here we are in full retreat.'

Reinhold Pabel also feared the grandiosity of Hitler's decision: 'So now the war has extended all over the globe. Everyone knows that over-mighty ambitions unleash an ever-escalating destruction,' he wrote. The big decisions were made by those far removed from conditions on the Eastern Front, and Pabel contrasted his present plight with conditions in his homeland:

In the battle-scarred ruins of the village we are in, there are just a few undamaged buildings, which we can use. We build bunk beds, find straw and make a shelter from the cold. At night snowstorms whip over the exposed ground on which our 'quarters' lie. The men are in a constant state of tension, with non-stop reconnaissance patrols, mine-laying and sentry duties. We know that the Russians are approaching.

The enemy air force is a frequent visitor and our own planes are scarcely to be seen. Food supplies and the post have all been severely disrupted, and only get through very occasionally. The days are short and the nights are mercilessly long. At around 3.30 p.m. it is already becoming dark, and we light broken lamps, but we are very short of fuel. We write and drink to while away the long evenings, and postpone the moment of going to bed, when the all-consuming battle with lice will be resumed. And in the meagre, flickering light our thoughts drift elsewhere. At home they will happily be preparing for Christmas – there are only fourteen days to go. Here – in a brief evening respite from this war – we scavenge to find a little bread, and celebrate that we still have half a tin of sardines to spread on it. And then we wait, until the full force of the winter's night descends upon us.

Hans von Greiffenberg believed a turning point had been reached: 'The Führer's almost pathological belief in his mission, which "providence" had imposed upon him, was now seriously inter-fering with his ability to make a clear judgement of the military situation.'

Surprisingly, some German soldiers still strove to find some decency and human values amidst the horror. Medical officer Wilhelm Hebestreit wrote on 13 December:

> In this country I find many people who could have come straight out of the novels of Tolstoy or Dostoevsky. They possess a remarkable, almost child-like innocence. Yes they are poor, and in our under-standing of things live in a backward and primitive condition. But it is a blessed kind of poverty, which brings out such tender feelings – the good-natured simple acts of kindness that I have witnessed – as if perhaps God was sharing some sort of secret with them. I came into their rough dwellings on sufferance, but very quickly began to see something very special is here. For the first time I am beginning to understand why human beings throughout the ages have renounced material possessions and embrace poverty and a simple life. Our cul-ture frowns upon those who still all cook, eat and sleep in one room. But I saw how it creates a sense of unity, and selfless common purpose that in truth we no longer know.

Hebestreit's sympathy was underscored by condescension and an inherent racism. The majority of Germans, however, were less generous even than this: 'I am reading the novels of Tolstoy and short stories of Leskov,' General Gotthard Heinrici wrote during the first terrible days of the retreat. 'Both these writers lived close to Tula,' he continued, 'and Tolstoy's home was briefly one of our military headquarters . . . Their books impress me very much. Leskov is a gifted storyteller. And one can only admire the descrip-tive skills of Tolstoy and the clarity of his characterisation.' But the novels were filtered through the distorting lens of Heinrici's own deep-seated prejudice. 'For me, fundamentally, they show why everything in Russia is so backward,' he then declaimed. 'The books show the Russian peasant in the same light that we find him today – good-natured, accommodating, but totally infuriating – lacking any sort of initiative, unwilling to undertake new endeav-ours and completely stuck in the well-worn groove of habit.'

A week after the start of the Soviet offensive, Stalin felt confident enough about the overall military situation to allow *Pravda* to run the headline: 'Defeat of the German army on the approaches to Moscow'. There were portraits of all the leading Red Army generals, with Georgi Zhukov taking pride of place in the centre of the page. On the same day Stalin ordered the removal of all demolition charges on Moscow's factories, bridges and public buildings. Overall, the first stage of the Russian counter-attack had been a considerable success.

Both wings of Army Group Centre were now in peril. To the south, many of the formations of the German Second Army – which had guarded Guderian's flank – were fighting for survival. Three infantry divisions – the 45th, 95th and 134th – had been surrounded by the Soviet Third and Thirteenth Armies. A German soldier from the 134th Division wrote: 'The troops are utterly depressed . . . our vehicles break down, then Russian air attacks destroy our horses and sledges. The enemy is everywhere.' The division's few remaining self-propelled assault guns could barely negotiate the ice and snowdrifts, and it was running out of petrol, ammunition and food.

On the night of 13 December the commander of the retreating 134th Division, Lieutenant General Conrad von Cochenhausen, was supposed to be leading his men in a breakout from Russian encirclement. Instead, shortly before midnight, the general drove to a deserted stretch of motor highway and shot himself in the head. The strain had become too much for him. The corps commander, General Hermann Metz, wrote a full report of the incident:

Cochenhausen had grown increasingly pessimistic about the military situation in the east and was extremely concerned about the combat fatigue of his division. A strong enemy attack on our south-western flank, and the complete failure of our supply lines, had made our position at Yelets untenable, so Cochenhausen was forced to retreat from the town. And on 13 December his division was trapped by the enemy. He told me that the Russians had brought up many tanks, and were placing his troops under heavy artillery bombardment. His men were desperately short of ammunition and were struggling to move their guns in the deep snow. They pulled back westwards in pitch darkness, braving icy winds, extreme cold and terrible road conditions. Everyone was under enormous strain. At 10.30 p.m. his troops were brought to a halt by a ravine. The Russians opened up on them with heavy machine guns and rocket launchers.

In September 1939 Cochenhausen had stood with Hitler surveying the German bombardment of Warsaw. 'The Führer was deeply moved,' he remembered with pride. Cochenhausen had been an enthusiastic advocate of Hitler's mission to create *Lebensraum* in the east. But now he had reached the limits of human endurance and was simply unable to go on.

A Soviet combat report was succinct. 'The commander of the 134th Infantry Division is dead. The division has been forced to abandon nearly all of its equipment, which is no longer functioning in the extreme cold.' German technological superiority was collapsing under the impact of the Russian climate. 'It is insanely cold,' Leopold Höglinger wrote on 13 December. 'We begin to drive, lose our way, get stuck in the snow.' A day later, artilleryman Gerhard Bopp's solitary radio truck also broke down: 'At 8.00 a.m. we halted by a ford. We tried to get the truck over it – but in vain. We put wooden slats over the frozen river and tried again, but the steering mechanism had frozen up and we could not shift the wheels. We thawed out the steering and the wheels, only to find that the engine refused to start – the gasoline feed pipe was now frozen.'

Bopp and his comrades struggled on. 'We made a fire under the truck. Again no gasoline was being pumped through. Perhaps the pump itself was defective.' Eventually they gave up. The truck was blown up, excess equipment destroyed and a horse and cart procured. At 4.00 p.m. they moved over the ford. And then the cart got stuck. Bopp's tale of woe continued: 'Night was falling, and the passing columns of our infantry – hurrying to reach their accommodation, did not help us. We loaded what we could onto the horse and began carrying the rest. Eventually another cart was found in the next village, and all our remaining radio equipment retrieved. That night,' Bopp concluded, 'we all slept extremely well.'

The night of 14 December was less peaceful for artilleryman Josef Deck. 'A snowstorm began that evening,' he remembered:

> but one very different from those we had experienced at home. It did not lessen the cold, it intensified it. And as we moved out into this blizzard our reconnaissance troops lost all sense of direction. One unit, sent to procure a village for us later that night, never returned, and we assumed they were now in the Russians' 'safe-keeping'. We attempted to drive westwards nonetheless. Connecting pipes broke, oil froze, engines refused to start. Our slow progress was illuminated by burning villages, completely devoid of life – all human beings and animals had been driven away. The ice had hardened on the road, and we skidded helplessly from one side to the other. It became a drive through hell.

Eventually Deck and his comrades found a solitary house, abandoned by its inhabitants, which still lay intact amidst the snowdrifts. They parked their truck, clambered into the building, laboriously started the stove and began to warm themselves up. The men fell into a fitful sleep. It was short-lived: 'Around 4.00 a.m. I suddenly woke up. Our accommodation was in flames around us – the stove had burst. We fled the building.' They drove off at a speed of 5 mph. Their toes were now frostbitten.

On 14 December Hans Meier-Welcker reflected back on the evening of entertainment that he had so much enjoyed six days earlier. It seemed like a memento from a bygone age: 'The performance that I witnessed could not be repeated – as originally intended – for many others in the division. In rapid marches, over ice and snowdrifts, we had to move to a threatened point on the front, and were immediately thrown in at a place where the enemy was about to break through.' The German troops performed well, and amidst so much dispiriting news Meier-Welcker was moved to witness his division's professionalism and resilience. He continued proudly: 'In our counter-attack fifteen guns were captured, at least ten tanks destroyed and many more damaged. The Russian troops were fresh reinforcements, and they had not yet experienced the German army in this war.'

Other German units were in terrible shape. Heinz Otto Fausten remembered the retreat of the 1st Panzer Division from Klin on 14 December:

> There was a sudden, dramatic explosion as I saw Klin's most prominent landmark – a big water tower – being detonated by German engineers. It collapsed into a pile of rubble. A panic-stricken throng of disbanded tank crews, artillerymen without guns, rear service people who had never fought and officers who no longer had any units left the town that evening. We formed a long column – some on horse-drawn sledges and carts, the rest walking. As we followed a track along the edge of a forest everything was burning: villages, supply dumps and abandoned vehicles. Engineers blew up the route behind us, blocking it with fallen trees.

Hastily formed battle groups from the 1st Panzer and 36th Motorised Divisions were holding open the fragile escape route. The Thirteenth Army forces under Soviet Major General Dmitry Lelyushenko broke into Klin the same night, overwhelming the last few German defenders. Although the Russians had not encircled all the enemy divisions as planned, they had inflicted grievous losses on them – in both men and equipment. The following day Fausten's column was overtaken by the Red Army. A ski battalion outflanked them, with tanks following up behind: 'They attacked from all sides,' Fausten recalled, 'and most of our soldiers and horses were killed outright in that first barrage of fire. I ran into the knee-deep snow towards the forest. When I turned, I saw those who had remained by the side of the road being hunted down and bayoneted by the Russians.'

On 15 December Georgi Osadchinsky's Red Army unit reached the outskirts of the village of Krivtsovo, south-west of Solnechnogorsk. They had not slept for two days, nor eaten for twenty-four hours. Their orders were to push the enemy hard, not allowing him a chance to regroup. The Germans were only a quarter of a mile ahead of them, having fortified several brick buildings, which lay around a ruined church.

The Red Army soldiers fanned out. Night was falling, and visibility was poor.

Then the Germans saw them. There were several bursts of machine-gun fire, and then everything was set alight to cover their retreat: 'A terrible fire, fanned by the wind, raged through the houses. Roofs collapsed, brands flew in all directions, thick clouds of smoke billowed up into the night sky. The Germans had doused the cottages and sheds with gasoline so that they flared up instantly,' recalled Osadchinsky. When the flames had died down he and his comrades entered the burnt-out village. 'All that was left were the Russian stoves with their crumbled pipes, the ruins of the church and the frames of the brick buildings. In the last one we found more than a hundred corpses of Red Army prisoners and civilians. All had been shot.'

On the evening of 15 December Josef Deck at last reached the safety of Mtensk, north of Orel: 'A mass of vehicles was converging on the town,' Deck recalled. 'Field police directed us to a side road, next to a brickyard, where many staff officers were standing. There, in the midst of them, stood Colonel General Guderian, grey in the face and exhausted, and only holding himself upright with difficulty. Yet he greeted each one of us, every single vehicle, as we pulled over. He lifted his hand to his cap and saluted the survivors of his army.'

Things could not carry on like this. The German Army was fighting for its life. Its commander, Field Marshal von Bock, was now complaining of health problems and hinting that he would like to be relieved of his command. He no longer had a clear idea of what to do, and on 16 December passed the following report to Hitler, effectively abdicating all personal responsibilities: 'The Führer must decide for himself whether my army group should stand and fight, thereby risking its total destruction, or retreat, entailing precisely the same risk. If he decides on retreat, then he must realise that it is unlikely that enough troops will ever get back to the new line to hold it.' Bock then added for emphasis, if any were needed, that when pulling back earlier that day one infantry division – the 267th – had been forced to abandon its entire artillery.

Luftwaffe commander Wolfram von Richthofen had decided to appeal to Hitler in person: 'I kept emphasising to him what matters now is keeping our troops alive and fighting where they are. The front lacks infantrymen, winter gear and food – but above all the will to stand fast . . . I stressed the need for him to appeal to each soldier . . . The Führer listened with enormous interest and concentration. He is planning a major proclamation.'

Adolf Hitler was about to make a major intervention on the Eastern Front. He had resolved to take personal responsibility for halting the retreat.

6

Stand Fast!

WITHIN THE WEHRMACHT was a sense of mounting crisis. German forces on Moscow's northern and southern flanks – at Klin and Livny – had almost been encircled, and the troops had been forced to retreat with massive losses in equipment. At Livny the German 45th Division had to abandon most of its artillery. The commander of the German Army, Field Marshal Walther von Brauchitsch – who had been ill – did not seem to have an answer to the deteriorating situation.

Alarming reports were coming in. On Army Group Centre's northern flank, as General Reinhardt's Third Panzer Group pulled out of Klin, army discipline began to break down. One report stated: 'More and more soldiers are streaming westwards, having abandoned their weapons. One can be seen leading a cow, on a rope, another pulling a sledge laden with potatoes. The road is under constant Russian air attack, and those being killed by the bombs are no longer being buried . . . The Panzer group is in a dismal state.'

'The effect of the air attacks was devastating,' Colonel Hans von Luck of the 7th Panzer Division recalled. 'In great haste, we cleared a retreat route from Klin. Vast mountains of snow were piled up on either side of the road – making it difficult for us to run for cover quickly. Russian planes would appear behind our retreating columns, strafing the infantry and bombing the horse-drawn supply and artillery units. Soon, the narrow roads were choked with the corpses of men and horses. Those that escaped the carnage were usually finished off by Russian ski patrols.'

On the southern wing, things were little better. The Wehrmacht's

Second Army had been badly hit by the Soviet counteroffensive, and its remnants – struggling to extricate themselves from Red Army encirclement – retreated in disarray. German soldier Willy Reese made a succession of night marches with the battered 95th Division: 'We were trying to slip a noose that Russian forces had almost drawn around us,' Reese remembered:

> The march back began without sleep, mute, in an atmosphere of unexpressed despair. The moonlight shone down on our silent column of fugitives, slowly making its way through the snow – reeling, slithering and stumbling westwards. Behind us were the pursuing Russians. We were dog-tired – this was already our third night without sleep . . . Our eyes closed, our legs went mechanically on for a few seconds, then our knees buckled. We keeled over, awoke with the pain of the fall, pulled ourselves up – and with the last of our strength tottered on. 'The Russians are coming!' – the warning worked like the crack of a whip.

Finally, Reese's unit took shelter in a village. It was allowed a one-hour rest period. 'I slunk into a house and collapsed in a corner,' Reese said. 'I was asleep before I touched the floor. When I awoke, I was all alone. I'd been forgotten about – but some of my strength had returned. I dashed outside. There was no one, neither friend nor foe. I hurried up a nearby hill, and from it saw my comrades in the distance – tiny dots in the snowscape. I set off after them. Hours later, I caught up with the column.'

Reese recalled a bitter, dull-witted apathy settling over the troops. Men lay down in the snow and refused to get up, resisting kicks and rifle prods from their comrades. The neighbouring German 45th Division was in equally dire straits. When it was attacked by Soviet planes, exhausted and starving soldiers – with the bodies of the dead and wounded scattered all around them – ignored the bombing, built massive fires and began to roast the carcasses of the horses from their supply column. The scene resembled the making of a funeral pyre.

'Morale and discipline have become the chief victims of this retreat,' wrote Lieutenant Kurt Grumann of the 87th Infantry Division. 'All along the road we see smashed-up vehicles and abandoned goods and equipment. Sometimes we see piles of ammunition, jettisoned in such haste that it has not even been blown up to prevent the enemy using it against us. These scenes are really shocking.'

'The overall situation was now extremely serious,' recorded Major General Hans von Greiffenberg, Army Group Centre's chief of staff. 'Intercepted radio messages showed that the Soviet high command – buoyed up by its success – was now hoping to destroy a substantial part of our forces in the snow and ice outside Moscow. In the first ten days of the retreat, the Red Army had flung at least thirty fresh infantry divisions and six new armoured brigades against us. More and more were appearing. For the first time, our combat reports referred to "tank fright" and "encirclement fear" among our troops – discipline was beginning to crack.'

An increasingly infuriated Hitler sent Brauchitsch out to the front on 14 December. The head of the German Army returned, overwhelmed by the scale of the crisis, and was promptly summoned to report to the Führer. Hitler's own record of their meeting is as follows: 'I had to act ruthlessly. I had to send even my closest generals packing, army generals whose strength was gone, who were at the end of their tether. One of them [Brauchitsch] came to me and announced: "*Mein Führer*, we can't hold on any longer, we've got to retreat." I asked him: "Where are you thinking of retreating to, how far?" He replied: "Well, I don't really know."'

Hitler continued: 'If you dropped back 30 miles, do you think it would be any less cold there? Do you imagine your supply and transport problems would be reduced? And if you retreat, will you be able to take your heavy weapons with you?' When Brauchitsch said they would have to be abandoned, the Führer responded in exasperation: 'So you are planning to leave them to the Russians then – how do you intend to fight further back with no heavy weapons?' Brauchitsch replied that the choice was now between preserving the artillery or the army. Hitler concluded that he no longer had the will to continue the fight.

On 16 December Brauchitsch was dismissed as head of the German Army and replaced by Hitler himself. Some German soldiers, swayed by the Führer's charisma, still trusted their leader enough to welcome the change. 'Hitler has taken over the supreme command of the army!' Hans Jürgen Hartmann wrote. 'It is clear that von Brauchitsch simply wasn't up to the tremendous nervous tension demanded by the war. Perhaps Hitler – in the very highest position – can make a better estimate of what can or cannot be undertaken on a daily basis. Everyone hopes that this crisis can be mastered soon.' Hartmann was well aware of what was at stake. 'Outside, on Kharkhov's Red Square, the remnants of our tank force have assembled,' he continued. 'Apparently they are to be sent north, to Belgorod, where bloody fighting is underway. It is clear that the whole front is in danger.'

'I am hardly surprised by the dismissal of von Brauchitsch,' wrote Lieutenant Ludwig von Heyl. 'He badly mismanaged the push on Moscow in mid-November, left the provision of supplies and ammunition in utter chaos and of all those who "talked up" the chances of this last assault, he was without doubt the worst offender.' Heyl concluded with bitter sarcasm: 'And now we hear that Brauchitsch is unwell. Apparently, his health is not good. Meanwhile, the soldiers he has sent into the depths of Russia are enjoying a pleasant "rest cure". At times we are experiencing a little fatigue, or occasional hunger pangs, but in general our condition remains excellent.'

Brauchitsch was not popular within the army, but some still viewed the timing of his dismissal with suspicion. Philipp von Boeselager of the 86th Infantry Division said bluntly: 'Hitler needed a scapegoat for this winter disaster, and so deliberately dismissed the army commander-in-chief, as if to say: "If I'd been in charge, it would have been different." That's what lay behind the decision.' General Heinrici remarked simply: 'Brauchitsch has resigned, and the Führer taken over, but I doubt whether he will be able to turn things around.'

Brauchitsch was not Hitler's first dismissal. At the beginning of December, Field Marshal Gerd von Rundstedt had been removed from his post as head of Army Group South after German troops were forced to retreat from Rostov. The Wehrmacht's position in Rostov had become vulnerable, and Soviet forces around the city were too strong but the Führer needed somebody to blame for the setback. Lieutenant Otto Bente, a company commander in the German 76th Infantry Division, felt that both decisions were unjust: 'Von Rundstedt was sacrificed because of the retreat from Rostov,' Bente wrote, 'and now von Brauchitsch – another well-educated general – is to go because of the failure to capture Moscow. Adolf Hitler – who has no military qualifications at all – is to take over as supreme commander. What sort of effect is this supposed to have on our officer corps?'

'Now the Führer has taken our fate into his own hands,' German soldier Albert Neuhaus wrote from Russia. Hitler had announced to his troops: 'Our country's struggle is reaching its climax. We are faced with world shaking decisions. The principal bearer of this struggle is the army – and I have therefore taken command myself. As a soldier in many battles of World War One, I share deeply with you the determination to win through.'

The suffering of German soldiers continued unabated. On 17 December Helmut Fuchs witnessed masses of wounded Germans, who had been evacuated from the front, being registered for hospital treatment at Smolensk:

Inside one large building – which is now serving as a processing area – a massive queue snakes back from two tables, past a hall and down a large staircase and into the biting cold outside. Many of our troops are so badly frostbitten that they are unable to stand, and support themselves on the shoulders of their comrades. It is a picture of utter misery, and I am reminded of pictures of the collapse of Napoleon's *Grande Armée*. The flood of wounded, sick and frostbitten soldiers never ceases. On the road outside, I hear the constant noise of motor vehicles bringing in fresh casualties.

Colonel Martin Gareis of the German 98th Division added:

We have completely underestimated Russia – the country's resources, strength and will to resist simply have not been understood. We are bedevilled with constant mechanical failures – the roads are littered with our broken-down vehicles. And we have just been informed that the divisional workshops are so overstretched they can only cover a tenth of all essential repairs. One workshop has come to a complete halt because of the lack of spare parts. No doubt they are all stuck in supply depots hundreds of kilometres to our rear. However, there is one piece of good news. To combat the infestations of lice, each regiment is now to receive an iron!

On 17 December the German Ninth Army abandoned Kalinin, 100 miles north-west of Moscow. Hans Meier-Welcker noted a day later: 'We are not able to sleep any more – we just try to catch a few minutes here and there during the night. The enemy is continually attacking us. They have brought up fresh divisions, which are of full combat strength, while our own ranks are thinning rapidly.' He concluded: 'We have been badly punished for overestimating our chances in this campaign. If there is one lesson from the past two months – that is it.'

'Our ranks are growing thinner and thinner,' wrote Lieutenant Gustav Schrodek of the 11th Panzer Division. 'Today we received an astonishing order – to excavate the graves of our dead, and remove them – so that we can conceal the extent of our losses from the Russians. This is hardly a morale-raising exercise – and more easily said than done in such freezing conditions. We ended up carrying back the marker crosses, designating our comrades' names and units.'

Hitler's decision to take over command of the German Army was followed by a draconian order for his troops to stand fast against the Russians, wherever they were. It was named the 'Stand Fast!' order, and it demanded that 'the front be defended down to the last man'. On 18 December German officers and soldiers were told: 'Large-scale withdrawals will no longer be made. They lead to catastrophic loss of heavy weapons and equipment. Commanding generals, commanders and officers are to take personal charge of compelling the troops in their positions to put up an absolute resistance, without regard to enemy

Christmas 1941 in Russia

German soldiers hold distinctly muted Christmas celebrations: some look pensive, others are clearly thinking of home

A German sentry stands on duty, New Year 1942

The wings of a Russian plane provide makeshift protection from the wind

The horror: German troops find a group of comrades frozen to death in the snow, mid January 1942

The front begins to solidify: German machine gun post, early February 1942

A German reconnaissance plane stands in front of a church.
Accurate aerial photography helped slow the Soviet counteroffensive

A Wehrmacht defence line

German troops start to adapt to winter warfare

After an attack: Red Army forces suffer increasing casualties, mid February 1942

A knocked-out Russian T-26 tank

Russian civilians flee the war zone

'Will it be possible to atone for the crimes we are committing?' German Army priest Josef Perau photographs a mass grave of Russian POWs, Roslavl, 19 February 1942

At long last, proper winter equipment arrives: a Wehrmacht
MG34 machine gunner in winter camouflage, March 1942

A relieved German
soldier with skis and a
sheepskin coat

The war goes on. A German grave on the steppe
during the spring thaw, April 1942

breakthroughs in the flanks or rear. This is the only way to gain time to bring up the reinforcements from the west that I have ordered.'

Victor Klemperer, a German Jew living in Dresden, took a dispassionate view of the rhetoric employed by Hitler in his proclamations. 'A few weeks ago,' he remarked, 'the Russians had been officially "annihilated". Now they are to be "annihilated" later. Instead, the Wehrmacht is to hold on "absolutely" to what it has already conquered.' The German Army was now 'heroically resisting' an enemy that had supposedly been obliterated. Klemperer was struck by Hitler's use of language, and the repetition of such words as 'absolute' and 'tenacious'. 'Behind them,' he observed perceptively, 'one senses uncertainty and fear. The phrase "heroic resistance" already sounds like an obituary.'

Within the Führer's circle, General Alfred Jodl, chief of staff of the German Armed Forces, commented approvingly on Hitler's action: 'I was amazed at his confidence and energy in taking measures to shore up the Eastern Front. A catastrophe of the scale of 1812 was in the offing.' Carl Wagener, operations officer with the Third Panzer Group, was less enthusiastic: 'With this order,' he stated, 'any major retreat was prohibited, and we lost the right to make independent judgements of the battle situation. The chance for our armies to move quickly and rapidly away from the enemy had been forfeited; instead, we were permitted only small, piecemeal withdrawals. Our troops' already battered confidence in the leadership waned even further, for all military logic dictated a substantial pull-back from the Russians.'

On 19 December, Hitler appointed a new commander to Army Group Centre. The Führer replaced Field Marshal von Bock, who was now complaining of health problems, with Field Marshal von Kluge, who had previously led the German Fourth Army. Fifty-nine-year-old Field Marshal Günther von Kluge was an able and ambitious general. He was also arrogant and unscrupulous. He shared the Führer's view that the army group should hold its present position, stating emphatically: 'Our soldiers must realise that beginning a large-scale retreat is a certain death sentence – the

Russians will harry our forces mercilessly, and not allow them any breathing space to regroup.'

But Kluge was not trusted by his fellow generals. His nickname within the army was 'Clever Hans', a reference to a circus horse famed for performing astonishing tricks. Lieutenant General Faber du Faur recalled his impressions of Kluge at this time: 'I met with the Field Marshal at Smolensk,' he said. 'He is clearly an intelligent man, and evidently believes that what he is saying is right. But he no longer pursues anything except his own advancement. The saying "La gloire à tout prix" could have been coined for him. In terms of his own interests, he knows exactly what is possible and what is not, and acts accordingly.' General Rudolf Schmidt, who took over command of the German Second Army in November 1941, believed that Kluge's ambition was having a damaging influence on German war policy. 'He needs to be kept more firmly in check by our high command,' he said bluntly. 'There has been too much pandering to his wishes.'

When Field Marshal von Kluge took over Army Group Centre he was scarcely on speaking terms with two of its most important commanders. In mid-December Colonel General Erich Hoepner had been given overall charge of all the Panzer forces north of Moscow. Hoepner held Kluge responsible for the final failure at the gates of the Russian capital, and after a blazing row communicated with him only via his chief of staff. On the southern flank of Army Group Centre, relations with Colonel General Heinz Guderian, who had been given overall charge of the German Second Infantry Army alongside his own Panzers, were little better. Guderian, who referred dismissively to Kluge as 'the high and mighty one', could not stand him either.

Faced with such antipathy, Kluge buttressed his position with slavish obedience to the Führer's wishes. Unsurprisingly therefore, Kluge's chief of staff, Günther Blumentritt, praised Hitler's decree: 'The Führer's fanatical order that the troops must hold fast regardless – in every position – was undoubtedly correct. Hitler realised instinctively that any retreat across the snow and ice would lead to a collapse of the front within days, and if this happened, the Wehrmacht would suffer the same fate as Napoleon's *Grande Armée*.'

But the views of Kluge and Blumentritt were not shared by most of their Wehrmacht comrades. Colonel General Adolf Strauss, commander of the German Ninth Army, launched a strong rebuttal:

> The military initiative has been lost to the Russians. We will not regain it by ordering our soldiers to sacrifice themselves in unprepared positions that cannot be properly defended. We will simply lose most of our troops and equipment. There is little shortage of determination to remedy this situation, either among our officers or our men, but at present our defences are too weak for such resolve to make itself felt. We will only stabilise the situation by moving our forces back to a shorter combat line that can be effectively held against the enemy.

Colonel General Hoepner declaimed bluntly. 'Fanatical will, alone, cannot change the situation – the will is there, but the strength is lacking. Standing and fighting is only possible when men have adequate supplies of ammunition and weapons that actually fire.' Colonel General Guderian added: 'A rigid interpretation of the Führer's directive forces our troops to meet the enemy's attacks in positions that are downright disadvantageous to them.' Kluge and Blumentritt's support for Hitler's stand was ferociously criticised even by staff officers in their own army: 'We are engaged in heavy defensive fighting, which our exhausted soldiers can no longer sustain,' wrote staff officer Hellmuth Stieff. 'There are no reserves whatsoever, and our supplies are repeatedly cut off by the winter weather . . . If the Führer does not rescind his insane injunction that we have to hold out, regardless of enemy breakthroughs, the Fourth Army is unlikely to last another week.'

The Third Panzer Group was bearing the brunt of Russian attacks north-west of Moscow. Carl Wagener, one of its operations staff, complained:

> The troops are at a loss to understand why, at this late stage of the campaign, 'absolute resistance' is suddenly expected of them. Dogmatic instructions will not prevent the enemy from attacking all

along the front, and our soldiers will pay for it with high losses. Even if a body of our troops is able to 'resist absolutely', it will be forced – sooner or later – to pull back, when the Russians break through on the flanks and cut off supplies. Because this cannot be done voluntarily, with sufficient time and space, it will never be possible to shake off the enemy – which is the essential precondition for any successful retreat.

But Hitler did not want to retreat at all. Guderian was summoned to the Führer's headquarters and warned that he needed to step back from the suffering of his soldiers and take a more dispassionate view of events. On 20 December, in his first situation conference as head of the German Army, Hitler firmly grasped the reins of power, telling Colonel General Franz Halder, the army chief of staff, that 'the will to hold out must be brought home to every unit'. A ruthless scorched-earth policy would be maintained, the ground would be contested inch by inch, and any village that had to be vacated by German forces would be burnt down, regardless of the fate of its inhabitants. Warm winter clothing would be confiscated from Russian civilians.

Hitler concluded: 'The phrase "Napoleonic Retreat" is threatening to become a reality. One thing must be stressed to officers and men: a retreating army will face a far crueller winter than an army that holds out where it is. The Russians will follow hard on the heels of any withdrawing army, allowing it no respite, attacking it again and again; nor will such an army come to a halt, as it lacks any kind of prepared position in the rear.' But this decision was imposed on army generals and officers who largely disagreed with it. 'The Führer's decree does not offer us a way out of our difficulties,' Hellmuth Stieff wrote. 'Instead, we are likely to see our armies disintegrate before our eyes. This is not real leadership – we badly need fresh input from a qualified military commander.'

Hitler believed that draconian discipline would restore army cohesion and morale. In practice, it was often arbitrary and unjust. 'One sentry who collapsed in a haystack, passing out through sheer exhaustion, was immediately court-martialled and shot,' said German soldier Willy Reese. 'Another was unable to find the unit to which he was taking a message in the darkness, and was sentenced to death for cowardice in the face of the enemy. Remaining Red Army prisoners of war were taken out of the camps and strung up on trees – apparently this order was intended to frighten off the Russians. It was all murder – the war had become insane.'

Colonel Martin Gareis of the German 98th Infantry Division observed: 'Those issuing such orders – in conditions of comfort and safety, more than 1,000 kilometres from the front – were insulated from the terrible reality of what was happening. The enemy was properly prepared and equipped for the extreme winter weather. We froze and froze. We had no real protection against the terrible snowstorms – no warm clothing, no felt boots. The cold undermined our will to carry on. Our soldiers were fighting for their lives.'

The Führer imagined that his opponents would impale themselves upon a series of well-defended German strongpoints while he transferred fresh forces to the Eastern Front, but he badly underestimated the strength and resourcefulness of the Soviet counteroffensive. In many places, Russian troops were already bypassing the Wehrmacht's positions and striking behind its lines. 'Hitler has forbidden all further retreat,' declared Colonel General Hoepner. 'But the Russians are using ski battalions and Cossack cavalry to get behind our defence lines and attack our supply depots. His underestimation of the enemy's strength will lead to a catastrophe here.' 'Today enemy ski troops have appeared again,' German soldier Reinhold Pabel wrote nervously on 19 December. 'We saw them moving past our village, along the edge of the forest. The whole of our company is supposed to settle here, but whether we will be able to stay for long now looks highly unlikely.'

Hitler had announced that fresh troops were on their way, but there were precious few of them. Kurt Grumann's 87th Infantry Division received news of the 'Stand Fast!' decree with very mixed feelings: 'There is to be no further retreat,' he wrote:

and we are to hold our lines to the last man. We are feverishly working on our defence positions. However the ground is frozen solid, and there is no proper digging equipment. We need pickaxes and spades – but none are available. We cannot even obtain barbed wire, or lay out mines. It is enough to make one howl in frustration. And despite the assurances of the Führer, we have received little in the way of reinforcement. Two hundred so-called "replacements" did arrive, recruited from veterinary companies and transport services, but most cannot even handle a rifle properly.

Grumann added:

The Führer himself has taken charge, but our troops walk around as if they were doomed. Our soldiers hack at the frozen ground, but the heaviest blows yield only enough earth to fill one's fingernails. Our strength is decreasing every day. We were told that more reinforcements would be sent to us by plane, but the first batch arrived at a completely different unit and now the weather is too bad to allow any flying. There is a feeling among the men that they have been put on sentry duty and no one has remembered to send in the relief. All this should have been anticipated months ago.

Meanwhile, Russian civilians in the path of the German forces were suffering terribly. As the Soviet counteroffensive began, Hitler had made it clear that 'in order to facilitate our military operations, there is to be no respect whatsoever for the native population'. Encouraged by this ruthless statement, many Wehrmacht troops were already burning towns and villages as they retreated. Now, on 20 December, the Führer decreed that a 'scorched-earth' policy would be adopted by the entire German Army, and ordered that all farmsteads and peasants' houses vacated by the troops must be burnt immediately. Hitler added: 'Strip prisoners and inhabitants of winter clothing – regardless of the consequences.'

'A Führer order has come through,' Leopold Höglinger noted. 'All towns and villages are to be destroyed. Shortly afterwards, we see the first flames rising nearby – that's war!' 'We torched all the villages we passed through,' said Willy Reese, retreating with the German 95th Division. 'We had been ordered to spread devastation – to deny our pursuers shelter. We obeyed.

Women wailed, children froze in the snow, curses followed us. But our self-loathing faded. We no longer questioned what we were doing. And when we were issued with fresh cigarettes, we lit them at the burning houses – then marched dully on our way.'

Reese observed that 'men drugged themselves with cruelty', yet some did not entirely succumb to it. 'I am sitting in a house that will be up in flames in half an hour,' wrote Werner Pott on 19 December, from a village near Kalinin, north-west of Moscow. 'Day after day we are in action, without a break, marching through snowstorms, filthy and covered in vermin, with frozen noses and feet so bad it makes you cry when you take your boots off. These are the burdens we carry as we try to "hold fast" at the front.' Pott continued: 'And yet, amidst all these strains, it is the plight of the civilians which moves me the most. We destroy their houses as we retreat, condemning them to death by hunger or freezing cold. How cruel this war is!'

Pott and his comrades left the village and began to move off into the dusk: 'A snowstorm is whipping up over the fields, and it is hard to keep a foothold on these icy tracks,' he continued. 'The village is already burning from end to end. Red tongues of flame shoot greedily upwards as if they want to devour the heavens – the world seems on fire. Stooping old men and mothers with little children hurry by, with bundles on their backs, carrying off their last belongings. Behind us our engineers are blowing up bridges and houses.'

'Each time we leave a village, we set it alight,' wrote Panzer Lieutenant Gustav Schrodek. 'It is a primitive form of self-defence, and the Russians hate us for it. Yet its grim military logic is clear – to deny our pursuing opponents shelter in the terrible cold.' One night Schrodek and his comrades in the 11th Panzer Division – retreating towards the Russian town of Volokolamsk, north-west of Moscow – found some houses reasonably intact, and wondered whether they might get a few hours' sleep, even though the beds were infested with lice. They dosed off, only to be dramatically reawoken.

'One of our sergeants had sought out "alternative accommodation" in the cattle shed,' Schrodek recalled. 'But he had not escaped the lice, and enraged, he sprayed his surroundings with a flame thrower. The lice were well and truly roasted – but the entire shed also went up in flames. That got us up quickly – but our troubles had only just begun. Nearby Russian units had spotted the fire, and believing that we were deliberately setting light to the village, and about to abandon it, launched a frenzied attack. We could not get our tanks to start in the cold, and had to pull out rapidly, jettisoning most of our armour.' Schrodek concluded laconically: 'When you think everything has been taken into account, war will always surprise you.'

By mid-December the Wehrmacht had been pushed back all along the Eastern Front. Its chances of suddenly holding off the mass of new Soviet forces did not look strong. Army Group North had abandoned the town of Tikhvin on 9 December and its commander, Field Marshal Wilhelm Ritter von Leeb, was now afraid that Russian troops would attempt to breach the siege of Leningrad. His soldiers watched the great city from their trenches and dugouts. On 19 December artilleryman Wolfgang Buff wrote to his wife: 'We wonder about conditions in Leningrad, Russia's window to the west, which we have held under siege for more than three months. Its food supplies have dwindled and deaths through starvation are rapidly accelerating. What will happen now, in the extreme cold? The city is under daily bombardment from our artillery.' Buff paused, as if suddenly conscious of what he was truly saying. 'There is something I would like to straighten out with you,' he continued. 'When I said in previous letters that our heavy artillery is deliberately firing into residential parts of Leningrad, you may have believed my own battery was involved in this. This is not the case. My guns are situated further south, at a point where the Russians are trying to break through our siege lines.'

Hitler still preferred to blame the winter weather than to acknowledge the fighting performance of the Red Army. 'Russian troops are still nowhere near as good as ours,' he announced. But some of the Germans were seriously reassessing their opponents. 'The Russians hold the advantage at the moment because of the greater mobility of their army units,' said German officer Helmut von Harnack:

> Unlike us, they are far less dependent on the motor vehicle. And we have totally underestimated the quality of their soldiers – who are showing a mixture of extraordinary resilience and tremendous strength. They are a different opponent from that faced by us at the onset of Operation Typhoon. Over the last few months they have developed their fighting education in a number of key areas. Their junior officers are now showing much more combat initiative, they are gaining greater skill in the use of modern weaponry and are showing considerable tactical awareness.

Harnack took a broader view: 'The Soviet high command still wastes too many of its troops on mass attacks, and bleeds its units dry – and that remains a major fault. But the greatest compliment one can bestow is that they have managed, in a very short space of time, to raise, equip and throw into the fight a whole series of new armies. Mastering these logistical challenges is a colossal achievement.' He then turned to the key issue:

> The most striking improvement in our opponent's combat performance has come through the deliberate introduction – at a crisis point in the war – of a sense of national consciousness. Russia draws its strength from its historical past. Before the defeat of Napoleon, it was Peter the Great – in the early eighteenth century – who first spoke of a great patriotic war of self-defence. He understood the power of such an idea, and how it could lift the morale of Russian soldiers. Stalin and his high command are now following suit. For fighting with special distinction, they are rewarding army units – renaming them as Guards Divisions and giving them special uniforms and banners.

Harnack concluded: 'The fact that we did not bring this campaign to a finish, and go on to take Moscow, is a massive blow for us. The lack of foresight about the weather, and its effect on our military operations, is of course an important reason for this failure. But the truth is we totally underestimated our opponent. He showed a strength and resilience we did not believe him capable of – indeed, resilience greater than most of us imagined humanly possible.'

Red Army soldiers were fighting with growing skill and confidence. 'Our counteroffensive was developing successfully,' Soviet Major General Konstantin Rokossovsky wrote:

> We maintained our momentum, making particularly good use of mobile strike groups, supported by artillery. We did not want to allow the enemy time to disengage from our pursuit and organise his defences. More and more frequently we came across large sections of roadway cluttered with their abandoned equipment – tanks, self-propelled guns and crates of ammunition. We made extensive use of ski units to accelerate our advance. And then we learnt, from captured documents and prisoner of war interrogations, that Hitler had ordered his troops to hold fast. Their task was to halt us – at any cost. As we approached the town of Volokolamsk, we realised that the Germans were preparing to make a stand there.

On 20 December Georgi Osadchinsky's Soviet 35th Rifle Brigade reached the outskirts of Volokolamsk. 'In the course of our counteroffensive, we had already covered about 120 kilometres,' Osadchinsky recalled:

> We kept pushing forward – we did not want to allow the Germans time to regroup. As they retreated, the enemy burned everything behind them. Sometimes we were able to take a village quickly, before the Germans had time to fully destroy it, and our soldiers huddled together in those huts still standing. But mostly we slept in the remnants of ruined, burnt-down houses, or out in the open, in 'beds' made from fir tree branches. Yet all the time we were gaining in combat experience, and becoming tougher and better soldiers.

Lieutenant Gustav Schrodek and troops from the German 11th Panzer Division had reached Volokolamsk a few days earlier. 'We have been ordered to take up "well-fortified" defences in the town and resist the enemy,' Schrodek stated. 'But the positions were a joke – there were no machine-gun nests, properly dug trenches or artillery placements. We did what we could – in a terrible rush. But we did not have the strength to stop the Russians for long.'

Increasing German respect for their opponents was reciprocated. On the morning of 20 December, Soviet reconnaissance patrols reported considerable German military activity in Volokolamsk. Osadchinsky's unit took up positions in a field, north of the town's railway station. There was a snowstorm, and visibility was limited. Then all hell broke loose. 'Suddenly, the enemy unleashed a hurricane of fire,' Osadchinsky said. 'First their artillery opened up, followed by their mortars and heavy machine guns – they were throwing everything they could at us. Our own guns responded, and then our infantry began crawling forward in the snow. It was hard to see how our attack was developing. But we heard reports that the enemy was not pulling back, and we had to overcome the defenders in hand-to-hand fighting.'

Osadchinsky and his comrades reached a German forward position. 'Before us was a scene of utter carnage,' he continued. 'There were bodies of our soldiers, entangled in the barbed wire, and those of the enemy, littering the trenches, bayoneted or ripped apart by grenades.' Osadchinsky had fought the Germans with a burning hatred in his heart, and had shown their soldiers no mercy. But now, to his surprise, he felt a grudging respect for them. 'They have followed the orders of their high command,' he thought, 'and fought and died where they stood. What iron discipline! But what is the point of such senseless sacrifice? These men have shown real heroism – but I doubt whether their heroic deeds will ever be known or appreciated.'

The Red Army capture of Volokolamsk – an important transport junction 65 miles north-west of Moscow – put Colonel General Hoepner's entire Panzer force in jeopardy. 'We are now dangerously overextended,' Hoepner wrote grimly. 'The Russians have now brought up ten fresh divisions and several new armoured brigades against my weakened formations. Hitler's halt order will be a death sentence for most of my men.'

The situation on Army Group Centre's southern flank was even worse. The Red Army had torn a hole between Guderian's forces and the German Fourth Army, and there were hardly any troops to plug the gap. Kluge and Guderian had a major row, and eventually two regiments from the 137th Infantry Division, commanded by Lieutenant General Friedrich Bergmann, were sent to Guderian's assistance. But on the morning of 21 December they collided with vastly superior Soviet forces.

Bergmann was a well-respected commander, who had particularly impressed his men in the difficult days of the Russian counteroffensive. One of his officers wrote of him: 'I was struck by our general's presence of mind and personal courage, at a time when others around him were simply overwhelmed by mental and physical stress.' To stop the advancing Russians from reaching the town of Kaluga, 100 miles south-west of Moscow, Bergmann had to drive the enemy out of the village of Sjavki, and gain access to the motor highway. Hitler believed that commanding generals had a personal responsibility to ensure acts of 'absolute resistance' from their soldiers. But Sjavki revealed the fallacy behind the Führer's injunction.

Early on the morning of 21 December Bergmann moved his troops forward. His formations were desperately under strength. Artillery became stuck in the snowdrifts, incapable of supporting the attack. German troops pushed on into the village and took the houses in hand-to-hand fighting. But then Russian tanks appeared. The Germans in the village were overwhelmed, and the support forces were pinned down by enemy fire and unable to move. Bergmann left his command post on the edge of the forest, formed up a combat squad out of his divisional staff and personally led his men into battle.

But the situation was hopeless. The Germans had no tanks or armoured vehicles, and their artillery still had not arrived. An entire Soviet armoured brigade was in the vicinity. One of Bergmann's staff officers, Lieutenant Rudolf Goppelt, recorded his commander's words as he urged the small group forward. 'The eyes of the world are upon you,' he exhorted. Goppelt added a laconic inscription. 'It was hard to believe that,' he wrote. Minutes later, two Russian tanks advanced on Bergmann's tiny force and the commander was killed by fragments from an exploding shell. Shortly afterwards, all his troops had to abandon their positions.

'A tragic blow,' Leopold Höglinger of the 137th Infantry Division wrote in his diary. 'Bergmann was killed. Now we truly understand the senselessness of this war.' Hitler was asking too much of the German Army. Major General Hans von Greiffenberg, chief of staff of Army Group Centre, said: 'It is highly doubtful whether the Führer's order to stand fast – whatever the cost – was justified from a military point of view. He was determined to withstand the enemy – but the losses forced on our troops by making such a stand were extremely high. Hitler was strongly influenced by the example of Napoleon in 1812. But there was no proof whatsoever that a retreat, once started, *had* to lead to the collapse and disintegration of the entire front.'

Then Greiffenberg observed: 'Hitler did not *want* to realise what was really happening. Instead, he began to believe that all difficulties could be overcome by sheer, unbending willpower. This was the moment when the Führer finally lost touch with the realities of the war in the east.'

7

'This Is All There Really Is'

'OUR COMPANY HAS re-formed,' Heinz Otto Fausten of the 1st Panzer Division remarked grimly on 24 December 1941, 'if one can call a shattered duty sergeant, a few supply wagons and a handful of stragglers by such a name. From my original group only Paul is left, but he is scarcely recognisable any more – he cannot speak, and is a confused, twitching bundle of nerves. The sergeant is at a loss – the army medics can do nothing with him, so our only hope is that a doctor at a military hospital might be able to help.'

There was little time for Christmas celebrations. That night Siberians attacked the village where Fausten and his tired and hungry comrades were quartered, setting a number of the houses alight. They were eventually driven off. It was close to midnight when Fausten and his fellows made a reconnaissance patrol beyond the village's outskirts. There they found the artillery unit that had been posted at the entry road. 'It was a tableau,' said Fausten simply, 'but there was nothing festive about it. The men had frozen to death in the positions they had been firing from. Three or four of them were kneeling behind the gun – one had been looking through the observation slit, the others loading – and all were now blocks of solid ice.'

At Christmas 1941, German troops all along the Eastern Front thought of their fellow soldiers outside Moscow. Private Wolf Dose and the 58th Infantry Division celebrated Christmas in siege lines around Leningrad. 'In the communal shelter my comrades had specially prepared a fir tree, which was nicely decorated, its candles casting a beautiful light,' Dose recalled. 'Beyond it stood tables covered with gifts and extra rations. As we enjoyed the warmth of our shelter, sang Christmas carols and took delight in swapping presents a burst of machine-gun fire rattled close by. There was a sudden silence. The sound reminded us all of what was happening near Moscow. There our comrades were celebrating a very different Christmas, one of a starkly martial kind.'

Hans Jürgen Hartmann, who was stationed in Kharkov, had been granted leave and was on a train carrying him westwards:

> It is warm and quiet in the compartment. The wheels slide easily over the snow-covered tracks, as if they do not want to disturb me. The pressure dial moves in a steady rhythm. The train drives onwards – and outside, the wind swirls around its carriages. I wonder whether our soldiers in front of Moscow are enjoying any warmth and quiet this evening. The Russians – knowing the day's special significance to us – will no doubt launch a fresh wave of attacks. Will another German unit perform a back-flip this evening, pushed further away from the Russian capital by well-equipped Siberian divisions?

Hartmann reflected uneasily on the unfolding struggle in the east. 'How brutal this war is becoming,' he thought. 'It is now a total war, a war against women, children and old people – and that is the greatest horror.' Hartmann decided it was better not to think about it. He drank a little and remembered happier times, when things were more simple and straightforward: 'The windows are thickly encrusted with ice, and it is difficult to wipe a hole in the patina of glittering crystal and view the world. As we roll onwards, I remember how our troops struggled towards Kharkov, tormented by mud and savage fighting. We captured the city, and then were halted by the enemy. For several months this drama has been played out, but now it all seems long ago, in the distant past. Outside the wind is howling – it tugs and rattles against the windows.' Hartmann concluded:

> I have often wondered what this Christmas might be like. I always cast out the war from my imaginary picture, or at least pushed it to the very edges. I conjured up special words for the occasion: Christmas, homeland, longing, joy and hope. Yet these words, always sincere and heartfelt, became increasingly strange and empty to me. They evoked something timeless, precious – and yet, in the conditions of the Eastern

Front, seemed scarcely believable any more. But now this train is carrying me back, smoothly and warmly, through night and snow, to the west. A reprieve has been granted to me – and I shall not forget it.

A spirit of comradeship in adversity sprung up, as different German formations were flung together in the chaos of the retreat from Moscow. Franz Leiprecht's unit began pulling back towards Maloyaroslavets, 70 miles south-west of the capital, at around 3.00 p.m. on 24 December. By 5.00 p.m. it had joined a long column, snaking along the motor highway. 'Apparently we are making "a correction to the front",' Leiprecht said. 'I was able to get a place on a truck for this drive, but the vehicle was in a terrible state – and kept breaking down, again and again.'

As night fell Leiprecht and his fellows could not find the village in which they were supposed to be quartered. They marched around in the darkness, and then saw lights in the distance. They came from a different village, but some makeshift accommodation was provided there. Leiprecht's unit unpacked its belongings. Then, suddenly, a connecting door opened. 'In a large Russian room about twenty German soldiers sat around a tree laden with burning candles,' Leiprecht recalled. 'With wonderful solemnity, "Silent Night, Holy Night" rang out, with someone accompanying the carol on harmonica. We stood quietly at the door, not wanting to disturb the moment. Within this simple circle of men was a most extraordinary atmosphere, far more powerful than anything I had experienced in a church.'

As the singing died away, Leiprecht spoke: 'I asked whether we might come in and warm up, and was gladly welcomed, and given a cup of coffee and some grog . . . So, I had managed to celebrate this holy evening after all, and the vast forest surrounding our village had granted us peace and shelter. My thoughts went out to my loved ones back home.'

Lieutenant Erich Mende of the 84th Infantry Regiment was also in transit. On the evening of 24 December his battalion boarded a military train. 'It was bitterly cold,' Mende remembered, 'with the temperature dropping below −35 degrees Celsius. The train was shrouded in snow. Our infantry was split up – about 50 men in each goods wagon – with straw for them to lie on. I entered my wagon and saw, to my surprise, the soldiers had found some candles and were propping up a little tree. We sat around it. Each wagon was heated by a small, portable stove – but it was still freezing.'

The 84th Infantry Regiment was being sent south, from Vyazma to Kaluga. Despite the cold, Mende never forgot the next few hours. 'As our train moved off into the night, our exhausted soldiers still managed – in wagon after wagon – to celebrate Christmas. From one wagon I heard the sounds of a harmonica being played, from another men singing "O Tannenbaum", from a third "Silent Night". Who could have imagined that on a rattling goods train, in such icy winter weather, Christmas could be so memorable?'

As Army Group Centre reeled from the blows of the Soviet counteroffensive, 'Silent Night' particularly touched German soldiers. 'On Christmas Eve we reached a small town,' remembered Franz Peters of the 23rd Infantry Division. 'It was deserted – but we found a little church. Inside it, where the altar should have been, there was only a large hole in the ground – the Bolsheviks had ripped it out. But our soldiers gathered around that hole, lit a fire and began to sing carols. And I have never heard "Silent Night" sung with such fervour – it was quite incredible. Many of us were moved to tears.'

Peters and the battered remnants of the German 23rd Infantry Division had assembled at the small town of Vladychino, west of Volokolamsk. That evening the divisional commander Major General Heinz Hellmich made a heartfelt appeal to his men: 'Somehow, we must recover our self-belief and hold the enemy at bay. The present crisis must be overcome. We are fighting for our very survival.' 'A parcel arrived from my mother,' recalled Karl-Gottfried Vierkorn of the 23rd Infantry Division. 'There was some marble cake – which I shared with my comrades. Then they asked me to read out the card my mother had sent. When I finished, there was complete silence. Far away from this terrible disaster – which no one imagined possible when we first entered Russia – something else still existed. Was there still a Christmas somewhere, where people peacefully exchanged gifts, gathered around the tree and went to Midnight Mass? Or was it just an illusion?'

For some German units, there was time for careful preparation. 'We are celebrating Christmas reasonably well,' wrote Lieutenant Ludwig von Heyl of the 36th Motorised Infantry Division, quartered in the village of Frolovskoye. 'Our house is clean and fairly warm. We have cooked and eaten a chicken, which we carried back with us on our retreat, and enjoyed three bars of chocolate, two half-bottles of red wine and a bottle of sparkling wine, rounded off with a little cognac.' After inscribing this careful inventory, which Heyl wrote out on the back of a captured Russian map, he added: 'We gave thanks to God for simply being alive.'

On 24 December artilleryman Gerhard Bopp rose early. 'At 8.00 a.m. I got up and started to organise things,' Bopp wrote. 'First I managed to procure some bacon. Then I went over to the nearby village and bartered for some potatoes, milk, five chickens and a small Christmas tree. I returned to our lodgings and began to put up decorations. We then cut out stars from the silver paper in our cigarette packets, and some of the local inhabitants gave us candles, which we fastened to the branches of the tree. It looked like a proper Christmas – and on the table were chicken legs, serviettes and cutlery, and a dessert of rice pudding that someone had miraculously conjured up.'

That evening Bopp and his unit enjoyed their meal together, and then turned out the lights, leaving the room illuminated by the candles on the tree. Bopp had prepared a small Christmas gift for each of his comrades, and to his delight found that every single man had done the same. It was a heart-warming occasion, yet Bopp was taken aback by what followed it: 'With the exchange of presents I felt a real Christmas spirit, but in its wake came a sudden, overwhelming loneliness, as if a place inside my heart now lay cold and empty. It was the saddest moment that I ever had experienced.'

Colonel August Schmidt, a regimental commander with the German 10th Motorised Infantry Division, was amazed at his soldiers' gift for improvisation: 'Around midday on 24 December we moved into new defence lines,' Schmidt recalled. 'Within hours, there was a most extraordinary transformation. Little Christmas trees appeared at every Company HQ, decorations were fashioned out of cigarette packets and candles were lit. Small gifts, pieces of chocolate or pastry were carefully set out underneath. It was simple, yet deeply moving.'

For radio operator Wilhelm Schröder's 10th Panzer Division, however, everything seemed to be going wrong. 'We took over a cold room in a little house,' Schröder remembered, 'and began to get it ready. We found a small iron stove in the village, which we took back and installed, and soon had it burning merrily. Then we decorated the room, put up a Christmas tree and covered the walls with newspaper. But some officers came in and confiscated our radio, saying they wanted to have some festive music of their own, and then our chickens – which we had acquired by bartering most of our cigarettes – burned in the pot.'

Worse was to follow. There was an alarming smell of charred wood, for the heat from the stove had set the floorboards alight. The Germans joined forces with the Russian owner of the house, a garrulous old man, in a rapid rescue operation – some breaking the ice that had formed over the village well, others carrying buckets of water, in relays. Schröder was struck by the antics of their Russian host: 'The old man rushed around the room, trying to take charge of everything at the same time,' he recalled. 'He crept under the stove, and then climbed over it, sweating like a bull, and his frantic activities were accompanied by a babbling commentary that grew more and more ludicrous. Our soldiers – carrying in pails of water – began to smile, for the first time in weeks. After an hour of communal "fire fighting" we were able to celebrate Christmas Eve together. The old man poured us glasses of vodka. There was food and wine on the table – and a sense of peace and calm spread through the room. It was wonderful to see everyone laughing again.'

The spirit of comradeship was not, however, universal. 'Advent for the doomed,' Willy Reese wrote, surveying the wreckage of the German 95th Division. 'Our conversations revolved around the themes of home leave – the perpetual delusion – and flight from our positions . . . We were all sick and irritable. Outbursts of rage and hate, envy, fistfights, sarcasm and mockery replaced what would once have been camaraderie. We didn't attend to our dead, and didn't bury them either – we just plundered their coats and gloves. Things and values changed. Money had become meaningless. We used paper money for cigarettes, or gambled it away indifferently.' Reese concluded: 'Only a few sought intimacy, most took refuge in superficialities – gambling, cruelty, hatred . . . Life had become a kind of crying without tears.'

Many German soldiers were unable to enjoy either food and laughter or gambling and distraction. On 24 December Corporal Alois Scheuer's 197th Infantry Division was given orders to pull back beyond the front line, and in the early evening the men began to move out of their positions. They waded through high snowdrifts, which sometimes came up above their waists, and past ruined, abandoned villages. 'For the last few weeks we have been in close proximity to the enemy,' Scheuer wrote, 'and have suffered heavy casualties as a result. My original company scarcely exists any more – nearly all are dead, wounded or missing. I am one of the few survivors.' Later that evening, the men reached their new quarters. 'To our intense disappointment,' Scheuer continued, 'no Christmas deliveries had reached us – no food, alcohol or post from home. We were left with our iron rations. And there was no news about when leave might be expected.' He concluded sadly: 'In the present military situation I doubt whether it will be any time soon.'

When Fritz Hübner took a small supply train into an abandoned Russian village on the evening of 24 December, he and his fellows made themselves as comfortable as they could in the ruined houses. They had no vehicles left, and were completely dependent on their horses, which were quartered in makeshift stables. The German unit decorated a small fir tree and procured some hot coffee from the army kitchen when they heard Russian tank fire. Red Army soldiers were about half a mile away, and the village had to be quickly evacuated. Hübner's diary entries reflect the practical details of their march – the time they left the village, temperature readings, distances covered and the time taken to reach their new quarters the following day. Hübner noted how at night, in the middle of a snowstorm, they orientated themselves by following the telegraph lines westwards. The men's clothing was utterly inadequate, and they suffered dreadfully.

Years later, with these records as an aide-memoire, Hübner returned to one specific incident. A pile of snowdrifts blocked the road for about a hundred yards, and the teams of horses, tethered to carts and sledges, were unable to surmount them. It was vital not to abandon the supplies. The Germans urged their horses forward, and once again they floundered in the snow. 'It was dreadful to see how they were suffering,' recalled Hübner. 'The poor creatures refused to go on, and had to be beaten harshly before they continued.' Then he said: 'Many years have passed, but this one image of Christmas 1941 has lodged in my mind – having to beat these poor helpless animals, struggling in the full force of a Russian winter snowstorm.'

Radio operator Leopold Höglinger's 137th Infantry Division spent the night marching towards the town of Kaluga, 100 miles south-west of Moscow. His diary entries were terse as Russian troops were all around them: 'Burning torches light our route,' Höglinger wrote, 'as we stumble onwards, through a jumble of vehicles and men – eventually finding accommodation in the front room of a small hut. We will attempt to celebrate Christmas here. It is very cold, and I don't think we will get much sleep.'

General Zhukov had now committed three fresh Soviet armies – the Thirty-Third, Forty-Third and Forty-Ninth – attacking the German Fourth Army along a broad front. Private Huber's company, part of the German 98th Infantry Division, also retreated on Christmas Eve, and the men fared even worse than Höglinger and his comrades: 'At 7.00 p.m. we began our withdrawal,' Huber recalled:

Our column wound along the snowy landscape, and I thought of 1812, and the long lines of the French soldiers, struggling against the winter cold. The temperature dropped steadily. The moon seemed almost glassy, and the stars sparkled with vivid clarity in the night sky. We looked back, and high on the hillside could see a small chapel, surrounded by countless wooden crosses and steel helmets. This was the last resting place of many of our comrades, who had died in this desolate spot repelling repeated Russian attacks, with the roar of artillery reverberating overhead. Now we were leaving it.

At 2.00 a.m. the men reached their destination. They looked around in bewilderment. The map coordinates were correct, but there were no quarters for them. In fact, there was nothing at all. 'It is early on Christmas morning,' Huber continued. 'We are on the edge of a forest clearing, trying to construct some form of shelter. Around me thirty indistinct shapes – a blur of frostbitten faces, threadbare coats and ripped gloves and boots – are fumbling around in the darkness. We are surrounded by deep snow, which covers the fields and ditches. A biting wind swirls around us – coating our steel helmets with a thin layer of ice. It grows in strength, until it becomes a blinding snowstorm, through which our surroundings are scarcely visible at all. All we need now is for the Russians to pay us a visit!' The men saved themselves by building makeshift 'dwellings' out of packed snow, in hollows protected from the wind, and then swathing themselves in every piece of clothing they could get their hands on. 'As the sun rose on Christmas Day there we all were,' said Huber, 'peeping out from our "snow castles".'

Others had to spend Christmas in constant fighting. On 24 December Private Gerhard vom Bruch and troops from the German 6th Panzer Division were sent to plug a gap in the front west of Volokolamsk, defending their position in temperatures below −30 degrees Celsius. On Christmas Day Bruch wrote: 'Things look bad – in fact catastrophic. The cold is growing worse, and the wind drives sharp flecks of ice into our faces. None of our heavy machine guns are working properly.' The men pulled back towards a nearby village, but the Russians had got there before them. 'The enemy had already breached our defences,' Bruch recalled, 'and some of our comrades were desperately holding out in the far end of the village. They were men scraped together from security detachments and our rear service personnel. We joined them – but were unable to stop the Russians. We suffered terrible losses and had to retreat again, in the bitter cold, leaving behind most of our dead and our wounded.'

The survivors regrouped in a hamlet, atop a hill. 'We are trying to set up fortifications,' Bruch continued, 'but have no more heavy weapons – and our machine guns and grenade launchers will not be enough to stop the enemy. If the Russians attack in strength, they will overwhelm us.' The few houses were crammed with men. 'Sixty soldiers are in our hut,' Bruch added. 'There will be no chance of sleep tonight – there is no room to lie down anywhere. Our company is physically and mentally at the end of its tether. On Christmas Eve our unit was 170 strong; a day later, we can scarcely muster twenty men.' Bruch concluded: 'A tragedy is taking place that is difficult to describe. Our army is facing the darkest days in its history.'

But the unfolding tragedy was not confined to German soldiers. On 25 December Red Army troops were rapidly approaching the town of Kaluga, and a decision was made to evacuate the town's POW camp. Gustav Wetter and his German comrades were stationed nearby, and they witnessed what followed. 'On this day,' Wetter wrote, 'in temperatures dropping below −35 degrees Celsius, 3,000 exhausted Russian prisoners of war were taken out of the camp and force marched to Roslavl. Many, weak from hunger, fell by the roadside and were immediately shot. Soon the route was littered with countless bodies. A number of prisoners were seen carrying bits of human flesh – parts of an arm or leg – which they were trying to eat. If one of them stumbled, others would immediately fall upon him and strip him of clothing and possessions. They all appeared starving and in a terrible condition – and they had an animal look about them.'

The suffering of these men was scarcely imaginable. 'We were struggling to survive in hell,' said Red Army prisoner Nikolai Obryn'ba. 'It was hard to remain a human being. We were threatened not only with physical obliteration, but also a moral annihilation as well. The Nazis were deliberately trying to destroy our dignity and our faith in everything that was good.'

Men were being pushed to their very limits. 'This is the best Christmas of my life!' German Private Willi Thomas wrote with bitter irony. 'The enemy attacked in overwhelming strength the whole day. We had no defence against their tanks. When we crawled out from under the rubble we saw our entire position had been reduced to soot and ashes. Our company is being torn to pieces – and in the morning it will start up all over again. And this was supposed to be the triumphal conclusion of our campaign.'

'Whenever one believes the war could not get any worse,' wrote Helmut von Harnack, 'again and again it does. On Christmas Eve enemy attacks reached a new level of ferocity, as Russians reck-lessly charged forward, heedless of losses. I took command of an amalgamated company of infantry, tanks and self-propelled guns and we were always in the thick of the action. There was one unforgettable moment. We smashed through enemy forces and rescued an encircled German battalion. The relieved commander looked over at me, and then shouted across the hubbub of battle: "My best Christmas present ever!"'

Occasionally, German troops managed to turn the tables on their Red Army pursuers. A small group from the 20th Panzer Division was defending three fortified houses at the far end of the village of Aristovo, south of Naro-Fominsk. Most of the settlement was in Russian hands. The men pooled their rations – a little tea and a tiny amount of alcohol – and realising this was inadequate for even the humblest of celebrations, resolved to capture some provisions from the Russians. As dusk fell, the last remaining German tank advanced along the village street, followed by about thirty infan-trymen, throwing incendiaries at the straw roofs and setting them ablaze. Then the infantry opened up with their machine guns. It was a desperate act of bravado, but the much larger Red Army force was taken by surprise and fled into the forest. That night festivities took place after all.

Elsewhere, Russian pressure was unremitting. The combat

journal of the German 134th Infantry Division recorded a series of Red Army assaults on 24 December. At 8.30 a.m. the enemy engaged with the 439th Infantry Regiment. It then switched targets, pushing towards the supply and ammunition depot. At 4.30 p.m. it was attacking the 446th Infantry Regiment. Patrols were sent out to probe other sections of the German lines. As dusk fell, the Russians increased their artillery fire and began to pressurise the whole front. The combat journal concluded: 'With one assault following another, it appears that the enemy's main intent is to systematically disrupt our Christmas celebrations.'

On Army Group Centre's northern flank, there was heavy fighting around Heinrich Haape's 6th Infantry Division. On the morning of 24 December a Russian attack was repulsed with heavy losses. The cold was so intense that when Haape and his comrades went out onto the battlefield, to plunder the enemy's quilted coats and felt-lined boots, they found them frozen onto the dead bodies and impossible to remove. That afternoon they learnt of a Russian breakthrough in a neighbouring section of the front, and there was now a danger of encirclement. Yet Haape was still able to recall the evening's almost magical light: 'The sun was sinking on the western horizon, blood red, like a huge Chinese lantern and with as little warmth. Its vivid, dying colours reflected over the wide expanse of snow. Icicles, hanging from the snow-laden fir trees, caught its rays and their translucent beauty gave us an ironic reminder that it was Christmas Eve. In spite of everything, the spirit of Christmas was in the air.'

The new divisional commander, Colonel Horst Grossmann, remembered this. 'The ice shone with a strangely beautiful light,' he recalled, 'one of the effects of the extreme cold – and the snow drifts shimmered with a rose-pink hue.' Then he added: 'Nothing else that evening would create a Christmas mood for us.' Grossmann never forgot his impressions as he assumed command that day:

> Everything was mixed up – infantry regiments were mingled with artillery units, engineers and flak companies with rear service personnel – and everyone was utterly exhausted. For the last week the troops had been marching, fighting and retreating in temperatures between

−30 and −40 degrees Celsius and the enormous strain had pushed them to breaking point. The day I took over command two men from an artillery unit collapsed and died while marching. Our soldiers lacked any sort of warm accommodation and were still without proper winter uniform in the bitingly cold weather. They struggled on − in tattered uniforms, thin greatcoats and inadequate footwear − attempting to hold positions lacking proper trenches and defensive obstacles against a numerically superior foe.

Grossmann added angrily:

The enemy we face is properly equipped for winter warfare, has warm clothing, felt boots, and white outer garments, which give him camouflage against the snow. The Russian is able to attack at night, and under the cover of snowstorms, with effective supporting fire from a whole variety of weapons, properly lubricated against the extreme cold. The Soviet commanders push their soldiers forward, towards our lines, again and again. And because we have to conserve our ammunition, our artillerymen are unable to lay down a heavy barrage on these massed attacks, as they long to do.

He then described the consequences of this situation:

Imagine this scene. The Russians rise up. A thin German line stands against their serried ranks. The defending battalion consists of less than a hundred men. With fingers so cold they can scarcely grip rifles or machine guns, our men hold their fire as the Russians charge forward. Because of the extreme cold, there is no guarantee that the heavy machine guns will work properly. And if they seize up, even if we destroy the first wave of the enemy, the remainder will overrun our position, killing everybody. Our waiting soldiers know this.

That evening Grossmann was struck by an ominous increase in Russian artillery fire. A fresh attack was in the offing.

The central section of the German line was held by the 37th Infantry Regiment. At 10.00 p.m. the Russians launched a night attack on its positions. The regiment had spent two days and a night without proper shelter − and the prolonged exposure to intense cold produced a bizarre emotional reaction from some of its soldiers. They became completely indifferent to danger. As the attack began, groups of men gathered around a burning barn and began to sing carols. Russian gunners quickly pinpointed the blazing target, and shell after shell exploded around them. But the men carried on singing, shouting and cheering, even as some were being hit by shrapnel. No one made any attempt to take cover. 'They were filled with a lunatic ecstasy,' Haape said, 'as if the cold, the strain, the constant exposure to danger had produced a mass longing for death. They sang and died without knowing what they were doing. At last an officer intervened and sanity was restored. Meekly they obeyed his commands, as if in a trance, and picked up their weapons again.'

At 12.45 a.m. on Christmas Day the Russians surrounded the regimental HQ in the village of Bukontovo. There was fierce hand-to-hand fighting around the village church, where a last stand was made. The battle swung backwards and forwards as the terrified horses of the artillery and supply trains, tethered in the churchyard, tried to break free from their fastenings. The regimental commander, already wounded twice, stayed in the front line, pistol in hand, organising the resistance. Eventually, the Russians broke into the church, fought their way up to the bell tower – which the Germans were using as an artillery spotting point – and overwhelmed its defenders. At 2.00 a.m. the remainder of the division had to abandon its positions to avoid encirclement.

'Most of us were now walking perilously along a border line between sanity and madness,' Haape said. 'Laughter was never far from tears; optimism rubbed shoulders with black despair. Death marched side by side with us in our ranks. Nothing normal remained.'

Soviet troops were well aware of the special significance of Christmas to German soldiers. It became almost a point of honour to disrupt the enemy's celebrations. The 25th of December held no special significance for them. The Russian Orthodox Church celebrated Christmas early in the New Year, on 7 January, following the old, Julian system of dating, and in any case, the Christian calendar was not officially acknowledged by the atheist Bolshevik regime. It is interesting to note, however, that Stalin was toying at this time with the idea of reopening a few churches, as a propaganda gesture – building on the idea of a patriotic struggle against the German invader – and, with the United States of America entering the war, as a sop to western opinion.

In the wake of the German retreat, Stalin had ordered a propaganda film to be made. It was entitled *Why We Fight*, and was shot largely in December 1941. It presented the Soviet counteroffensive at Moscow in full flow, with Red Army tanks, cavalry units and ski troops advancing at speed, with Russian planes in the sky above them. Shivering German soldiers were shown surrendering en masse. The film also briefly featured a service in a Russian Orthodox church.

One of the battle scenes was filmed during the liberation of Solnechnogorsk on 11 December, and Georgi Osadchinsky's Siberian 35th Rifle Brigade – which took part in the engagement – later chatted to the film crew, which was in the town. 'They asked us about the fighting,' said Osadchinsky, 'although we were too exhausted to say anything much. But our soldiers learnt, to their considerable amusement, that Stalin had ordered this stage-managed church celebration of a Russian Orthodox Christmas.' One cameraman confessed: 'It has to be in the film, although we have set it up several weeks too early.' There was general laughter, and then one Red Army soldier quipped: 'Comrade Stalin's religious observances are clearly a little rusty. Perhaps he has become confused by the Germans' festivities.'

'We knew that the Germans wanted to celebrate Christmas on the 24th and 25th of December,' said Soviet artilleryman Pavel Ossipov. 'This became clear to us from the Christmas trees and other decorations found in villages liberated from the enemy. Hoping the enemy's alertness would be dulled by indulgence, we pursued him even harder during this period.' Then Ossipov added: 'It was exhausting for our troops to be marching more than 15 kilometres every day. We entrenched ourselves, fired at the enemy, waited for our infantry to catch up, moved forward, took up fresh positions and fired again. We never had time to celebrate anything. We fought on the move, prepared our weapons on the move, slept on the move. That was how our soldiers fought in the Moscow counteroffensive.'

The Christmas festivities did have some impact. Soviet Lieutenant Ivan Savenko would never forget the spoiling raid his unit conducted on the evening of 24 December. Their target was a German unit stationed near Belev, 50 miles south of Kaluga. That morning they watched through their binoculars as a large column of provisions arrived at the enemy camp. They saw the Germans happily unloading crates of wine, chocolate and cigarettes. 'It was a mouth-watering prospect,' Savenko said. 'We had nothing in our food bags except a little hard, broken bread.' Over the last few weeks, as the Russian troops had continued to advance, their supply train had become increasingly overstretched, and the men were down to basic rations. The prospect of robbing the Germans of their Christmas fare was particularly enticing.

Savenko and his comrades had noticed that the enemy disliked night fighting in the harsh winter conditions, so they waited until dusk before launching their attack. But the Germans had anticipated this, and the Russians blundered straight into a trap: 'We advanced into the village,' Savenko recalled. 'Strangely the Germans retreated without offering us much resistance. We imagined that they were already somewhat the worse for wear after their Christmas celebrations, and pushed on to the supply column. Some of the wagons had been unloaded, but one in the centre was still full and we rushed over and began plundering it. Suddenly flares lit up the whole area. The Germans had set up firing positions on the surrounding roof tops, and they cut us down with heavy machine-gun fire. They annihilated our unit. I was wounded in the arm, but some of my comrades dragged me to safety.'

German commanders on the Eastern Front felt the calamitous turn in their army's fortunes keenly. 'The disaster continues,' General Heinrici wrote to his wife on 24 December, 'but in Berlin, at the very top, nobody wants to admit it . . . They refuse to rec-ognise that the Russians can do such a thing to us.' Heinrici knew that if the Wehrmacht's forces before Moscow were destroyed, it would deliver Germany a mortal blow. He continued: 'Each day the noose tightens around our neck . . . there are brief moments of respite, and then the onslaught starts all over again. Heinrici's thoughts turned back to Christmas: 'Thank you for your kind gifts,' he added. 'I have taken the packages straight to our little celebration. I look at the pretty wrappings, and long to be at home with you. It is hard to carry on, feeling like this.'

On Christmas Day Heinrici wrote home again: 'My thoughts are with you,' he began. 'I am living this day with you in spirit. Here we face unwelcome developments, and our situation is growing ever more difficult.' Heinrici's army corps was withdrawing towards Kaluga. 'We are able to repel the Russian frontal attacks,' he added, 'but they are continuously infiltrating our flanks and making particularly good use of ski patrols. Finally we have received permission to pull back, but the orders were given far too late. Our vehicles are skidding along the icy roads, our guns slipping into ditches – impossible to extricate again. In all my years as a soldier, I have never experienced such difficulties.'

Heinrici believed that Hitler's increasing fear of losing prestige prevented him from grasping what was truly happening in Russia: 'The Führer does not want to believe it,' he commented. 'For propaganda reasons, our high command refuses to admit that the army before Moscow is in jeopardy.' But the full extent of the disaster was becoming clear to him. Admiral Wilhelm von Canaris, head of German military intelligence, described the sombre mood at Hitler's headquarters on 24 December: 'The Führer's principal adjutant, Rudolf Schmundt, is drawing comparisons with 1812,' Canaris began, 'and talking of the moment of truth for National Socialism. The equipment losses we have suffered are colossal: trucks, guns and aircraft have to be destroyed because we lack the fuel to bring them back. And all this has had a grim effect on our soldiers' fighting morale.'

Then Canaris said candidly: 'Our mistreatment of Russian prisoners is having awful consequences. In our retreat from Moscow we have had to abandon German field hospitals. The Russians then dragged out our sick and injured, hanged them upside down, poured gasoline over them and set them on fire.' This callous murder of the Wehrmacht's wounded, lying helpless in field hospitals abandoned during the retreat, features in a number of German soldiers' accounts. What is striking is Canaris's acceptance of moral responsibility for it, acknowledging that German mistreatment of Russian POWs had made the war as brutal as this. However, he made no formal protest over the issue, either to Hitler or the German high command.

As has been seen, many German soldiers attempted to mark Christmas in any way that they could. Now, at this time of crisis, the Nazi regime – although highly distrustful of Christianity and the Christian Church – chose to embrace the Christmas festival officially. Its hopes of a rapid victory against the Soviet Union had been rudely dashed. But it saw an opportunity to distract the German public from the growing military disaster in the east. It decided to depict its soldiers in Russia as heroic protectors of the German homeland, announcing that Christmas in Germany could be spent safe and secure from the Bolshevik hordes because the Wehrmacht was standing guard on the distant eastern frontier. However, newsreels were careful not to show either the severity of the fighting or the suffering of the soldiers. Instead, they offered a sentimental view, filming German troops cutting down fir trees and carrying them into their living quarters, and happily receiving post from home.

Propaganda Minister Joseph Goebbels gave a Christmas Eve radio broadcast to the German nation. He paid tribute to the 'sacrifices' made by the Wehrmacht in the winter campaign. Their 'devotion to duty' had saved the homeland from the horrors of war. 'This war has only made us stronger,' Goebbels said. 'We will not win it now through weakness.' He added: 'There are few presents around our Christmas trees this year. We have sent our candles to the Eastern Front, where our soldiers need them more than we do.'

Lieutenant Wilhelm Prüller was an ardent National Socialist. 'I know full well the sacrifices that must be borne in Russia,' he wrote on Christmas Eve, 'for they are sacrifices made for a greater cause. Because of our fight, millions of our people can celebrate this – the most German of all holidays – in peace and security.' But the Nazi message received a cynical reception from most Wehrmacht troops.

'On 24 December we put up a Christmas tree and heard a radio broadcast from Hitler,' said German soldier Josef Deck:

> in which, from the security of his distant headquarters, he pledged his personal resolve to defend the homeland. We quickly forgot about it – we had more pressing concerns. We did urgent repair work on the roads in the freezing cold. The front line was now 10 kilometres from Mtensk. Behind it our high command had ordered the creation of a 'dead zone', where everything was burnt to the ground. Because of this brutal action, Russian farmers armed with pitchforks and scythes are now attacking our positions alongside regular Red Army soldiers. We all long for a chance to escape from this terrible war.

Hitler made a specific request to his people: 'If the German nation wishes to make a present to its soldiers at Christmas,' he urged, 'it should be warm winter clothing.' Germans were asked to provide fur-lined boots, warm woollen coats, jackets and undergarments, protective headgear and thick winter gloves. 'The news of the winter clothes collection was received with bitterness rather than joy,' said Ulrich de Maizière, an officer in the 18th Panzer Division. 'It showed only how poorly prepared our high command had been.' Franz Peters, a soldier in the 23rd Infantry Division, added: 'None of it ever reached us when we needed it. The winter clothing finally arrived at my unit in May 1942, when the temperature had risen to 22 degrees Celsius. By then most of our comrades had long since frozen to death.'

Although Hitler now spoke of the Christmas festival, he tolerated the presence of Christian ministers within the Wehrmacht only reluctantly. German Army chaplain Josef Perau wrestled with the dilemma of being a priest under Hitler's National Socialist regime, deep in the heart of Bolshevik Russia. 'In the chaos of this struggle,' he wrote, 'it is for us to see the good amidst the horror, and to take hold of it.' To seek out the good in Germany's war with Russia was indeed a herculean task. The search for meaning transcends race or nation, and at this time of war Perau knew many factors could prompt it: 'A wounded German lieutenant joyfully greeted me,' he noted. 'He grasped my cross, and for a long time held it up to his lips. Such religious enthusiasm may be the result of combat stress – but who am I to judge whether it is sincere or not?'

Perau was deeply moved by the simple Christmas service he held at Yukhnov, 120 miles south-west of Moscow. 'For the main service on Christmas morning between 300 and 400 soldiers had come,' Perau wrote in his diary. 'No bells summoned them, and they found no festive church adorned with decorations, with beautiful music playing. They came into a cold, dark barn, with a makeshift altar, at which a solitary priest stood. That was all. But they understood that this is all there really is. Their lusty, heartfelt singing moved me more deeply than the finest choral recital.'

Another divisional chaplain wrote on 24 December: 'Slept well in a dirty room. Next to me are potato peelings and other refuse. I visited the men in their quarters. They look awful – ragged, covered in bedbug bites, entire bodies bloody, emaciated and dirty. Russian mortar shelling is coming closer. One man is blown up right in front of the church. The church must have been magnificent once – now gold-brocaded robes serve as curtains for the broken windows. We hear the enemy shooting from the woods, nearby. But that evening I return to the men in their crowded basement room, and we talk. Then, they ask me to read the Christmas story from the Bible.'

Yet, any search for meaning was confronted by relentless hatred and pain, spawned by Hitler's war in the east. Marie Avinov worked as an interpreter for the Wehrmacht in German-occupied Zubtsov. On Christmas Eve the military police apprehended a gang of Russian teenage boys. They had stolen some Christmas parcels being brought to German soldiers. Avinov was asked to interview the ringleader, a boy of about thirteen with wavy golden hair and piercing blue eyes. The Germans believed that he was working for black-market speculators, but Avinov sensed something different. She warned him that the gang was risking execution: death was the usual punishment for such offences. 'The boy's eyes fixed themselves on me in a most disconcerting way,' she recalled. 'I felt increasingly self-conscious – and began speaking too fast and too loud. He said little in response.'

Avinov was cooperating with the German regime. She justified her stance by her hatred of Bolshevism and Stalin's repression, but she was left shaken by her encounter. 'I was struck by the courage of this tough little boy. He did not seem to be motivated by profit or gain. Instead, I realised that he saw his theft as an act of genuine patriotic sabotage – denying the invader gifts that gave solace and encouragement to his cause – and no amount of punishment would deter him.' The boy was given a brutal whipping, and then released. Shortly afterwards, his gang was again caught red-handed attempting to steal Christmas packages from a sledge. All eight were hanged the same night.

Christmas was marked by the exchange of cards and messages, and with the Germans' expansionist ambitions in mind, Stalin's regime came up with a darkly witty twist. On 24 December 1941 Russian planes flew over enemy lines dropping sacks of 'Christmas cards'. They offered the Wehrmacht seasonal greetings from the Soviet Union. A snow-covered field was depicted, full of crosses topped with German helmets. The caption declared simply: 'Living space in the east'.

Yet occasionally, amidst the horror of this war, opposing ideologies could be bridged in the most remarkable of ways. On the evening of 24 December Lieutenant Hans Schäufler's unit – the 5th Panzer Brigade – moved into prepared positions in the small town of Kromy, near Orel. In the midst of the town was a half-ruined Orthodox church. In the aftermath of the Russian Revolution the Bolsheviks had attempted to blow it up. Later, they had used it as a storage area. When German troops entered it the snow lay knee-deep in the interior. Icicles hung from the broken windows and a thick hoarfrost covered the shattered remnants of the dome. An icy wind was blowing inside, yet the Germans were determined to hold an impromptu service. Schäufler said: 'After weeks of desperate fighting, we simply wanted to thank God we were still alive.'

The men set to work. They cleared the snow as best they could, carried two spruce trees into the building and began decorating them with candles and hangings. Some of the soldiers pulled up the floorboards from a side room and made a rough-hewn altar and communion table. In the midst of these preparations, Schäufler was passed an urgent radiogram message. It read: 'A Russian Cossack regiment is advancing on Kromy, and there is also partisan activity near the town.' Schäufler knew that if he read out the message – thereby formally acknowledging it – the men would have to take up battle stations and the planned Christmas service would be abandoned. The warning was serious, yet Schäufler and his comrades desperately wanted to celebrate Christmas. 'I could not believe the Russians would attack so quickly,' he said. 'I discussed the situation with a friend, and we decided to disregard the message.'

The divisional chaplain had arrived to conduct the service, and around eighty German soldiers settled into the vast interior of the church as Mass began: 'The priest stood before us at the makeshift altar,' Schäufler recalled, 'lit by the ghostly light of flickering candles. Snowflakes were quietly falling through the broken church roof and onto his shoulders.' And then, looking round, Schäufler could scarcely believe his eyes:

> Standing behind our small group was a mass of faces – the inhabitants of Kromy. Rough-looking men, with leather strapping entwined around their leg-wear, and women in scraped sheep furs and dark-coloured head cloths had joined us. Their clothes were humble, and yet I could not recall a more festive-looking gathering of people. Their eyes were shining in anticipation – and the thought struck me: 'How long has it been since these people were allowed to participate in a religious ceremony?' The men and women of Kromy, unable to understand a word of our service, wanted to be here nonetheless.

The service continued. Wehrmacht soldiers stood up and gave readings. There was an air of unreality about it all. In the midst of one of the most terrible wars in human history, the German invader – who had brought so much destruction in his wake – was honouring God on high, and wishing peace and goodwill to all humans on earth.

Schäufler looked around again, and then shuddered: 'In the background of the church I caught sight of a group of young Russian men, not joining with the others but standing aloof. Their fur hats remained on their heads. I looked straight at them and saw in their eyes an expression of uncanny, burning hatred. And then it struck me with the force of a blow – the radiogram warning!'

The men were Red Army soldiers or partisans. Transfixed in horror, Schäufler noticed one of them standing a little apart from the others. He had strong, intelligent features, and was probably their leader. The Russians were watching him too, as if waiting for a sign. A Russian grandmother with snow-white hair slowly went forward to the makeshift communion table, knelt with great difficulty and then, with a trembling, outstretched hand, reached forward and touched the cross. As she returned to her seat, Schäufler noted:

I felt a change among the sinister group, standing in the darkness. Some were looking towards the altar, some were smiling. As everyone else was kneeling, I was able to see that the distinguished-looking man in their midst wore well-cut officer's boots under his fur coat.

The priest was giving the concluding blessing. Unaware that Red Army soldiers were now in the church, he lifted the cross and moved it from side to side, over the whole congregation, over Russian and German, over friend and enemy. And then the group's leader stepped forward, carefully removed his fur cap and slowly lowered his head. Nervously, as if fearing some sort of punishment, his men followed his example – hesitantly, but all did it, without exception.

Two harmonicas struck up the tune for a Christmas carol. The Red Army soldiers had now left the building. 'Silent night, holy night' was sung resoundingly by the snow-covered assembly, and the wind carried the sound of the refrain out of the open roof. A cloud of white breath hung momentarily over the congregation – and then dissolved into the darkness above.

Slowly, the place of worship emptied. Schäufler was the last to leave. Outside, the man with the officer's boots was standing by the porch. There was no one else around. Schäufler remembered:

We looked at each other, looked into each other's eyes, for a long time. Then he said in halting German, first to himself, and then – solemnly – to me: '*Christ ist geboren!*' – 'Christ is born!' Quite spontaneously he held out his hand. I clasped it, and matched the firmness of his grip.

Then he was gone, into the dark Russian night – not along the path the others had used, but confidently, in a different direction, through the knee-deep snow.

8

Looking into the Abyss

As December 1941 drew to a close, Stalin and the Soviet high command were presiding over an extraordinary success. A month earlier, the German Wehrmacht had reached the outskirts of Moscow. Now its armies had been forced to retreat, in utter disarray, suffering catastrophic losses in men and equipment. It was a stunning turnaround in fortunes.

'Our victory at Livny, on the southern flank of the German advance, was a cause of great celebration,' Nikita Khrushchev said. 'So many of the enemy were killed or taken prisoner there. The troops that we captured were a sorry sight – shivering and demoralised, with completely inadequate clothing and footwear.' The Germans on Army Group Centre's northern flank had been equally firmly rebuffed. When Khrushchev travelled to Solnechnogorsk, to the north-west of Moscow, he found the Germans had retreated so hastily that their dead were simply left under a covering of snow. As the corpses were unearthed, Red Army soldiers viewed the remains with grim satisfaction.

Soviet armies had pushed back both flanks of the German Army Group Centre, safeguarding the Russian capital. They had recaptured Klin, Kalinin and Volokolamsk, freed Tula from near-encirclement and regained Kaluga. In the first few weeks of the counteroffensive, German Panzer forces had been hard hit. Now their Fourth and Ninth Infantry Armies were under increasing pressure, and between the towns of Yukhnov and Sukhinici south-west of Moscow a gap had been torn in their front. 'We are dangerously overextended,' wrote the German Army's chief of staff, Colonel General Franz Halder, 'our troops are utterly exhausted, and the enemy hammers incessantly at our positions, bringing up more and more troops.'

On New Year's Day 1942, Lieutenant Vladimir Goncharov, a company commander in the Soviet Thirty-Third Army surveyed a village liberated from the Germans. 'We undertook a night march of 15 kilometres,' he wrote, 'and then launched a surprise attack on the enemy. They fled, leaving behind their Christmas trees, wine and food. They did not have time to burn the village down, and most of its houses are still standing. Our advance is gaining momentum.' Goncharov continued: 'A captured German soldier stands before us. Despite all the enemy has done to our country – and the hatred we feel for him – I cannot help but feel pity for this man. He is poorly clothed, utterly exhausted and has badly frostbitten feet. Before the war he was a carpenter – in his kitbag he has a picture of his young wife and baby daughter.'

Goncharov and his comrades felt unable to predict whether the Germans opposing them would fight fiercely, retreat or simply surrender. 'The temperature is dropping again,' he noted. 'The enemy still does not have proper winter clothing and equipment. Most of the prisoners we take are badly frostbitten. As we push forward, we find the sides of the road littered with dead horses, abandoned motor vehicles and tanks. The Germans' weapons malfunction in the cold, and fresh ammunition and supplies rarely reach them. The extreme winter temperatures, inadequate clothing and lack of proper food are all having an effect. What cruelty to leave an army in this condition!'

Captured Germans were utterly demoralised. They complained angrily: 'Hitler is warm – we are freezing.' Enemy soldiers said in prisoner interrogations: 'We have children at home too – we have all had enough of this war!' The Wehrmacht appeared close to disintegration. 'The enemy's morale is dropping rapidly,' Goncharov wrote, 'and a mood of bitter disillusionment is spreading among their troops. We must keep pushing forward.'

As Red Army troops freed towns and villages from German occupation, Stalin's foreign minister, Viacheslav Molotov, brought out a pamphlet detailing enemy atrocities uncovered there.

Goncharov had a copy in front of him: 'After reading a few pages one's hair stands on end,' he said. 'This is the animal claw wielded by the Nazis. But we are uncovering countless little tragedies of our own. In the small village we have just taken,' Goncharov continued, 'the Germans shot all its male inhabitants. And yesterday we found some Russian POWs, who had managed to escape from a nearby camp – they are telling us horrifying stories about conditions there.'

'When I talk with the villagers we have liberated,' Goncharov said, 'it is often small things that reveal most about this so-called "master race". The Germans strip off their clothes to get rid of lice, unconcerned that there are Russian women in the same room, and arrogantly order people to prepare meals for them, treating everybody as if they were servants. Nazi values lack all sensitivity to others and those that uphold them are brutal and crass.'

As the year turned, in the German siege positions outside Leningrad, artilleryman Wolfgang Buff listened to a curiously muted address from the Führer: 'Soldiers – you stand on the eastern frontier. Through your fight, you are holding back the enemy.' A Wehrmacht communiqué was equally cautious, stating: 'If the Russians hope with the advantage of winter to penetrate our front, we will ensure that they do not succeed'. Buff's New Year was a simple affair, interrupted by a brief artillery duel with Red Army forces. He and his comrades chatted together, and reminisced about happier times. 'Last year we celebrated the New Year in Le Havre,' Buff recalled. 'The occasion was full of pomp and swagger. Our armies had, after all, been victorious all over Europe. What a difference a year can make!'

At midnight gunshots and flares were let off, and the men gathered together and sang. The following morning temperatures had dropped to −34 degrees Celsius. Buff and his comrades stepped outside, and enjoyed the brief reprieve from the fighting. 'It is an ugly war,' Buff said. 'But this morning, in the sunlight, our snow-covered, winter world glitters as if we are in a fairy tale.' Others briefly appreciated the year's beginning. German medical officer Wilhelm Hebestreit wrote: 'We are quartered in a gently rolling landscape. In a nearby hollow, under the ice, a brook is flowing and the far side of the incline is dotted with peasant huts. Everything is covered in deep snow and glitters as the sun comes up. It is a magical winter's day.'

At Vorotynsk, south-west of Kaluga, Lieutenant Erich Mende and his comrades of the 84th Infantry Regiment had fought their way out of Russian encirclement, surviving on iron rations, a few potatoes and a jar of pickled cucumbers which they had found hidden in a peasant hut. Hungry but relieved, they assembled at midnight outside the battalion HQ. Someone produced a small bottle of vodka and passed it around. The commander joined his men and spoke to them. 'He praised our courage,' Mende recalled, 'congratulated us on escaping the enemy and wished us good fortune. Then he asked us to hold a minute's silence for our dead friends. I have never experienced such deep, all-embracing quietness.'

Heinrich Haape's German 6th Infantry Division was pulling back from positions near Kalinin, with the Red Army hard on their heels. On the evening of 31 December the men reached the town of Staritsa. It was in flames, and most Wehrmacht units had already left, but more than a thousand wounded had not been evacuated. Haape and his comrades were furious to find them there – the Russians would show them no mercy – and resolved that these men would not be abandoned. They commandeered every vehicle they could find – lorries, sledges and even gun carriages – and packed them with wounded soldiers. Men with broken bones were given shots of morphine, wrapped in blankets and placed on artillery wagons. No one was left behind.

By saving their wounded comrades, Haape and his fellows reaffirmed a sense of solidarity and common cause. But as the relentless pressure of the Soviet counteroffensive continued, others succumbed to panic or sheer indifference. On 31 December Private Gerhard vom Bruch's 6th Panzer Division was driven out of its positions by strong Russian forces. That evening Bruch's unit searched for shelter, and eventually found a peasant hut that was still partially intact. Inside was a heap of dead German soldiers.

Bruch guessed from their injuries that they had been caught in an enemy artillery bombardment. The bodies had been left jumbled on the floor, and the men's identity papers had not even been removed. 'It was a dreadful sight,' Bruch said. Yet, although genuinely shocked, Bruch and his fellows did nothing either. 'We were too numbed by the events of the last few days to respond with any human decency,' Bruch acknowledged honestly. 'We simply shoved the dead soldiers outside and began to heat the room up. Then we passed around a bottle of wine and shared a little cake, in a derelict hut surrounded by a mass of corpses.'

Fritz Hübner recalled a similar incident. 'On the afternoon of 31 December our company pulled back from the frontline,' Hübner said:

> We gathered our equipment together and our exhausted, hungry soldiers moved off. But as we marched westwards, an odd shape became visible. At first its details were indistinct, and as we came closer it appeared to be a large pile of clothes. Then, as we gathered around it we made out a mass of bodies. About a hundred of our dead comrades were lying in the snow. Around them were tyre marks, and we assumed that they had been driven to the spot for burial. But although wood had been thrown down for the coffins and marker crosses, the bodies had not even been laid out properly. Frozen solid, with arms and legs splayed out in different directions, the poor soldiers just lay there. It was a picture of utter horror. There was a moment of stunned silence and then the man next to me said: 'So this is what a hero's death really looks like.' No one felt able to answer.

The German Army had always taken great care over the burial of its dead, laying them to rest in carefully marked graves with proper military honours. This provision was a benchmark of the Wehrmacht's morale and cohesion, the collapse of which was an ominous portent.

'A growing uncertainty is taking hold,' wrote German Army chaplain Josef Perau, 'about which no one dares speak . . . We are hearing the confessions of many seriously wounded soldiers. Our military situation is critical, and it is abundantly clear that a serious setback has occurred. No warm winter clothing has arrived, and our troops are suffering appalling frostbite – and many emergency amputations are being performed. Russian bombers are reaching Yukhnov now, and each attack produces fresh casualties.'

Yet moments of genuine heroism could still be found. Colonel General Franz Halder, chief of staff of the German Army, was increasingly concerned about the position of Maloyaroslavets, 60 miles south-west of Moscow, on the central section of the front. The Soviet Thirty-Third Army had penetrated German lines north of the town. 'This breakthrough has split our position,' Halder said gloomily, 'and at the moment we can see no way to restore it.' Exhausted troops from the German 98th Infantry Division were flung into the breach, in an attempt to stave off the enemy. Maloyaroslavets lay astride the main road from Moscow to Roslavl. As Napoleon's army had fallen back from Moscow, French troops had fought a desperate rearguard action in the very same place, trying to buy time for their retreating comrades. History was about to repeat itself.

On 31 December, Colonel Martin Gareis's 98th Infantry Division took up its positions around Maloyaroslavets. Inside the town were scenes of chaos, as vehicles from three fleeing German divisions converged on it and Russian bombing and shelling increased dramatically. 'A thick cloud of smoke, with a red underbelly, was rising into the night sky,' Gareis remembered. 'On the roads, hundreds of vehicles were jammed together, constantly revving their engines in the icy cold, the sound rising to a terrible howl. They were all desperately trying to get out onto the road to Medyn. But the long queue only moved forward slowly, and above it a cloud of freezing vapour hung in the air. Meanwhile, the enemy was poised to storm our defences.'

At 11.00 p.m. Red Army troops overran German positions north-east of Maloyaroslavets. On the stroke of midnight Russian troops broke into the town, and another force swung west to cut off the escape route. The defenders fought back with desperate bravery. 'One last instinct united our men,' said Gareis, 'to somehow hold back the enemy, and allow time for our supplies and equipment to evade the trap.' Germans and Russians fought hand to hand in the streets, and a last divisional reserve, drawn from engineers and signals staff, defended the road to the west.

There were scenes of animal savagery. In the side streets of Maloyaroslavets, lit by the flames from the bombing and shelling, drunken Red Army soldiers smashed their way into the German medical station, knifed and shot the wounded, and flung the remainder – naked – out of the first-floor window. The temperature had fallen to −38 degrees Celsius.

At 5.00 a.m. on 1 January 1942, Russian combat groups armed with grenades and mortar launchers reached the centre of the town. They believed that resistance had collapsed, but Gareis and his men regrouped and for five vital hours held off Red Army forces attacking the exit road, while most of the convoy of German vehicles escaped the town. 'Our last stand saved much of our army's equipment,' Gareis concluded. 'The cost was the near annihilation of the division.' On the morning of 1 January, Colonel Gareis surveyed his remaining soldiers. Most had open wounds, torn and inadequate clothing, and frostbite on their noses, ears and cheeks. The 289th Infantry Regiment, which had begun the battle 2,000 men strong, was now reduced to 120, and was reformed as a company.

'Our forces have been hit extremely hard,' wrote German officer Helmut von Harnack, 'and we have only parried the enemy's blows with the last reserves of our strength. The Wehrmacht is a reeling boxer – and we are now right up against the ropes.'

Further south, a 50-mile gap in the German front had opened up between Kaluga and Belev, splitting the Fourth and Second Panzer Armies. In a desperate attempt to stem the Soviet advance, the German high command set up a breakwater, garrisoning the rail junction and ammunition depot of Sukhinici – 145 miles south-west of Moscow – with a scratch combat force and ordering it to hold out at all costs. On 3 January Sukhinici's commander, Major General Werner von Gilsa, created a 4,000-strong battle group from leading elements of the 216th Division and auxiliary and support personnel, and prepared to face the Soviet Tenth Army and 1st Cavalry Corps. He was immediately besieged by the

Red Army. In the first three days of savage fighting, Gilsa's casualties tallied 250 dead and over a thousand seriously wounded.

In conditions of terrible adversity, men were reassessing their beliefs. Lieutenant Otto Bente, a company commander in the German 76th Infantry Division, saw in the New Year accompanied by a Russian artillery bombardment. As he and his comrades toasted each other with sparkling wine, an enemy shell exploded, shattering the windowpanes. Two days later – unable to sleep because of the cold – Bente and his fellows sought to while away the time. One officer fetched the unit's war diary and began to make entries in it; another reread his letter of recommendation for a military award. Bente had a book with him on *Great Germanic Leaders*, but its message – pleasing in the early days of the Wehrmacht's advance into Russia – now rankled with him: 'I have come to distrust this idealisation of our Teutonic past,' Bente wrote. 'Truth is subordinated to propaganda, and there are a host of unwarranted assumptions. We are told that if a soldier's blood is shed for a noble cause, all will be well. But I have seen too many comrades die – I no longer believe this.'

Then someone pulled out a copy of Homer's *Odyssey* from his kitbag, and began reading some of its passages out loud. Men gathered around, spellbound: 'We thought we were invincible,' Bente said, 'but now, nothing was succeeding for us. Suddenly, we powerfully understood this tale from the past. We were a band of warriors, far from home, harried from place to place by merciless fate.'

Nikita Khrushchev recalled a remarkable change in Stalin's demeanour after the first successes of the Moscow counter-offensive. 'He straightened himself up,' Khrushchev said simply, 'and walked around confidently, as a commander and leader.' A major new Soviet offensive was in the offing, for now, and with the enemy in such disarray even greater victories seemed possible. 'Stalin will launch a fresh assault against us,' one German soldier wrote. 'He hopes to force a decision through winter fighting, as Russia did against Napoleon in 1812 – a strategy he clearly aims to repeat.'

The forecast proved correct. The new offensive was led by Soviet General Georgi Zhukov. On 6 January 1942 Stalin instructed Zhukov to bring up more armies, and break and then destroy the German Army Group Centre. The Soviet supremo wanted to deliver a knockout blow.

German staff officer Hans Meier-Welcker considered General Zhukov to be a formidable adversary. 'It is Zhukov's skill in planning military operations that I fear the most,' Meier-Welcker wrote on 6 January. 'From time to time captured Red Army documents arrive at my desk. Some are in Zhukov's own writing, which is methodical and evenly formed. Their contents show his intelligence and ability. He is forging the Russians into an impressive fighting force.'

The Red Army kept on advancing. 'Our next target was the village of Kashurino, which fell at dusk,' wrote Soviet Lieutenant Vladimir Goncharov, with the Thirty-Third Army, on 8 January. 'I stayed at the command post all day, supervising the assault. The military initiative is firmly in our hands.' Goncharov's force was now moving towards the key German stronghold of Yukhnov, 120 miles south-west of Moscow, and his soldiers felt that the enemy was on the run. 'Some of our men are saying our advance will continue all the way to Berlin,' he concluded.

In the midst of doubt and horror, some of the German Army still retained an instinctive deference to authority. On 8 January Heinrich Haape's 6th Infantry Division – on Army Group Centre's northern flank – was retreating towards Rzhev, 130 miles north-west of Moscow. Hitler's 'Stand Fast!' order prevented the men disengaging from the Russians, and they were fighting a succession of bitter rearguard actions. As they approached one village – Malakovo – exhaustion overwhelmed them. It did not seem possible to carry on, Haape said: 'A slouching, ragged band – icicles hanging from their hats and helmets – shuffled aimlessly towards Malakovo, out of line, out of step, bodies bent under the weight of ammunition and weapons. There was nothing military about their bearing any more. All the fight had been knocked out of them.'

Then from the front of the column came a whisper 'The commander!' The commander was standing by one of the village huts, waiting to greet his men. Word was passed down the line: 'The commander is with us!' And Haape remembered: 'There was an instinctive movement. Not a single word of command was given, but the men formed a proper marching order. They took up step. Rifles were placed on shoulders at the correct angle. They lifted their heads and looked straight to the front. And as one, they began singing: "From the mountain flows a stream, of sparkling wine so cool . . ."' The commander removed his hat and stood to attention – with his hand at the salute – as his men marched past, acknowledging the defiant marching song. Its last words rang out: 'Lucky is he who can forget the woe and sorrow he has met.'

However, firm conviction in the overarching power of the Führer was fading fast. In its place, German army chaplain Josef Perau, stationed in Yukhnov, felt a mounting sense of dread. On 10 January he wrote: 'Outside, a snowstorm is whipping around the houses. Its sound mingles with the growling of Russian artillery, which is drawing closer and closer. The sky is red from the fires of burning villages. Each night we sleep fully dressed, in case there is a full-scale alert. The military hospital has had to be evacuated by plane – but for the most seriously wounded, this movement will be fatal.' Perau continued: 'Our Russian house owners have been gone for a week now. One morning, they were overcome by a terrible fear. We watched in silence as they loaded their children and few possessions onto a cart. The mother and father briefly knelt before their icons and prayed, and then they disappeared into the white, cold vastness that surrounds us.'

'We have had snowstorms over the last few days,' wrote German staff officer Hellmuth Stieff with the Fourth Army on 10 January. 'Most of the roads are impassable to us. But Red Army troops – moving freely on skis and snowshoes – appear at will. Russian cavalry are trying to get behind our position and disrupt our supplies – they are drawn to us like filings to a magnet. Our forces between Medyn and Kaluga are about to run out of food and ammunition. A timely withdrawal would have avoided this – but the Führer forbade it. I watch events unfold with dull resignation.'

On 11 January German soldier Hans Jürgen Hartmann with Army Group South wrote from Kiev: 'I just feel lucky to have escaped any involvement in the chaos unfolding before Moscow, where hundreds of thousands have been killed or have gone missing, and where the most terrible mismanagement still continues. Our troops are being sacrificed in pointless military actions. Here at least my comrades and I are warm and safe.'

The Wehrmacht was going through a crisis of confidence, and its first casualty had been Colonel General Heinz Guderian. 'Guderian was the star in our firmament,' said Lieutenant Hans-Erdmann Schönbeck of the 11th Panzer Division, 'an incredibly popular general whose dynamism and drive inspired the whole army.' Luftwaffe operations officer Colonel Karl-Henning von Barsewisch added: 'Guderian was full of energy, restless, alert, always on the move. He was a remarkable leader, intelligent and charismatic, and when he took a decision it had the power and drama of Thor swinging his hammer – everyone jumped up immediately to transmit the order.'

Colonel General Guderian had been summoned to Hitler's headquarters on 20 December 1941 after ordering an unauthorised retreat. Guderian argued that commanders in the field should be able to make such decisions themselves, using their own judgement. The Führer had refused to accept this. When Guderian withdrew more troops four days later, Field Marshal von Kluge demanded this be prevented, and on 26 December Hitler had dismissed the brilliant Panzer leader. One of his officers, Joachim von Lehsten described the effect on the troops:

'All our commanders – at divisional, regimental and battalion level – were talking about it. It was an absolute disaster – our soldiers found Hitler's action incomprehensible. Everyone respected and admired this man: a remarkable leader of outstanding ability.' 'It was a catastrophe,' said Colonel August Schmidt of the 10th Motorised Infantry Division. 'Guderian was dismissed because he had the courage to stand up to Hitler and challenge his misguided halt order, an order which threatened to destroy our entire army.' Hans-Erdmann Schönbeck concurred: 'It was a terrible shock,' he said. 'The decision was completely unjust, and of course its timing – with our army in retreat – was awful:'

This was the watershed. Guderian was the creator of *Blitzkrieg* and the German Army's most outstanding tank commander. Joseph Goebbels put the view of Hitler and his entourage: 'Guderian lost all self-discipline,' Goebbels stated. 'In the winter of 1941–2 he ordered a retreat on his own initiative, putting the whole front in jeopardy. After he did this, other commanders followed suit. Our terrible crisis in the east began with this unauthorised action of Guderian's.' Goebbels then continued: 'The army generals completely lost their nerve at this time. They had previously only enjoyed a succession of victories, and were unable to cope with this sudden crisis. All they could think about was retreat.'

Guderian saw things differently: 'Our supreme command has completely overreached itself,' he said. 'It does not want to believe reports of the dwindling combat strength of our troops, and makes one unrealistic demand after another. It has been completely taken by surprise by the dramatic drop in temperatures, and has made no provision for fighting in such extreme conditions. It has seriously underestimated the strength of the enemy.'

The departure of Guderian was followed, in quick succession, by that of two Army Corps commanders, General Hans Felber, on 27 December, and General Otto Förster, on the 30th, both dismissed for withdrawing troops without permission. On 4 January 1942 Colonel General Erich Hoepner wrote: 'The list of jettisoned generals grows ever longer. Guderian's dismissal was quite astonishing. Hitler is now threatening Corps commanders, expressly forbidding any retreat – but his orders are only endangering more and more of our men. Our high command is making a series of fundamental errors and I am putting my head on the line by continuing to complain about them. There is a serious cost to one's nerves fighting against the enemy and one's own supreme commander at the same time.' On 8 January Hoepner was peremptorily sacked by the Führer, after pulling back troops threatened with encirclement.

General Gotthard Heinrici, commander of the 43rd Army Corps, saw the damaging effect of this:

> All suggestions for dealing with this crisis are rejected, through fear. Our new commanders are desperate not to antagonise Hitler, and everything is referred back to him. Kluge is absolutely terrified. And the Führer's rigid insistence that there will be no 'Napoleonic retreat' leaves us standing with unprotected flanks, allowing the enemy all the time he needs to encircle our positions. We have been promised fresh divisions. But these replacements are only coming in slowly, drop by drop, and they make little difference to us . . . Tomorrow our principal supply route will be lost. And what will happen then? We will probably be ordered to carry on fighting without food or ammunition!

Then Heinrici said: 'We have advanced more than 1,200 kilometres into Russia, yet our supreme commander – the Führer – refuses to surrender a scrap of land to the enemy. I believe a terrible price will be exacted for what is happening here.'

A report from Army Group Centre acknowledged: 'After a succession of orders from Hitler, intended to bolster our troops' determination to stand their ground, there has been no improvement in morale whatsoever – in fact quite the opposite.' It added:

> The mood among our commanders is one of intense bitterness, and there are grave worries about the future. Alongside innumerable complaints about the lack of winter equipment, the general tone of the criticism is: 'The catastrophe of this winter could have been avoided, if they had listened to us. Our warnings were clear, and either our high command did not read our reports or it failed to take them seriously. Nobody wants to know the truth.' The other reproach is about the 'Stand Fast!' order. Our officers say: 'We know how to defend ourselves, but our hands are now tied. We cannot act on our own initiative. The order to hold out at all costs – forcibly imposed on our troops – means that we cannot make an orderly withdrawal, and instead are pushed back, with the enemy always at our heels. The result has been irreplaceable losses in men and equipment.'

Army Group Centre inventoried some of these. On 10 January 1942 it reckoned that from the start of the retreat it had lost 7,319 lorries, 4,351 motorcycles and 3,643 cars. Luftwaffe commander Wolfram von Richthofen warned Field Marshal von Kluge that providing German troops with skis and snow-shoes was now an absolute priority. 'We have lost our mobility,' he said, 'and this will undermine our ability to resist. If a motor-ised force claims a battle complement of 10,000 men, usually only a thousand of them are ready for combat – the remainder are scattered along the motor highway, trying to catch up. Our forces are trying to create strongpoints to blunt the enemy's attacks, but at present we can neither equip nor reinforce such positions properly.'

After a series of desperate arguments with Hitler and Halder, Field Marshal von Kluge finally withdrew his support for the 'Stand Fast!' order and asked permission for Army Group Centre to pull away from the Russians. Hitler refused. On 11 January he summoned Kluge to his headquarters and told him that the enemy had to be fought to a standstill. But the Führer's army was now utterly demoralised.

'After the dismissal of Guderian and Hoepner, the mood of the troops sank alarmingly,' recalled German artilleryman Josef Deck. 'Wild rumours began circulating, that there would be peace negotiations and the war would be over soon – though who was supposed to be negotiating with whom no one could say. Things were a complete shambles – on one occasion German artillery and dive-bombers mistakenly attacked our own positions. The Stukas hit several of our tanks, putting them out of action – and then the Russians joined in, launching a massed infantry assault. We beat them off by firing our guns at point-blank range, with the barrels horizontal.'

Along the Lama river, west of Volokolamsk, Private Gerhard vom Bruch and his fellows from the 6th Panzer Division were manning a defence line formed from craters, blasted out of the frozen ground by explosives. 'It was a desperate task for our engin-eers to undertake,' Bruch wrote, 'but it seems to have worked.

The craters have been widened and deepened by us and made into a series of shelters. We have lined them with wood taken from ruined houses. Perhaps we can hold the enemy here.'

In early January 1941 the 6th Panzer divisional commander Colonel Erhard Raus had written: 'Our medical stations are reporting frostbite cases of 800 a day. At this rate, the division will cease to exist within a week.' In temperatures below −30 degrees Celsius no man could lie in a forward foxhole for more than an hour, unless he was wearing a sheepskin coat, felt boots, a fur cap and padded gloves. Raus's troops had now gained a brief reprieve, but on 11 January Russian T-34 tanks appeared out of the swirling snow and advanced on Private vom Bruch's crater, guns blazing. 'To the left of us, the soldiers suddenly fled,' Bruch said, 'and the Russians were all around our position. Fortunately, the tanks then swung off in a different direction.' Bruch and his comrades abandoned their makeshift shelter, and struggled westwards through the heavy snow.

'Stand fast − or die,' Lieutenant Kurt Grumann of the German 87th Infantry Division wrote on 11 January. 'There will be no withdrawal for our regiment, that's for sure − now the Russians are sending ski units behind our positions. A strong wind sweeps drifts of snow across the roads, and we are reduced to using our rifles as shovels. We must keep our supply route open, at all costs. Who could have imagined that our morale would drop so low − what on earth is happening to us?'

The 15th Panzer Regiment − part of the 11th Panzer Division − had led the attack on Moscow. It was now stationed over a hundred miles from the capital, in near impenetrable forest. 'Our few remaining tanks stood immobile behind our position, useless in the cold and snow,' said Hans-Erdmann Schönbeck. 'We sat within our foxholes, constantly on the watch for partisans. We were fighting as infantry, although we had no training for this kind of warfare. The soldiers were bitter, and believed that they had been abandoned by Hitler. Criticism of the Führer was made openly and discipline was in real jeopardy.'

Heinz Otto Fausten of the 1st Panzer Division watched military discipline collapsing around him. 'We were retreating westwards in loosely formed groups,' he remembered:

> The occasional food depots along our route were heavily guarded – to prevent theft by our own soldiers. Marching through the heavy snow, every step was absolute agony. We struggled against the icy wind with our last reserves of strength. Men staggered into the 'frostbite lane' along the side of the road. Some sat there, apathetic, chewing snow, again and again; others lay down and fell asleep. They would not wake up. To distract myself, and to keep on moving, I recited speeches and poetry I learnt as a child. I struck my fist into the air for emphasis, and when I reached passages I was no longer sure of I improvised vigorously.

Fausten reached the next halting point with a few of his comrades. They had heard that bands of renegade soldiers were now robbing and killing stragglers. The following morning they awoke to find their horse and cart stolen. Distraught, they hurried on, in a desperate attempt to overtake the thieves. 'After about ten kilometres we came across a chilling sight,' said Fausten. 'Our pony lay by the side of the road – shot in the head. From its flanks, large chunks of flesh were missing.'

On Army Group Centre's southern flank, Willy Reese's 95th Division was defending the village of Dubrovka, south-east of Roslavl. 'We had little food – and we could never get our quarters warm,' Reese recalled:

> There was the stink of frostbite, as men used the same bandage – pus-encrusted and stiff with scabs and rotted flesh – again and again. Some had long rags of blackened flesh hanging from their feet. It was snipped off. The bones were exposed, but with their feet wrapped in cloths and sacking, the men had to go on standing sentry duty and fighting . . . Everyone had diarrhoea, and one soldier was so enfeebled that he collapsed on the way to the doctor and froze to death. Older men developed rheumatism, and often screamed with pain. But we couldn't let anyone go.

One of Reese's comrades, searching for felt boots, found some on the frozen corpse of a Red Army soldier: 'He tugged at the

Russian's legs, but in vain,' Reese recorded. 'So he grabbed an axe and took the man off at the thighs. Fragments of flesh flew everywhere. Then he bundled the two stumps under his arm and set them down by the oven, next to our lunch. By the time the potatoes were done, the legs had thawed out and he pulled the bloody boots on.' Everyone then began to eat, indifferent to the mutilated body in their midst. Reese concluded: 'Our soldiers looked like ghosts – half living, half dead . . . Our existence has become one long complaint against the war.' The Russians maintained their pursuit, sensing that the Germans were almost finished.

Soviet Lieutenant Vladimir Goncharov and his men of the Thirty-Third Army were closing on the Moscow-Roslavl motor highway. 'We are on the right flank of our army,' Goncharov wrote on 11 January, 'moving cross-country, through deep snow. The temperature is below −30 degrees Celsius. But tonight – for the first time in weeks – we are quartered in warm outbuildings, and I am writing this by a stove. The houses in the village are full and our soldiers are also in the barns and cellars. The reconnaissance patrol is sleeping happily around me. For us, a bath, some tobacco, a little tea and a warm stove are indescribable pleasures.'

Goncharov related a couple of amusing incidents from their advance. 'In one liberated village – Kobyino – we found out that a married Russian woman had been having a relationship with a German soldier,' he remembered:

> As long as the Germans were in the village, the aggrieved husband could do little about her adultery. But when the enemy suddenly fled, he decided to put his house in order. As our soldiers moved into the village, he very publicly drove his wife out from their home, announcing – most dramatically – that she was a national traitor who was undermining the war effort. Then, to the growing amusement of our troops, the fellow began a vigorous cleaning operation, mopping his floor and washing down the walls, and declaring to the assembled onlookers that he had purged his house of 'Fascist filth'. Our men found this hilarious – and applauded vigorously.

The following morning, as breakfast was being prepared for the regimental staff, the same husband clambered into his attic to look for a pair of felt boots. Goncharov noted:

> The man was substantially overweight and under the stress of his massive bulk the main roof beam collapsed, and everything – petrified house owner, boards, earth and accumulated debris – fell right down on top of us. The typewriter was smashed, valuable documents scattered and most importantly, our precious soup was ruined. Two minutes later our commander appeared, and looked around in utter disbelief. Then, suppressing his laughter with difficulty, he complained: 'And now I will have to write a serious report on this "incident" for Army HQ.' But we were still mourning our soup.

Goncharov added: 'Laughter at such moments helped us to keep our sanity. We were witnessing such terrible things. Outside one house we found the body of a two-year-old child, killed by a mine. In another, lay a sixteen-year-old girl. The Germans had raped her – and then shot her.'

General Zhukov now decided to commit Soviet paratroopers to his offensive, dropping them ahead of the main advance. The 10,000-strong elite 4th Airborne Corps was brought into the battle. This was a bold, aggressive move, involving a series of night-time parachute drops close to enemy lines. Goncharov was impressed by such a tactic: 'Introducing airborne troops at this stage of the operation has had a considerable impact,' he observed. 'Our paratroopers are clearing the area in front of us. The Germans have been completely taken by surprise – and are fleeing so fast they do not even have time to burn villages.'

On 12 January Lieutenant Goncharov recorded that the Soviet Thirty-Third Army was attacking Medyn, north-west of Kaluga. The remnants of Colonel Martin Gareis's 98th Infantry Division were bravely defending the town. The divisional anti-tank company had been reduced to three guns, crewed by an officer and six men. They were unable to hold off the numerically superior Red Army forces.

Further north, on 14 January the 11th Panzer Regiment – part of the German 6th Panzer Division – was repelling a series of Russian infantry attacks. But when ordered to pull back, the men were unable to respond. Lieutenant Klaus Voss wrote: 'The mental and physical stress our soldiers are under is now so severe that some are incapable of coordinated military action.' The following day, a localised withdrawal was again postponed. 'The men are so exhausted,' said Voss, 'that further orders have been held back to allow them to snatch a few hours' rest.' 'For all of us caught in the hell of this retreat,' wrote Private Gerhard vom Bruch from the same division, 'there is only one remaining thought – self-preservation.'

Some German reinforcements were finally arriving from the west. In early January the Fourth Panzer Group reported: 'The troops are complaining that the replacements are arriving with inadequate equipment. Owing to their complete lack of winter clothing, these men – unaccustomed to the severe cold – are often completely exhausted before they even join battle.'

In December 1941 the German 81st Infantry Division had been stationed on the French Atlantic coast. On 27 December orders had come through for its 189th Regiment to be sent to Russia immediately. The following day the men clambered aboard a military train. They were not issued with any special food, winter clothing or equipment; the German high command seemed afflicted by a state of near paralysis. After ten days' uninterrupted travel the regiment arrived at Andreapol, 200 miles north-west of Moscow, clambering out into three-foot deep snow and a temperature below −30 degrees Celsius. The men did not have winter greatcoats, balaclavas or earmuffs and some succumbed to frostbite within hours of their arrival. A German supply officer recorded in astonishment: 'That an entire regiment of 3,000 men could be sent to us without any protection from the terrible winter weather defies description.'

The priority had to be for these men to be properly equipped and supplied before being sent to the front. But there was a fresh military crisis, as Soviet troops under Colonel General Andrei Yeremenko broke through a gap between Army Group Centre and Army Group North, and they were flung into battle at once. Their destination was the small railway town of Okhvat. On 11 January Lieutenant Dietrich Karsten's 1st Battalion took up defence positions along the edge of a frozen lake, on Okhvat's outskirts. A month earlier, Karsten had felt frustration at being in an easy billet in France, far away from the fighting on the Eastern Front. In a letter to his wife, he had described the German assault on Moscow in November 1941 as 'a real war', and complained of feeling 'very left out of these decisive events'. When he heard that his regiment would be sent to Russia he was excited, not fearful. 'Things are moving on,' he had written, 'and that is good. The soldier in me gets his way.'

Karsten was a brave officer, who had won the Iron Cross fighting in France, but he had no inkling of the horror awaiting him in Russia. At Andreapol he sought repeatedly to acquire proper winter clothing for his men. Nothing was available. The regiment then made a series of forced marches to Okhvat, suffering terribly from the cold. They arrived in the town at the same time as the advancing Russians, and had to fight hard to take possession of it. They were briefly successful, but on 13 January Colonel General Yeremenko flung in two more Russian divisions and overwhelmed the hapless reinforcements. Karsten died the following day, and most of his regiment was wiped out with him.

Army Group Centre could no longer contain intense Russian pressure along a front that extended for over 500 miles. German soldiers were now falling back everywhere. The scale of the crisis could no longer be denied, even by the Führer – who was at last forced to listen to his generals. On 15 January a reluctant Hitler modified his 'Stand Fast!' order, permitting a larger retreat. He stated: 'This is the first time in this war that I have given the order for a major withdrawal. I expect it to be carried out in a manner worthy of the German Army.' But the order was hedged with preconditions, and came much too late.

'When Hitler – after lengthy arguments with commanders on the ground – finally allowed a retreat to an agreed winter position,' said Carl Wagener, on the operations staff of the Third

Panzer Group, 'we were looking into the abyss. Nearly all our vehicles had been lost – and much of our artillery had also been destroyed. We were forced to carry our wounded back in horse-drawn carts, and inevitably, many succumbed to frostbite. Russian fighter planes hovered menacingly over our retreating columns, machine gunning them at will. Our supplies rarely reached us, and we were forced to rely on occasional air drops by the Luftwaffe.'

With food and ammunition running out, Lieutenant Erich Mende and his company had already abandoned their defence positions at Tikhonova Pustyn, 30 miles north-west of Kaluga, and retreated along snow-covered tracks into a forest. In the grip of total starvation, some of the men began to hallucinate: 'One soldier believed he had seen a pig,' Mende said, 'and ran off into the forest to try and slaughter it. Another claimed that freshly baked poppy cakes had emerged from a sheet of scrap metal.' As he marched, his mind increasingly affected by malnutrition, Mende fell into a reverie. He imagined he was back at home, and his mother was presenting him with a basket of freshly gath-ered strawberries. 'But then,' Mende recalled, 'I was overcome by desperate hunger. I did not use a spoon, or even my hands, but shoved my face hard into the basket. My mother watched in horror – it was as if I had become an animal. When I recovered my awareness of where I actually was, I still believed I had crushed strawberries on my cheeks.'

Hitler had permitted a withdrawal to a line that ran from Rzhev to Yukhnov, but German troops had already been flung back there. They were now on the brink of annihilation, as the Russians threatened to surround and overwhelm their remaining forces.

On 19 January the remnants of Fritz Langanke's SS *Das Reich* Division were covering the retreat to Rzhev. A bitterly cold wind was blowing from the east. They passed a large brick building, and something about it chilled even these hardened fighters. 'It was an abandoned German military hospital,' said Langanke. 'It had a most sinister atmosphere. Then, at the back of the house, we saw something that captured the merciless cruelty of this winter war.

Underneath the windowsill we found a large heap of amputated hands, feet, arms and legs. After operations for frostbite were performed, the men's limbs had simply been tossed outside, into the snow.'

Russian forces were poised for the kill. 'We now approach Yukhnov,' Soviet Lieutenant Vladimir Goncharov wrote, 'and can hear the sound of German vehicles moving along the road. The town is burning, and flames are rising into the night sky.' General Heinrici reported on 19 January: 'We are completely encircled in Yukhnov. Hitler's promised reinforcements never arrived. We are finished – unless a miracle happens. But although I have been crying out to God, so far he has not sent any assistance either. All this is the Führer's doing. He ordered us to stand fast – disregarding the advice of countless military professionals.'

Heinrici could no longer hold back his despair. 'Now the Grim Reaper mercilessly raises his sickle over our battle lines,' he said. 'Each day he cuts down more and more of our men. Soon it will all be over.'

9

Enter General Model

THERE NOW SEEMED to be nothing the Germans could do to arrest their headlong flight. Operation Typhoon had first stalled and then collapsed under the onslaught of winter, broken and failed supply lines, a divided leadership and a resurgent Red Army. The Russians were now resolutely driving the Germans back towards the west, and threatening to cut off and encircle many of the retreating defenders.

On 19 January 1942 Stalin made a dramatic intervention in the battle, removing Colonel General Kuznetsov's First Shock Army from the Russian offensive and ordering its immediate transfer to the army reserve. This major Red Army formation was in the midst of the fighting, but the Soviet leader declared that it was no longer needed at the front. When General Georgi Zhukov complained about this decision, warning that his troops were becoming overstretched, Stalin retorted that such caution was unnecessary: the Germans were almost finished.

The German position did indeed look close to collapse. On the night of 19 January Fritz Langanke's SS *Das Reich* Division was on the Moscow–Smolensk motor highway. Traffic had come to a halt in a blinding snowstorm and Wehrmacht military police were struggling to get the vehicles moving again. 'There was constant yelling and swearing,' Langanke recalled. 'A strong easterly wind was blowing, and temperatures had sunk to around −40 degrees Celsius. The lubricating grease in our armoured reconnaissance car had frozen solid, and we could only move the steering wheel with the greatest difficulty. Cars and trucks were repeatedly getting stuck in the snow, and when their engines were no longer able to start, the police simply pushed them off the road.'

At a sharp turning, Langanke's vehicle collided with a section of snow wall and juddered to a halt. 'It was bitterly cold,' he remembered, 'and staying inside our armoured car without the engine running was like sitting on a block of ice. The gunner and I got out and tried to warm ourselves up by jumping about. But the military police arrived, and despite our protests, tried to shove our vehicle into the ditch. Fortunately, it was too heavy for them. There was more cursing, and then, reluctantly, they helped get us moving again, pushing the car backwards and forwards while we revved the engine. Finally, it started – and our hellish journey continued.'

Langanke's depleted SS unit was redeploying to the town of Sychevka, south of Rzhev. A new crisis had blown up on Army Group Centre's battered front and troops from the SS *Das Reich* Division were being flung into the breach. As the men moved on through the night, they saw how desperate the German position now was. Defences were alarmingly thin, and behind them were scenes of utter chaos, with supply personnel milling about, unable to get food and ammunition up to the front. It seemed that one last, hard push from the Russians would bring the whole tottering edifice crashing down.

Early the following morning, Langanke reached the crest of a hill. Below, traffic had once more come to a standstill. 'All the columns ahead of us had halted,' he recalled, 'and drivers, crews and soldiers were standing by the side of the road, looking upwards. The snowstorm had died away and sunshine had replaced it – the snow glittered all around us. On that cold winter morning, two large rainbows had appeared in the sky – one atop the other. Their colours were radiant and thousands of German soldiers were gazing at the sight in wonder. For a moment, the war was completely forgotten.'

'More and more Russian villages are burning,' said German staff officer Carl Wagener of the Third Panzer Group, 'and at night the sky is stained blood red.' Many German troops became inured to the destruction. 'We continue to set villages alight,' said Lieutenant Kurt Grumann of the 87th Infantry Division. 'The inhabitants fled their homes, but later returned and begged for food. We drove them away. We cannot share our meagre reserves – we must be merciless.' Constant exposure to suffering deadened the senses of most, but some Wehrmacht soldiers were shaken by the cruelty of their battle orders. On 19 January staff officer Hans Meier-Welcker, retreating with the German Ninth Army, wrote: 'We arrived at a settlement, and some Russians were willing to help us, clearing tracks through the snow and providing rooms in their houses. They brought water for us to wash in and shared the last of their food. And then, after a stay of two days, we followed strict orders and burnt down their village. Old women and little children were flung out into the freezing winter. This "military necessity" – as it is described by our high command – is becoming unbearable for those soldiers not reduced to automatons by the fighting.'

On Army Group Centre's southern flank, the same scenes of destruction were repeated. Colonel General Rudolf Schmidt – promoted after taking command of Guderian's Second Panzer Army – spoke about the cumulative effect of such actions on his troops:

> As our divisions continued to retreat, the high command ordered that all prisoners held by us were to work day and night, clearing the roads. These unfortunates were starving and in rags, and this brutal decree quickly finished most of them off. We were instructed to burn every village we passed through, and drive the remaining inhabitants – in temperatures of −40 degrees Celsius – into the forest to face certain death. Many resort to slogans to justify this – slogans embracing the ideology of racial supremacy – that we are waging a pitiless struggle against the Jewish-Bolshevik *Untermenschen*. But others are torn apart by the suffering we are inflicting.

German soldier Wolfgang Borchert wrote starkly: 'A village is going up in flames. The people stand around their houses – they are clutching their children, and have jammed pots, pans and blankets under their arms. Some hold wooden pictures – small icons

– adorned in gold, silver and blue. There is a man to be seen on them, gentle and kind, with an oval face and brown beard. The inhabitants stare wildly into his eyes – but their houses keep on burning.'

Among the Wehrmacht, conscience pangs still stirred. Lieutenant Erich Mende's unit was deep inside the Russian forest. One morning they reached a clearing, and as they stepped forward Mende and his comrades could scarcely believe their eyes: 'In the open space before us was a monastery. It was on fire, but the tower and outer structure was still standing, and liquid lead ran off the roof and flowed – hissing – into the snow. Some local people were desperately trying to retrieve precious religious items from the flames.' Unthinkingly, the German soldiers – who had been torching houses for weeks – rushed in to help. It was an instinctive reaction, as if – suddenly – the war had ceased to exist. Some managed to save church books and icons, and handed them to the Russians. Others tried to contain the fire, emptying snow-filled buckets onto the roof. One man clutched Mende's arm and said: 'Thank God we have had the chance to do this. For a few brief moments, I felt a human being again.'

On 19 January, as Stalin withdrew the First Shock Army from the front, the German Ninth Infantry Army received a fresh leader. The previous commander, Colonel General Adolf Strauss, felt that his army's position was now hopeless. The German Army's chief of staff, Colonel General Franz Halder, noted in his diary: 'Strauss cannot carry on.' On the same day Halder added: 'Von Leeb [the commander of Army Group North] asks to be relieved of his post; von Reichenau [the commander of Army Group South] has had a stroke.' German command dispositions resembled a hospital bulletin board. And in this 'emergency ward' the plight of Army Group Centre had become critical. Luftwaffe pilot Peter Stahl witnessed the condition of many of the German troops struggling back to the Rzhev-Yukhnov line: 'It was a truly harrowing picture,' Stahl remembered. 'Long columns of our soldiers floundered through the snow. Abandoned vehicles were everywhere. As we flew over these men, at low altitude, we saw that most were almost

unconscious with fatigue. They paid no attention to us whatsoever. Villages were burning – the entire horizon was filled with
columns of black smoke. What a pitiless war!'

Soviet armies had broken the German front in numerous places.
The Wehrmacht clung to a series of strongpoints – at Kholm,
Rzhev, Yukhnov and Sukhinici – but around them, Russian
forces were pushing westwards. Stalin wanted to encircle and
destroy Army Group Centre and ordered his troops to gain possession of the Smolensk-Moscow motor highway and throttle its
fragile supply lines.

At Rzhev the position of the German Ninth Army was particularly hazardous, and it was hardly surprising that Colonel General
Strauss did not want to continue his command. Along his section of
the front no fewer than six Soviet armies had launched a concerted
attack. Strauss's own army was split into groups, each one fighting
for its very survival. On his northern flank, German lines had collapsed completely. Isolated garrisons were holding out at Demyansk
and Kholm, but Soviet armies had skirted around them, heading
towards the town of Vitebsk, 150 miles to the Ninth Army's rear.
General Hans-Georg Reinhardt's Third Panzer Group had been
grandly redesignated the Third Panzer Army, despite having lost
most of its tanks and motor vehicles. It was now pulled back to
plug the breach, assisted by Wehrmacht reinforcements from western Europe. Rzhev had thus become the linchpin of the German
position: if it fell, the entire front would collapse.

Substantial Soviet forces – including two armies, the Twenty-
Ninth and Thirty-Ninth – had broken through weak German
lines along the river Volga, north-west of Rzhev, getting behind
the bulk of the German Ninth Army. Somehow, this threat had
to be eliminated. 'In this winter war, firm and clearly defined
front-line positions no longer existed,' SS soldier Fritz Langanke
wrote bluntly. 'Outstanding leadership was now required, com-
bining a skill in improvisation with an unshakeable determination
to endure and beat the enemy. And at the nadir of our fortunes, a
new commander of the Ninth Army entered the stage – General
Model.'

Fifty-year-old General Walther Model had begun Operation Barbarossa in charge of a division, but his aggressive, attacking style had won him a series of promotions. This post would be his greatest test. His brief from Hitler and Colonel General Franz Halder, chief of staff of the German Army, was to halt the retreat and somehow wrest the military initiative from the Red Army. Colonel Horst Grossmann, commander of the German 6th Infantry Division — stationed north-east of Rzhev — recalled his new commander: 'Model was small but wiry, with close-cropped grey-black hair. He wore a large monocle, and had piercing blue eyes. He was tough, brave and direct. A firm mouth and jaw line showed stubborn determination; staccato, fast movements with his hands revealed an impulsive streak, and also a fiery temper.'

Model was a controversial figure. He was disliked by many members of German Army staff, who regarded him as an abusive leader, oblivious to the niceties of etiquette. Restless and impetuous, Model frequently countermanded existing orders, and would make rapid decisions without consulting his subordinates. When he took command of the 41st Panzer Corps during Operation Typhoon, the entire corps staff had asked to be transferred.

Ordinary soldiers under Model's command, however, respected his forcefulness, dynamism and willingness to share their hardships. Colonel Grossmann was struck by this: 'Model's most outstanding trait was an ability to deeply connect with front-line troops,' he said. 'He reached out to them and won their unswerving loyalty. He joined them in their foxholes and dugouts, sat with them in their makeshift defences, talked with them about their worries and fears, their concerns about their families back home. Model never stopped trying to improve conditions at the front. His heart belonged to his soldiers — and from this he won their trust, and was able to demand the utmost from them in the heavy fighting that lay ahead.'

Grossmann recalled: 'Model visited the front-line every day — travelling in his *Storch* reconnaissance plane, by car, on skis, on horseback or on foot. His physical and mental stamina was extraordinary. If there was a danger point along the front, if a crisis suddenly arose – he would appear there. He was more often on the battlefield than in his headquarters. He took considerable risks and gave of himself unsparingly, and was a shining example for his entire army.' Major Alexander Conrady, battalion commander of the 36th Motorised Infantry Division, said simply: 'Model was everywhere.'

Lieutenant General Hans Gollnick, the commander of the 36th Division, remembered one such front-line visit:

> General Model arrived at my HQ and was briefed on the battle situation. I showed him the front line from an observation post. That would have satisfied most commanders, but Model wanted to get up closer. So I accompanied him to a battalion in defence positions along the upper Volga river bank. To reach it, we had to cross a bridge that was within range of Russian artillery – and enemy anti-tank guns duly opened up on us. This did not prevent General Model racing across the bridge. When we arrived at the command post the men were in a large room, sleeping on piles of straw – they had just repelled a Red Army night attack. A company commander was still awake and, recovering from his surprise, described the combat situation to us. Then a sly wink from Model indicated that he had seen enough.

Model made an immediate difference. Within days of taking command of the Ninth Army he took an audacious gamble, one that would transform the situation on the Eastern Front. In a situation of dire emergency, he decided to launch an attack on the enemy. After declaring his 'unshakeable determination to withstand this crisis shoulder to shoulder with my troops', on 21 January Model went onto the offensive against the Soviet armies that had broken through German defences north-west of Rzhev. 'We will strike the Russian flank, and catch them in a stranglehold,' he declared. His staff officers were astounded by Model's optimism in a truly desperate position. 'And what, Herr General,' one asked him, 'have you brought us for this operation?' Substantial reinforcements were urgently needed, but none were at hand. Model regarded the man for a moment, and then replied with calm assurance: 'Myself!'

This was a remarkable, almost outrageous statement. But fighting on the Eastern Front was about to enter its most critical stage, and something quite exceptional was needed to rally demoralised German forces. Model had the defiant bravado of a man impervious to danger. During Operation Barbarossa he had cheated death on a whole series of occasions. Two days into the war in Russia, leading the 3rd Panzer Division, Model had leapt out of his armoured communications vehicle to see what was halting his tanks. Moments later, an enemy shell scored a direct hit on the vehicle, blowing it apart and killing all four crew members while Model stood by unscathed. The following day, when Model climbed out of his command tank to supervise an infantry assault, he escaped death in the very same way as his tank went up in flames behind him.

Model's run of luck continued. Later that summer as his 3rd Panzer Division moved south towards Kiev, Model held an impromptu briefing before an attack on Russian positions. A Soviet artillery commander spotted the gathering and fired on the group, killing several officers and wounding the battalion commander; again, Model was untouched. Sometimes he personally led attacks on enemy positions, and during the first weeks of the German retreat from Moscow, with Wehrmacht soldiers fleeing in disarray, he would stand at crossroads, pistol drawn, ordering the men back into position.

Model set a high personal standard, declaring: 'A man who leads troops has no right to think about himself.' His bravery had a powerful impact on German soldiers caught between Hitler's dogmatism and the pessimism of their commanders, overwhelmed by the difficulties they were facing. 'How is this battle supposed to be fought?' General Gotthard Heinrici had demanded. 'Are our men going to be senselessly sacrificed, ordered to hold their ground until they are wiped out by the Russians? First-rate regimental commanders have no idea what to say to their troops any more. Everybody must be told exactly what the plan is, and what is expected of them.' General Model now drew a line in the snow, recognising that the Wehrmacht's only chance of survival was to turn and confront its pursuers.

'At the beginning of the retreat, our soldiers had no idea whether they were supposed to defend or counter-attack,' wrote battalion commander Alexander Conrady. 'Things were in a constant state of flux. But with Model, there was one overarching goal – to defeat the Red Army and restore a continuous front.' Lieutenant Otto Weidinger of the SS *Das Reich* Division said: 'Even in the most hopeless situation, a determined, dynamic leader can change the course of a battle. Model brought us one fundamental principle – "Attack, regain the initiative and dictate the course of action to the enemy" – and, however unlikely that prospect seemed, at least it was something that every soldier could understand.'

Model won the confidence of the Ninth Army in one highly dramatic incident. As leading elements of the Soviet Thirty-Third Army pushed towards the town of Vyazma – south of Rzhev astride the vital Moscow-Smolensk motor highway – the Führer intervened, ordering forces Model had earmarked for his counteroffensive to block this threat instead. Model refused to accept these dispositions. 'This must not happen,' he declared. He then flew back to the Führer's headquarters and confronted him in person. When Hitler attempted to dismiss his objections, Model said bluntly: '*Mein Führer*, who commands the Ninth Army – you or I?' Taken aback by Model's sheer force of will, Hitler backed down.

It took real courage to challenge Hitler in such a fashion. Colonel Hasso von Manteuffel, commander of the German 7th Panzer Division, said: 'Model stood up to Hitler in a way hardly anyone else dared.' The Führer respected Model's bluntness, and also his toughness. 'I distrust generals prone to over-theoretical thinking,' he remarked shortly afterwards. 'I'd like to know what happens to their theories in a moment of crisis. But when an officer shows himself worthy of command, he deserves the prerogatives of decision-making that go with it.'

In return, Model strongly supported Hitler's war in the east. He sought to denigrate recent Soviet battle achievements, telling his officers that they had been overly intimidated by Russian 'bushcraft techniques'. The inherent racism of this statement revealed

Model's underlying sympathy for the Führer's National Socialist ideology. An adept tactician, with an outstanding gift for improvisation in difficult situations, Model now demanded that the war be waged with utter ruthlessness towards the Red Army, partisans and the Russian native population. On 21 January his forces moved onto the offensive.

Model's first objective was to attack west and east of the Soviet breakthrough point along the Volga north-west of Rzhev, and reforge a continuous front line. The Russians were taken by surprise, and their confident surge forward lost the momentum that had begun to seem unstoppable. Model formed up battle groups, provided his troops with as much supporting artillery fire as he could muster and summoned the Luftwaffe's Stuka dive-bombers to support the attack.

The Germans – whose loss of air superiority was felt keenly in the early days of the Soviet counteroffensive – now used an array of novel approaches to keep their planes in the air. Luftwaffe pilot Hermann Plocher said: 'Aircraft engines that had been stopped overnight in the extreme cold were difficult, if not impossible, to start. Warming ovens and all sorts of expedients were devised in an effort to solve this problem. Planes on standby were often placed with their noses in "alert boxes" – heated shacks, which kept the engines warm enough to start at short notice.'

These tactics proved successful. Luftwaffe bombers and fighters reappeared in the skies above Model's advancing troops, attacking the enemy. The breach in the German line north-west of Rzhev was repaired. On 23 January, Luftwaffe commander Wolfram von Richthofen wrote: 'The first stage of the Rzhev offensive has been completed – we have sealed the gap in our lines. We caught the Russians by surprise, and have cut off the two armies which had broken through to the west of our forces.' Richthofen knew that these Soviet armies – the Twenty-Ninth and Thirty-Ninth – still posed a considerable threat, and German resources were thin. But he sensed an opportunity to turn the tables on the enemy.

'The Russians are no longer devising carefully crafted operations,' he added, 'but are pushing forward with everything at their

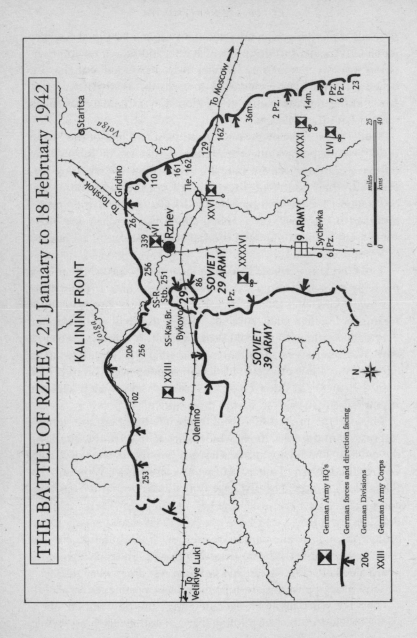

THE BATTLE OF RZHEV, 21 January to 18 February 1942

KALININ FRONT

Staritsa

Volga

To Torshok

Gridino

To Moscow

36m.
2 Pz.
14m.
7 Pz.
6 Pz.
23

XXXXI

LVI

162
129
161
110
6
26
Tle. 162

XXVI

9 ARMY

Sychevka
6. Pz.

Rzhev
LVI
339
256

SS-R.
Stb. 251
SS-Kav.Br.
Bykovo
86

SOVIET
29 ARMY
29

XXXXVI

1 Pz.

206
256

Volga

XXIII

253

102

Olenino

SOVIET
39 ARMY

N

To
Velikiye Luki

miles   25
kms   40
0   0

German Army HQ's

German forces and direction facing

German Divisions

German Army Corps

206

XXIII

256

disposal. They believe – after the disasters suffered by us at Klin and Livny – that our entire position is about to disintegrate. So they press on, as fast as they can, hoping to destroy all our forces in one great encirclement battle. They are in such haste that they do not properly consolidate their positions – and this is giving us the chance to counter-attack.'

The Germans' fresh offensive continued. On 26 January Model ordered his troops to surround the Soviet Twenty-Ninth Army, which lay behind his own forces. In the operation's first phase, the SS *Das Reich* Division moved out from Sychevka, captured a series of Russian-held villages and established a strongly protected perimeter around the town. 'During the day, strong winds whirled up the snow, and temperatures dropped to below −40 degrees Celsius,' recalled SS soldier Fritz Langanke. 'In the extreme cold, it was not possible to fight continuous military actions; instead, there were short bursts of savage fighting, and improvisation became the order of the day. We used captured Russian equipment, skis, sledges and anything else that came to hand. And we created strongpoints for our troops – heated houses or snow shelters – where our soldiers could recuperate. Our riflemen in their snow holes had to be relieved at regular intervals, for anyone unable to warm up in a house after several hours of combat had little chance of surviving.'

Further north, Soviet Lieutenant General Ivan Konev was now trying desperately to break through and re-establish contact with the Twenty-Ninth Army. Georgi Osadchinsky's 35th Rifle Brigade was one of the Red Army units flung against the German lines. Osadchinsky was now a platoon commander:

The fighting against the Rzhev salient was bloody and cruel. But our attacks were not properly prepared and the enemy had organised his defences well. On 27 January we advanced against his positions, trudging through knee-deep snow. We were met by a hail of fire, and ahead of us our way was blocked by barbed wire and minefields. The Germans opened up on us from the flanks, pinning our battalion down – and their snipers began to pick off our machine gunners. Our commanding lieutenant tried to summon artillery support, but none came. I saw him crying in rage and frustration. We were caught in a death trap. Our brigade – which had repelled the Germans from Moscow and fought so bravely in the counteroffensive – was now being torn to pieces.

The Germans raked the Red Army force with machine-gun and mortar fire. At nightfall a few scattered Russian survivors retreated from the battlefield. Osadchinsky stumbled back, dizzy and nauseous. Others were not so fortunate. 'Behind us,' he recalled, 'we heard the sounds of sporadic shooting. The Germans were finishing off the wounded whom we had been forced to leave behind.'

On 29 January General Model launched the next stage of his operation. German battle groups assembled at Sychevka would now strike north, aiming to drive a wedge between the Soviet Twenty-Ninth and Thirty-Ninth Armies, and then encircle the Twenty-Ninth. The struggle was bitter. Units on both sides fought to the last man and prisoners were rarely taken. 'Combat in the Rzhev salient has degenerated into a slugging match, a total free-for-all,' wrote the German Army's chief of staff, Colonel General Franz Halder. 'The front line is in a constant state of flux,' staff officer Hans Meier-Welcker complained. 'The Russians threaten to encircle our forces, and then we are ordered to surround those encircling us. It is extremely difficult to plan and execute military operations any more.'

Certain factors were clear enough. The Rzhev salient formed a bulge jutting into the advancing Soviet front, running north of the major railway line from Velikiye Luki to Rzhev, adjoining the Volga river for a stretch of 20 miles and then swinging to the north and east of it, protecting the German-held towns of Rzhev and Zubtsov. The key to the salient's importance was its rail links – the supply lifeline of the Wehrmacht's Ninth Army. Rzhev was the junction point of the railway from Velikiye Luki, bringing supplies in from the west, and Vyazma, carrying food, ammunition and reinforcements from the south. Astride the rail link from Rzhev to Vyazma was the town of Sychevka, the crucial assembly point for Model's offensive.

In the second week of January, when Russian forces had broken through the German salient, two Soviet armies had pushed west of Model's Ninth Army. The Soviet Thirty-Ninth Army was based around the small town of Vasilevka, 20 miles north-west of Sychevka. North of the Thirty-Ninth Army, the Twenty-Ninth was positioned around the town of Manchalovo, 15 miles west of Rzhev. The Soviet Twenty-Ninth Army posed the greatest threat to the Germans, because it was cutting both the road and rail links running westwards out of Rzhev, and for this reason Model had boldly resolved to destroy it.

Logistics were the key to successful winter fighting, and the foundation stones of Model's offensive. His first steps were to cut the supply routes of the Soviet Twenty-Ninth and Thirty-Ninth Armies by rejoining broken German lines along the Volga, north-west of Rzhev, and to strongly protect his own at Sychevka. 'General Model understood that the railway line that ran from Rzhev through Sychevka to Vyazma was the key to our entire position,' said Heinrich Haape, a German doctor with Colonel Grossmann's 6th Infantry Division. 'If it was captured by the enemy, our army would run out of ammunition and food. Model organised makeshift units equipped with anti-tank guns and heavy machine guns and ordered them to defend the railway to the death.'

The railway line was held, and Model built up army morale by ensuring little luxuries were delivered to the troops. Haape continued: 'Gift packs containing cigarettes, cigars, alcohol and coffee reached the division. In the midst of this terrible winter battle, real coffee was now simmering on our fireplace.' The Wehrmacht was coming back to life. From Sychevka, troops and supplies were funnelled north, to buttress the strongholds at Zubtsov and Rzhev, and to strike against the Russian armies in the rear of the German positions. It was a tribute to Model's energy and drive that he immediately got a firm grip on the Wehrmacht's faltering supply system, and improved the situation so quickly.

General Model's military tactics defied the ordered logic of the German Army Staff map room. He took command of the Ninth

Infantry Army but augmented it with Panzer formations, created mobile groups by amalgamating a variety of different units and used them piecemeal to deal with a confused and rapidly changing battle situation. A German unit shown on situation maps defending the front south-east of Zubtsov would suddenly reappear in a battle group gathering at Sychevka and then move off in an entirely different direction, attacking to the north-west. It was perhaps not surprising that Colonel General Franz Halder – a conservative and traditional military thinker and planner – simply could not understand what was happening, describing the battle as a 'free-for-all' and wringing his hands in bewilderment.

Orthodoxy demanded a consolidation of the struggling German position before any further aggressive move could be attempted. But Model's aggressive tactics were working, nonetheless. There are situations in which military planning is beyond any conventional response, for when everything is collapsing, morale is broken and conviction is gone, mere adjustments will not fix them. A radical solution is then the only option, providing as it does a chance of jolting people out of a defeated frame of mind.

Model instinctively realised this. 'He tenaciously held to his plan,' Colonel Horst Grossmann observed, 'despite violent enemy counter-attacks on our flanks, which at times threatened to bring down our entire position.' Model used aerial reconnaissance photographs and intercepted Russian radio signals to anticipate his opponent's movements and retain the battle initiative. The German advance continued through waist-high snowdrifts, and in extreme cold that dropped below −40 degrees Celsius.

'The struggle is see-sawing backwards and forwards,' Fritz Langanke wrote. 'We wait for our Stuka dive-bombers to attack, and then move forward again. There are fierce hand-to-hand clashes with the enemy, in which no quarter is given or received. We do not have vehicles to evacuate our wounded, so they are brought out of the combat zone by horse-drawn sledges. We wrap the men in blankets, but most perish in the freezing cold before they can reach a first aid station.' Langanke recalled a particularly disturbing incident. 'Our armoured car drove over the bodies of several dead Russians,' he said, 'and one of then became wedged under the vehicle. I was unable to pull him out – he was caught in one of the wheels, almost as if he was clinging on to it – so I grabbed a saw, wriggled underneath and began cutting away his arms. As I did this, our two faces came close together and with the sawing motion he suddenly began to move. I froze in horror. It was only in response to the saw's action, but it seemed for a moment he was shaking his head at me.'

Fighting was savage. 'Casualties on both sides are rising steadily,' Hans Meier-Welcker wrote from Zubtsov, 15 miles south-east of Rzhev, at the end of January. German forces east of the town were repelling ever more desperate Red Army assaults, for Lieutenant General Konev was making attempt after attempt to reach the endangered Soviet Twenty-Ninth Army. The Russians, unable to break through, sometimes resorted to shocking tactics. Marie Avinov, an interpreter for the Wehrmacht's military police in Zubtsov, recalled a conversation with a German officer, Heinrich von Lange, after one clash with the enemy. What happened had so profoundly disturbed Lange that he asked for the divisional chaplain to be present:

> Our unit was posted on the outskirts of a village. Ahead of us lay a meadow, and then a forest – from which we were expecting a Russian attack. It was snowing heavily. Suddenly, a group of small figures emerged from the trees and began walking slowly towards our positions. As the group drew nearer, we saw that it consisted of about fifty young boys, none older than six or seven. We realised to our horror that the Russians were using these children as decoys, while they prepared to attack – and were moving up behind them. Every second counted. I was in charge of the heavy machine guns – and I gave the order to fire. In moments, every boy was mown down.

Lange struggled to continue. 'They lay there in the snow, like little puppets. Then, when the Russians attacked, we fought like savages – we didn't leave a man alive. We took no prisoners – we even killed those who surrendered and begged for mercy.' Lange began pounding the table with his fist. 'Damn the Russians! Damn this war! Damn, damn, damn us all!' There was an uneasy silence.

Then Lange looked hard at the chaplain and said: 'Did we, or did we not, commit an unforgivable crime?'

The chaplain began to talk about a soldier's duty, about how the Bolsheviks had sent the children out – and that they alone were guilty. Lange interrupted him. 'No, Father, they are not the only ones to blame. I might have ordered my men to shoot in the air, above their heads – and those little kids would have run off like frightened rabbits.' He stopped again, and then said despairingly: 'Oh, what's the use? A crime is a crime – you can't talk yourself out of it.'

The greatest threat of a Soviet link-up with the Twenty-Ninth Army was across the river Volga, north-west of Rzhev. General Model had ordered the SS Infantry Regiment *Der Führer* to guard this section of the front, but the regiment was under strength and the Volga heavily frozen over; the ice was even capable of supporting Russian tanks. On 30 January Lieutenant General Konev assembled rifle divisions and tank brigades from another Soviet army, the Thirtieth, and ordered them to breach the German line and join with the Twenty-Ninth at all costs. The Russians hurled wave after wave of attacks across the river, but somehow Model's defences held.

As Soviet relief efforts were thwarted, the German attack gained momentum. General Model formed the remnants of Heinz Otto Fausten's 1st Panzer Division into a combat group at Sychevka and threw it into the battle. 'Our task was to strike at the Soviet Twenty-Ninth Army from the south,' Fausten said, 'wheel round the enemy's position and link up with Model's main force at Rzhev. We knew that if we accomplished this, we would surround an entire Russian army – and its strength would fast bleed away.'

Amidst the horror of the fighting, there were still occasional flashes of human decency. As his group closed in on the Twenty-Ninth Army, Fausten and his comrades discovered a small military hospital, recently abandoned by the Russians. 'We had gone out on a reconnaissance patrol,' Fausten recalled. 'There were vehicle marks on the snow-covered tracks, signs that the enemy had made a hurried withdrawal – and everything was strangely silent. Then we came across a large farmhouse, hidden from view among some trees. Inside it, we found badly wounded Soviet soldiers, lying in the straw.' Fausten moved from makeshift bed to bed. 'I lifted up the covering over one soldier and saw a trap door, presumably the hiding place for the doctor or nurse. I let the cover fall back down.' The Russians watched Fausten in silence. Two days earlier, Red Army soldiers had deliberately targeted a German medical station in a nearby village. In this battle, both sides were ruthlessly killing the opponent's wounded.

Fausten paused. A memory came to him. In it, Red Army soldiers were on the attack, and Fausten's unit was hurriedly pulling back from a burning village. One of his closest friends had fallen, wounded. He was hit in the leg and could no longer move, and he cried out desperately for help. But Fausten could not reach him, for the village was swarming with the enemy. The friend kept calling out to him, 'Otto, Otto,' until the Russians finished him off.

'Let's set this place alight,' Fausten thought. But as he moved to act, a dying Russian soldier begged for water. Fausten, touched by his suffering, could not help but respond. As he did so, he wondered: 'Are we so very different?' Fausten made his decision. He reached into his pocket, pulled out a packet of cigarettes and passed them round. The tension lifted, and brief but heartfelt words were exchanged between German and Russian: '*Spassibo – danke!*' Fausten and his comrades left the hospital intact.

As the 1st Panzer Division closed its trap, Soviet losses were rising steadily. Beyond the military hospital, grim evidence of this awaited Fausten. Behind the building he found a large pile of near-naked Russian bodies. 'It was a corpse mountain,' said Fausten. 'Here lay the enemy's dead from the recent fighting. They were awaiting a mass funeral and burial.'

It was a bold manoeuvre to send the 1st Panzer Division north to encircle the Soviet Twenty-Ninth Army, for there were Russian forces on both sides – to the west and the east – of the German corridor running from Sychevka to Rzhev. But the SS *Das Reich* Division anchored Sychevka's defence, beating off frequent Russian assaults, and its determined resistance freed up more and more German troops. To support the advance of the 1st Panzer Division, General Model now ordered Colonel Erhard Raus's 6th Panzer Division to move up from Sychevka and push back the Soviet Thirty-Ninth Army, which lay to the west of the town. Model wanted to split the two Soviet armies and completely isolate the Twenty-Ninth further north, which was the main target of his attack.

Colonel Raus's division was seriously under strength, but he worked wonders with the limited resources at his disposal. Raus kept the advantage of surprise, ensuring transport and troop movements took place at night and employing a maximum concentration of fire on every target. As storming parties captured an objective, the area was consolidated, Russian counter-attacks dealt with and fresh supplies brought in. German progress was slow but steady – soldiers nicknamed it the 'snail offensive' – but these tactics were highly effective against a numerically superior opponent. By 5 February Raus had captured more than eighty villages from the Russians and pushed the Soviet Thirty-Ninth Army away from its neighbour, allowing the Twenty-Ninth to be fully encircled by Model's remaining forces.

General Model had despatched the 86th Infantry Division from Rzhev to join with the 1st Panzer Division, and an entire Soviet army was now caught between the German pincers. All along Army Group Centre's front, Wehrmacht commanders drew inspiration from Model's offensive. To the north, Reinhardt's Third Panzer Army successfully held off advancing Soviet forces, preventing them from reaching the Moscow-Smolensk motor highway. To the south, Schmidt's Second Panzer Army pushed forward from Orel, driving the Russians eastwards. At Yukhnov, General Gotthard Heinrici – promoted to commander of the German Fourth Army – defied the Soviet forces encircling the town, counter-attacked and linked up with the neighbouring Fourth Panzer Group (now redesignated the Fourth Panzer Army).

In little more than two weeks, a German front had been reforged. The Wehrmacht had ceased to fall back and had gathered itself once again into a coherent force. Astonishingly, the Soviet advance was faltering.

Lieutenant Vladimir Goncharov's Soviet Thirty-Third Army had swung past Yukhnov, its forward units pushing the Germans back further west, towards Vyazma. The Soviet high command hoped that the Thirty-Third Army would join up with Russian forces approaching Vyazma from the north, surround the town and establish a hold on the Moscow-Smolensk motor highway behind Army Group Centre's forward position. But in the last week of January 1942 the German retreat halted. Model was making his presence felt. 'The Luftwaffe has reappeared in strength,' Goncharov wrote on 23 January, 'and is inflicting substantial damage. The advance has slowed considerably – the enemy is holding his line more firmly and we are running low on ammunition and food.' He added with feeling: 'Our soup tastes like water now.'

On 26 January Goncharov's company attacked a German-held village, but they were beaten off. 'Casualties are mounting,' he wrote. 'Our latest operation failed because we had insufficient strength to coordinate our push effectively. The Germans were able to separate our forces and destroy them piecemeal.' On 30 January Goncharov noted: 'The enemy is now counter-attacking with tanks and infantry and the Luftwaffe is flying over our positions. A coherent action to repel the invader no longer exists – it is a struggle for strongpoints, roads and railways. The battle is in swirling flux all around us.'

It would probably have been more effective for the Soviet high command to have called off its attack on Vyazma here, and concentrated on extricating its armies from the threat of German encirclement. But Stalin – still believing a major victory was within his grasp – did not fully realise the danger. 'We overestimated the capabilities of our troops and underestimated the enemy's,' General Georgi Zhukov confessed. 'Our forces – increasingly overstretched – were finding it more and more difficult to push the Germans back. They were proving a far tougher nut to crack than we had anticipated. Our military efforts at Rzhev, Yukhnov and Vyazma were failing.'

German General Gotthard Henrici arrived at Yukhnov to encourage his men personally. 'To get there,' he wrote to his wife on 5 February, 'I had to drive through a 400-metre stretch of road held by the Russians. Fortunately, they were taken by surprise, and I managed to get through. But two vehicles behind me were destroyed by mortar fire.' Heinrici spent the night with his soldiers. 'We lay huddled together, in a small timber outbuilding, listening to the roar of explosions as the enemy bombed our positions. A nearby house was completely destroyed in one blast.'

Throughout the German retreat, General Heinrici had regularly visited his soldiers' front-line positions. A tough but compassionate commander, he won his soldiers' trust at a time when many had lost faith in the Wehrmacht's high command. Now his dramatic appearance at the front electrified his troops. German Fourth Army staff officer Hellmuth Stieff, who made the journey with him, said: 'We still held Yukhnov but it was coming under nonstop Russian air attack – Red Army forces had already surrounded the town. And then our army commander suddenly arrived! The men were overjoyed that Heinrici was with them – and their determination to hold out against the enemy grew stronger.'

As Yukhnov's defenders tied down Russian forces, Heinrici prepared a surprise German flank attack north of the town. 'At the end of January, we advanced on Red Army positions in the villages north of the Yukhnov-Medyn motor highway,' recalled General Lothar Rendulic, commander of the 52nd Infantry Division. 'Our strength was badly depleted – our two remaining regiments consisted of only 300 men each – but we massed all available artillery to provide covering fire and attacked at night. We drove the Russians out.' Radio operator Leopold Höglinger's 137th Division was also involved in the offensive. 'An infantry attack, supported by artillery fire, has taken another village,' he wrote. 'The fighting was savage. The buildings are still burning – dead Russians are lying everywhere.'

Heinrici's flank assault was successful. His troops linked up with the forces of the Fourth Panzer Army to the north, and another breach in the German lines was repaired. 'A wonderful morning,'

Höglinger noted on 3 February. 'Our Stukas smashed the Russian positions, and then our tanks broke through and joined us. The motor highway is jammed with military traffic and our planes are flying overhead. It feels as though we have new impetus.' Soviet Lieutenant Vladimir Goncharov wrote the same day: 'The Germans have suddenly pulled themselves together. They have moved onto the attack once more. Today we heard news that our forces near Vyazma are cut off – we will have to attempt a breakout. The morale of our soldiers has slumped. At the beginning of our counteroffensive men were eager to hit back against the enemy; now our commanders have to maintain discipline by threats and intimidation.' Goncharov added: 'Bread has been replaced by small scraps of horsemeat. Our soldiers are growing weaker.'

General Heinrici found the change in his army's fortunes to be near miraculous. 'If the Russians had concentrated all of their forces on a few key objectives, they could have destroyed us,' he wrote. 'But they became over-ambitious – and tried to do everything at once. They forgot the wisdom of the saying: "A bird in the hand is worth two in the bush."' Heinrici understood the reason for this. 'The enemy thought we were finished,' he added. 'He did not think it possible that we could pull a scratch battle group out of the line and use it against his flanks. But we have succeeded. And now – at last – proper reinforcements are reaching us.' Hellmuth Stieff believed that yet another turning point had been reached, and that the outcome of Typhoon might not be as catastrophic as previously feared. 'The Russians are no longer threatening to destroy us,' he declared on 6 February. 'Our troops are now managing to adapt to this winter war and have overcome the shock of the first weeks of retreat. For the first time, we are dealing with the enemy's threats.'

'The decision to continue our attack on Vyazma was a serious mistake,' acknowledged Soviet General Georgi Zhukov. 'The Germans pinched off the base of the Thirty-Third Army's position along the river Ugra, and surrounded our forces. They brought up substantial reserves and greatly strengthened their position.'

'We have a serious emergency!' Lieutenant Vladimir Goncharov recorded in his diary on 7 February. 'The Germans are on the Ugra, only one kilometre away from us.' The following day he wrote a single line: 'The enemy are attacking.' He died repelling the assault. Wehrmacht troops recovered his notebook later that day.

In Rzhev, General Model now brought up security detachments and military police to reinforce his battle lines and to combat the threat from Russian partisan groups, working actively with the Soviet forces to the rear of his own Ninth Army. Model ordered the newly arrived German security police to crack down hard on the native population. 'A large white house on the town's main street has been taken over by the Gestapo,' wrote one of the Rzhev's inhabitants, Nina Semonova. 'We are afraid even to pass it. It has been given the nickname "The House of the Devil". After entering, no one emerges again. We know of hundreds who have disappeared there – their fate is discussed in whispers.' A report of these activities was smuggled out to the Soviet high command. 'In the town of Rzhev there is a concentration camp with fifteen thousand captured Red Army soldiers and five thousand civilians,' it began. 'They are held in unheated huts, and scavenge for one or two frozen potatoes. Occasionally the Germans throw some rotting meat over the barbed wire. Every day people are dying – the ones who are too ill to work are immediately shot.'

Starvation was increasing among the town's inhabitants. 'Hunger torments us,' Semonova added. 'For two days we have had nothing at all to eat. My baby cries all the time – she is desperate to be fed. I hold her to my breast, but cannot produce any milk.' On 15 February Semonova wrote: 'There is no light, no water and no bread. We try and get water from the Volga, but the German soldiers shoot at us. When my father went to the river, they let him draw water through a gap in the ice and then shot his bucket full of holes. Then they fired around him – forcing him to crawl away on his hands and knees.' Semonova concluded: 'We hear reports that the Germans have turned the tables on our troops. I cannot bear this!'

On 15 February Red Army commanders, now aware of the

atrocities being committed at the Rzhev prisoner-of-war camp, warned their men that General Model was shooting Russian prisoners. The encirclement battle west of Rzhev was reaching a terrible climax. Knowing what awaited them, many Soviet units – although now in a hopeless situation – fought to the last man rather than surrender.

'There has been more hard fighting,' Luftwaffe commander Wolfram von Richthofen wrote on 16 February. 'We are steadily destroying the trapped Soviet Twenty-Ninth Army. Its forces are making a last stand in a series of deep trenches and dugouts.' On 17 February the surrounded Russian army launched its final, desperate attacks. One point in the German line – held by the 256th Division – came close to buckling, but Model arrived at the danger spot with reinforcements, and fought alongside his men until the crisis passed.

Model's vigorous reorganisation of the Wehrmacht's supply system was at last bringing much-needed winter equipment to the Rzhev battleground. On the night of 17 February a bizarre incident occurred. A German specialist ski unit (another of Model's achievements) was sent to reinforce the 6th Panzer Division's position. Approaching along the same stretch of forest track was a Russian ski detachment, ordered to support a Red Army breakout attempt. Both wore near-identical winter clothing, and carried similar equipment. Unwittingly, the Soviet force joined the staggered march column. Both sides trudged alongside each other, carrying their skis. The men had fur-lined collars turned up against the cold, and were moving forward without speaking. Neither Germans nor Russians recognised each other.

The 'combined assault force' finally reached the outskirts of a Wehrmacht-held village. The Russians stopped to prepare an attack. A German officer – not understanding the reason for the halt – complained that precious time was being wasted. A Red Army officer – taken aback to hear one of his men suddenly speaking German – assumed this was some sort of drunken prank, and struck him in the face. Tempers flared, others pitched in to help and a confused fist fight developed along the length of the column. As men began swearing and yelling in different languages, it became clear that something was seriously amiss. Eventually the Red Army unit fled into the forest. The German force stood rooted to the spot in bewilderment.

Russian attempts to smash their way out of the trap failed. On 18 February the action report of the German Ninth Army stated: 'The Soviet Twenty-Ninth Army – compressed into an ever-shrinking area – has launched wave after wave of mass assaults, but suffered extraordinarily high losses. Only six Russian tanks managed to break through our lines, but they were promptly destroyed by artillery fire.' General Model sent out an Order of the Day at the conclusion of the fighting: 'Soldiers of the Ninth Army,' the commander enjoined, 'proven warriors of the Eastern Front, you have crushed the enemy's army – every officer and every soldier has contributed to this exceptional feat of arms!'

At the end of the Rzhev battle, the Germans claimed that six Soviet divisions had been destroyed and another four scattered, around 26,000 Russians killed, and 180 tanks and 340 guns captured or destroyed. This was a modest tally compared to earlier Wehrmacht successes, but it was quite remarkable that a victory, even a modest one, had been won in such desperate circumstances. The Soviet Twenty-Ninth Army had been destroyed and the Thirty-Ninth was now trapped. Further south, between Vyazma and Yukhnov, the Soviet Thirty-Third Army was fighting for its survival. The Russian advance had been powerfully undermined and the German front saved. The spectre of Napoleon's terrible fate began to recede.

'The German Ninth Army attacked the Russians through severe snowstorms, in temperatures as low as −40 degrees Celsius,' wrote Army Group Centre's chief of staff, Major General Hans von Greiffenberg. 'In vicious, see-saw fighting the Soviet forces were annihilated and Russian plans to destroy our entire northern flank were thwarted. At long last, we had regained freedom of action.' SS Lieutenant Otto Weidinger paid tribute to Model's achievement: 'We were staring total destruction in the face,' he said. 'The enemy had made a series of successful breakthroughs, and was poised to encircle all our forces. But somehow our dying army group pulled itself together. Remarkably, the German Ninth Army turned the tables on the enemy – and this astonishing success ensured the survival of Army Group Centre.'

'Our high command badly overestimated our chances,' said Soviet platoon commander Georgi Osadchinsky. 'The troops were ordered to push the Germans back, without proper reinforcement or rest. Our leaders did not think that the enemy could recover. They underestimated his resolve at a moment of crisis. And we paid for it.'

10

The First Butterfly of Spring

ON 19 FEBRUARY 1942, Wehrmacht priest Josef Perau wrote a stark entry in his diary: 'Will it be possible to atone for the crimes we are committing?' he began. 'On the outskirts of Roslavl, the dead from the Russian prisoner-of-war camp are being buried in enormous mass graves. Every day trucks unload hundreds more bodies. The guard on duty told me that there are already more than 19,000 of them. Apparently, these people died of disease and starvation because they were provided with nothing to eat. Soldiers tell me that some prisoners have resorted to cannibalism, becoming so hungry that they eat meat from the corpses of their dead fellows.'

Perau heard German administrators attempting to justify what had happened, blaming supply difficulties over the winter. 'It has been difficult enough to find food for our own troops,' he was told. But he had no doubt that the Wehrmacht bore responsibility for this tragedy, and that behind it lay the race doctrine of Hitler's regime. Perau stood on the very edge of the mass grave. 'People back home simply will not believe what is happening here,' he thought. He quickly took a photo of what lay in front of him: 'There are heaps of twisted bodies, their eyes wide open, their hands outstretched – in terrible accusation.'

Russian prisoner Nikolai Obryn'ba recalled a transit camp in Yartsevo, north-east of Smolensk. Its barbed-wire enclosure was overlooked by watchtowers on stilts that reminded him of huge spiders. On his arrival, Obryn'ba was greeted by a mass of faces, blue with cold, with hollow, sunken eyes. The only rations available for the thousands inside were a few small pieces of horsemeat.

The stench of rotting bodies was overwhelming. German Major Heinz Herre visited a POW camp at Stalino in the Ukraine's Donets Basin. A lieutenant from the camp staff asked him: 'Do you really want to see this menagerie?' Herre entered a warren of dilapidated buildings. 'A hellhole – filled with skeletal figures,' he wrote in his diary, 'the dead lie amidst the dying and frozen human urine and faeces are everywhere.' Typhus had broken out – and the camp's only doctor was fatally ill. '20,000 prisoners – all doomed to die,' Herre concluded. 'In neighbouring camps it is not disease, but starvation that is finishing everyone off.'

At the end of February Alfred Rosenberg, the minister for the occupied territories in the east, wrote to Field Marshal Wilhelm Keitel, head of the German Armed Forces, about the Soviet prisoners of war. Rosenberg stated:

> Of 3.6 million prisoners captured by us, the vast majority have already perished through starvation and disease. Most of these deaths were avoidable, for even in areas where there were genuine shortages, the Russian civilian population usually brought food for the prisoners to eat. Our camp commanders let them starve instead. A frequently heard comment was: 'The more of them that die, the better it will be for us.' The Soviet government is of course well aware of conditions in the camps, and ensures they are widely publicised throughout the Red Army.

Wilfried Strik-Strikfeldt, a liaison officer with Army Group Centre, added: 'The abject misery in the prisoner-of-war camps has passed all bounds. A number of officers – on their own initiative – are now releasing all prisoners, rather than deliver them to the collection points.' Others, however, had them shot. After one February battle, Max Kuhnert's unit captured eighteen Russian prisoners. His commanding officer told him: 'Take these men half a mile away from here – then finish them off.' Kuhnert marched them towards the woods, and recalled:

> One or two of the prisoners began glancing around, and giving me questioning looks. They were mostly older men. Their greatcoats hung loose, they had no belts and their felt boots were in tatters. I

shouted at them to stop and indicated with my machine gun that they should line up. I saw the alarm in their faces. One man pulled out a cross. But now I had had enough.

I had never disobeyed an order before, but abruptly I waved my hand in the direction of the wood, lowered my gun and began to walk away. When I turned back, no one was in sight. On my return – for the first time since I had joined the army – I did not submit a duty report. I was never asked for it.

Wilfried Strik-Strikfeldt recalled a meeting with Army Group Centre's commander, Field Marshal Günther von Kluge. 'He had every sympathy with the demand for proper treatment of Russian prisoners of war,' Strikfeldt recalled, 'and was highly critical of the way the occupied territories were being administered. But he was very much preoccupied by the military tasks at hand. "Let's talk about it later on," Kluge said.' The conversation never took place. Most Wehrmacht troops disengaged from the human tragedy unfolding around them. They had beaten off countless Russian attacks, and their positions were holding. That was enough. After the horror of the winter, many were simply relieved to be alive.

On 25 February a German lieutenant in the Fourth Army's 292nd Infantry Division noted: 'At last – after so much bitter fighting, we are enjoying a little calm and can take stock of things again. Those few weeks in January put us under the most terrible strain, and I feel fortunate to have survived them. The horror of that time will stay with me for the rest of my life – combat in temperatures below −45 degrees Celsius, the many severe cases of frostbite . . . It was the worst this war has demanded of us – but how much heroism it produced! And now, we have come through the worst of it.' Major General Hans von Greiffenberg, Army Group Centre's chief of staff, wrote: 'Our retreat had been conducted in the most terrible conditions, but it had not turned into the rout that the enemy was hoping for.' The German line was now stabilising.

At the conclusion of the Rzhev battle, Walther Model was promoted to the rank of Colonel General and awarded the Oak Leaves to the Knight's Cross by a grateful Hitler – a prestigious honour, granted for exceptional bravery and skill in command. 'I will wear the medal with pride in the military success of all my soldiers,' Model announced. 'I am fully confident that together we can deal with any threat from the enemy and successfully carry out the mission in the east that the Führer has entrusted to us. Our martial spirit has come to full fruition.'

On 28 February General Hans-Georg Reinhardt, commander of the Third Panzer Army, also received the Oak Leaves to the Knight's Cross from Hitler. Reinhardt was delighted. 'At 2.00 p.m. we went straight through to see the Führer,' Reinhardt wrote. 'He presented the awards with appreciation, taking particular care over each one of us.' On his return to the Eastern Front, on 2 March, Reinhardt sent out a rousing declaration to his troops. 'Combat in Russia has passed its crisis point,' he stated. 'Thanks to the strength of will and superhuman efforts of our soldiers, the Red Army has been brought to a halt. The objective of the Soviet leadership – the destruction of our entire army group in a winter counteroffensive – has been thwarted. The steadfastness of our troops at a time of grave danger will go down in the annals of warfare.'

Reinhardt had garrisoned a succession of fortified towns – Velikiye Luki, Velizh and Demidov – on Army Group Centre's north-western front. His forces – once so close to Moscow – had been pushed back 250 miles from the Russian capital. Now he hoped they would act as a breakwater, stemming the tide of the Red Army's advance. The strategy succeeded, but it was a close-run thing, as entries in the Third Panzer Army's combat diary made only too clear. On 3 February it was noted: 'The Red Army is cutting the road links behind our units. We are very short of artillery and the Army Group is unable to provide reinforcements. We live a hand-to-mouth existence – our position is desperate.' The Russians subsequently broke into Velizh and Demidov, and used ski troops and partisan formations to cut German communications. But Reinhardt's line held, and the Red Army was repulsed.

North of Reinhardt's Third Panzer Army, surrounded German strongholds at Demyansk and Kholm still fiercely resisted the enemy. 'A new mood is emerging among our troops,' wrote Hans Meier-Welcker on 2 March. 'We endure our fate stoically, fight with determination and endeavour to fulfil our duties – even when the orders given to us far exceed what is possible. We are Eastern-Front fighters – engaged in a struggle of such ferocity that battlegrounds elsewhere fade into insignificance. Despite the serious setbacks – which were not the fault of the troops, but rather of our high command – our soldiers have regained their pride and self-belief.'

German soldiers had gained experience in winter fighting. They had learnt how to prepare strongpoints, transforming houses into miniature fortresses, banking snow against the outer walls, reinforcing the structure and cutting out firing points – sometimes camouflaged with bedsheets, so they would blend against a white background. All remaining artillery – mortars, anti-tank guns and heavy machine guns – would be grouped together in specially prepared "nests", houses with the roofs purposefully torn off, floors reinforced and walls reduced to gun-barrel height. A barrage of fire would then be directed against enemy assembly areas.

A Wehrmacht unit would move into an area, quickly construct an outer defensive perimeter – a series of trenches and dugouts connecting the infantry's fighting positions – and behind them build bunkers in sheltered ground, heated by stoves and charcoal burners. Communication paths were cleared through the snow, and mines and obstacles set out. In February 1942 the German 10th Motorised Division, although reduced to the size of an infantry regiment, successfully defended a series of such strongpoints along a 30-mile section of the front against an estimated seven Red Army divisions.

Specialist winter equipment was at last getting through to the front-line soldiers. Major General Karl Becker, who brought the German 328th Infantry Division up to the Third Panzer Army's defence line in early March, deployed ski units, issued his men with camouflage suits and protective clothing, and used boat-shaped sledges to transport machine guns and ammunition more easily. As German confidence grew, aggressive counter-attacks were launched against Russian forces, and concentrated artillery and small-arms fire unleashed against their approaching infantry. The Wehrmacht's 35th Infantry Division noted happily that 'intense flurries of shells falling on Red Army assault units just at the moment of attack can stampede even the best of troops'.

Soviet General Zhukov was frustrated by a growing shortage of ammunition and poor cooperation between his artillery, infantry and armoured forces. 'We are not suppressing the enemy's defence systems,' he complained, 'and our troops are suffering very great losses as a result.' By the end of February 1942, Stalin's great offensive had lost much of its drive and momentum.

General Gotthard Heinrici visited Hitler to receive the German Cross in Gold. The medal, ranked just below the Knight's Cross, was awarded for bravery and resolute command. 'I am delighted for Heinrici,' staff officer Hellmuth Stieff commented. 'He fully deserves the honour – he is a superb soldier and leader.' Stieff added: 'An uneasy calm now prevails at the front – the Russians have been pushed back, but they are still capable of causing us trouble. More Soviet airborne troops are being dropped around our position.'

The immediate crisis had passed. But Heinrici knew the Russians still posed a threat and felt that a realistic appraisal of the situation remained overdue from the German high command. He met Hitler on 28 February: 'After a meal with the Führer, we discussed the military position,' Heinrici noted. 'I gave a full description of the state of the Fourth Army, and the vulnerability of our supply lifeline, the Roslavl–Moscow motor highway. I told Hitler that after our recent successes fresh Russian airborne troops had been committed to the fight, and that they were threatening to cut our road and rail links.'

Heinrici remained angry about the consequences of Hitler's 'Stand Fast!' order and wanted commanders in the field to be able to make their own decisions. He challenged the Führer directly: 'Why do you insist we cling on to strongholds such as Yukhnov, regardless of the military circumstances?' he asked. 'We need to conduct our operations more flexibly. Our priority must be to bring in more reserves and then free up our forces. If we focus all our energies on holding Yukhnov, the motor highway behind it – which is only defended by a small group of soldiers – will be taken by the enemy. And possession of the motor highway, not Yukhnov, is the crucial issue. The road is our lifeline – if we lose it, the army will die.'

Hitler was taken aback. 'It is no longer of particular importance whether our position is 10 kilometres east or west of Yukhnov,' he conceded. 'Now that the front is stabilising, we can afford – in certain places – to concede ground in order to straighten out our lines.' Then the Führer gathered himself. 'Let me talk about the bigger picture, for as you know, I took a tough stance over this issue. I believed that we were close to a total collapse, and that many of our generals – considering the situation hopeless – had lost the will to continue. So I issued my "Stand Fast!" order to prevent a general panic.'

General Heinrici was sceptical, and wrote of Hitler's comment: 'In general strategic terms, such a response was certainly justified. But as a concrete military directive, it was seriously flawed. It denied us any tactical flexibility in dealing with the enemy. And from this mistake, we suffered unnecessary losses and the crisis only worsened.' Heinrici summed up the general outlook: 'The view at the Führer's headquarters is that we are now over the worst of the Soviet winter offensive, and that by holding Russian forces at bay we have achieved a remarkable triumph – one that has considerably weakened the enemy. New-found optimism holds sway.'

However, little account was taken in all of this of the terrible losses in manpower and equipment suffered by the Wehrmacht. Heinrici found Hitler reluctant to engage with the human tragedy of the German retreat. Instead, he was struck by how much the Führer was absorbed by technical questions, such as the design details of anti-tank defences. 'It is in the realm of technology that he seems to be most comfortable,' Henrici concluded.

Soviet General Zhukov was making one last effort to push towards Vyazma. But the Russian paratroopers, dropped behind

German lines to galvanise the offensive, were suffering increasing casualties. On 28 February an attack by the Soviet 9th Airborne Brigade was defeated by the Germans, and the troops were forced to retreat through inhospitable terrain and deep snow. Max Kuhnert's unit was one of those fighting against the paratroopers: 'I remember the aftermath of one battle along the Ugra river,' he said. The ground around us resembled a slaughterhouse. Bodies were everywhere, some with their clothing torn off by the shell blasts. Limbs were strewn about. And as we picked our way through the carnage, the hard frozen bodies clinked like porcelain when accidentally knocked.'

All along the front, Russian attacks were being beaten back. Soviet machine gunner Mikhail Kuznetsov remembered fighting near Gzhatsk in the last week of February. The Red Army was trying to dislodge the German Fourth Panzer Army. 'We were increasingly hungry,' Kuznetsov recalled:

If we were lucky, we had a little bread, and some watery soup with a few tiny pieces of pasta. Mostly we survived on scraps of horsemeat. We were running low on supplies and ammunition, and German resistance was strengthening. Then we were ordered to make a night attack on a neighbouring village, which our commander believed was weakly defended by the enemy. But it was a trap. The Germans were hidden in the forest close by, and their guns – camouflaged among the trees – were trained on the village's main street. They let us break in, and then opened up on our soldiers. It was a massacre. Of my entire company, only four men got out alive.

Soviet soldier Alexander Rogachev was fighting near Staraya Russa, about 300 miles north-west of the Russian capital. 'The pressure on us was unremitting,' Rogachev said. 'We were never allowed any rest. We were ordered to capture Staraya Russa on 23 February, to coincide with Red Army Day, but our attack failed – the German position was too strong. There should have been a pause to resupply and reinforce our troops; instead, more and more attacks were ordered – three or four every day, and more at night. Our casualties were horrific.' Early on the morning of 28 February, Rogachev and his company crawled towards the Germans. They were spotted, and a mortar bombardment was unleashed against them. Rogachev was knocked out by an exploding shell. When he came to, he was able to crawl slowly away. Behind him, he heard the screams of the Russian wounded being bayoneted by the enemy.

Soviet Colonel Pavel Lopatin's 4th Guards Infantry Division was near Lyuban, 80 miles south-east of Leningrad, with the Second Shock Army of Lieutenant General Andrei Vlasov. Vlasov – awarded the Order of the Red Banner for his contribution to the defence of Moscow – had by now been despatched by Stalin to break the German siege of Leningrad. Forty-one-year-old Vlasov was one of Stalin's youngest and most promising commanders. His plan was to strike north along the Moscow-Leningrad railway line, but his army was short of artillery and ammunition, and desperately needed reinforcements; the enemy's positions were very strong. On 29 February Colonel Lopatin wrote: 'At night, the front line is lit by the glow from the Germans' rockets; during the day, we are under constant mortar fire. The shelling does not stop – the sky is shrouded in black smoke.' On 7 March he added: 'The enemy's planes dominate the sky. Our infantry attack the German lines without success. Our artillerymen are running low on shells and we do not have enough tanks.'

Stalin had launched his counteroffensive on a broad front – from the Leningrad region in the north to the Crimea in the south – but his armies were now in trouble. As the Germans fought back, the Red Army's supply train had buckled. 'By the beginning of March our unit had been without rations for two weeks,' Soviet artilleryman Mikhail Borisov said. 'We scavenged for food and drank melted snow – the Germans had poisoned all the wells. The Luftwaffe dominated the sky above us.' Stalin's high command still hoped that the Wehrmacht's forces would disintegrate, just as Napoleon's *Grande Armée* had done. Soviet propaganda posters showed Red Army troops fighting the Germans on Borodino Field under the watchful gaze of Field Marshal Mikhail Kutuzov, the hero of 1812. Many Red Army officers were swayed by this belief, and continued to urge their men forwards: 'In 1812 the Russian people rose up and defeated Napoleon,' Captain Andrei Zorin wrote. 'Only the pathetic remains of the French forces were able to retreat homewards. There can be no doubt that we will do the same to the Germans. Soviet platoon commander Georgi Osadchinsky said: 'Our leaders hoped that the collapse of Napoleon's army in 1812 would be repeated – but that expectation was becoming a mirage.'

'It is a brutal war,' German staff officer Hellmuth Stieff wrote, 'and both sides are waging it pitilessly.' Lieutenant Helmut Mauer of the Wehrmacht's 45th Infantry Division, on Army Group Centre's southern flank, recalled one incident in early March. 'The Russians had launched a night attack on our position,' Mauer recalled, 'and several of their T-34 tanks broke through our lines. Then they reversed, and deliberately rolled over the bodies of our wounded. I saw three tanks approach a medical tent – clearly marked with the Red Cross – and bulldoze it. Within seconds, it had been completely flattened.'

As Russian pressure waned, some German commanders began to think about the future shape of the war. On 12 March General Heinrici drew up a list of suggestions for proper treatment of Russian civilians. 'After the failure of our offensive against Moscow,' he began, 'no one knows how long this war will last. In these circumstances it is vital – for political and economic reasons – to secure the goodwill of the native population'. Heinrici's concern had come far too late. However, he continued: 'Much goodwill has already been lost through a succession of blunders on our side, including the wholesale requisitioning of food from local inhabitants and the complete lack of facilities for prisoners of war.' In place of this 'sorry catalogue of errors', Heinrici proposed a host of positive measures: sufficient food for the native population, land redistribution, support for local trade and commerce, limited political autonomy, freedom of religion, and the recruitment of auxiliary police and self-defence forces.

Heinrici's use of language was cautious, as he distanced himself from the full horror of the war, whether through indifference to the scale of the suffering or genuine remorse for the events whose reality he could not quite bring himself to face. His writings show that he still strongly supported Hitler's mission to create *Lebensraum* – living space – for the German people in the east. Heinrici declared that the fight against the 'Jewish–Bolshevik threat' should be carried forward with all the strength the Wehrmacht possessed. He believed that prisoners and civilians ought to be humanely treated, but not out of intrinsic sympathy for the Russian people; instead, because 'the German soldier in the east needs conditions of political and economic stability in the occupied territories in order to properly fulfil his military mission'. Heinrici's proposals were not acted upon. Although, as the German retreat ended, the wholesale burning of Russian villages did cease, inhumane treatment of civilians continued.

On 18 March Leopold Höglinger – radio operator with the German 137th Infantry Division – described a trip to the town of Roslavl, south-east of Smolensk. 'We travelled in a covered truck,' Höglinger began. 'The road was partially snowed under, and a group of Russians was struggling to clear it.' Höglinger's tone was matter-of-fact: he probably regarded these work details as fortunate, since they were either conscripted or even bribed with a tiny food ration, while most local people were starving. 'We reached the airport at Roslavl,' he continued, 'two Russians have been strung up there.' There was no comment on this either; such hangings were now a regular occurrence. Höglinger parked his truck, and made the last part of the journey on foot. He and his companions were unsure of the distance to their quarters, and became impatient: 'We took a Russian and his sledge, *against his will* [my italics], and loaded our baggage onto it.' Eventually accommodation was found; nothing more was said about the Russian. 'Dead tired but happy,' Höglinger concluded, 'we stuffed ourselves with food.'

A gulf in comprehension existed between these two peoples. As the cold weather lessened, Rudolf Gschöpf, chaplain of the Wehrmacht's 45th Infantry Division, described a telling incident. A Russian work detail was helping to bury German dead in a local cemetery. A small amount of food was offered to them, for it was backbreaking work as the ground was still frozen solid. German troops used explosives to blast a crater in the ground and then watched the Russians do the hard manual labour, hacking out individual graves with spades and pickaxes.

After several hours, a superficial camaraderie developed. Songs were sung by each contingent – first by the Germans, then by the Russians. 'Then some of our soldiers began to criticise the Russian songs,' Gschöpf recalled. 'They found them lacking in melody and judged them inferior to our own music.' One of the Russian women knew a little German, and was angered by the soldiers' tactlessness. But Gschöpf was bewildered by her display of emotion. 'It is extraordinary how a casual remark – perhaps a little thoughtless – can cause so much offence,' the chaplain said. 'Somehow, the woman took it as criticism of Russian national culture – a complete overreaction.'

The Führer regarded these occupied territories as a German colony, and ruthlessly plundered them. His sole concession was to introduce a minimal food ration for Soviet prisoners, in order to exploit them better as a workforce. For most of the Red Army soldiers captured by the Wehrmacht, this measure came far too late to have any meaningful effect.

Hitler now took the credit for recent military achievements, and blamed others for the failure at Moscow. The hapless Field Marshal Walther von Brauchitsch, former head of the German Army, was singled out for special abuse. On 19 March Goebbels wrote in his diary: 'Hitler described to me how close we were – these past few months – to a Napoleonic winter. Most of the blame for this lies with Brauchitsch. The Führer has only words of contempt for him – a vain, cowardly wretch, unable to grasp what was happening, much less master it. By his constant interfering and disobedience he completely wrecked the entire plan of campaign in the east, which had been devised with crystal clarity by Hitler.' Goebbels glossed over the fact that Hitler's directives were often confused and contradictory, and that his leader – after authorising Operation Typhoon – had confidently expected Moscow to fall.

History would now be presented differently. 'The Führer had no intention whatsoever of aiming for Moscow,' Goebbels continued. 'Instead, he wanted to cut off the Caucasus [from the rest of Russia] thus hitting the Soviet state at its most vulnerable point. But Brauchitsch and his general staff knew better. Brauchitsch kept hammering on about Moscow. He wanted prestige victories instead of real ones.'

Wilfried Strik-Strikfeldt, staff officer with Army Group Centre, wrote: 'The failure in front of Moscow might have opened Hitler's eyes. For the strategist, a serious setback does not necessarily mean ultimate defeat: it is an occasion to reconsider, to correct past errors, to formulate new and better plans. But with the Führer, ideological fantasy now prevailed over common sense.'

Wehrmacht troops remembered Hitler's bombastic Order of the Day at the start of Operation Typhoon. When he issued a medal to all those who had survived the winter fighting, it was derisively nicknamed 'the Order of the Frozen Flesh'. The Führer had lost the respect of many of his troops. 'One of our comrades has brought us some amusing lyrics', artilleryman Gerhard Bopp wrote on 20 March. 'They are to be sung to the refrain from 'Lili Marleen':

> *At the gates of Moscow, a lone battalion stands*
> *The once-proud remnants of our fighting band*
> *Although the Kremlin they could see*
> *Suddenly they had to flee*
> *Just like Napoleon*
> *Just like Napoleon.*

The Germans had indeed suffered a Napoleonic retreat, but there would be no catastrophe at the end of it: Stalin's great offensive was petering out. 'Our troops had not been properly reinforced, and they were running low on supplies,' Soviet platoon commander Georgi Osadchinsky acknowledged. Stalin had committed his forces over too wide a front. 'Two or three more armies in the central sector would have made all the difference,' General Zhukov said ruefully. At Rzhev, the Russians were now only able to launch sporadic, small-scale attacks, and these posed little threat to Model's troops.

On 25 March German doctor Heinrich Haape remembered a three-hour thaw at midday. 'It made a real impression on us,' he recalled. 'It was the first sign of the approaching spring. And ironically, the very next day a mass of clothing arrived: huge quantities of fur coats, woollens, and fur-lined boots – the fruits of Goebbels's winter appeal to the German people. We left most of it in the command post stables. How useful it all would have been four months earlier. But now only twenty-eight of the battalion's original eight hundred were alive to see it.'

The military efforts of both sides were subsiding, and front-line positions had solidified. German soldier Heinz Otto Fausten and his comrades from the 1st Panzer Division watched the enemy from an observation post in a disused barn, on the crest of a hill. 'We could hear artillery fire in the distance,' Fausten recalled, 'but the scene in the Russian-held village ahead of us was peaceful. Red Army soldiers stayed inside their houses, and the rising smoke from the chimneys was shimmering in the sunlight. After the terrible winter fighting, the front was quiet.'

Once, while Fausten was on duty, there was a bizarre interlude. He heard a horse and cart clattering along the roadway. It was Fausten's duty sergeant, accompanied by a young Russian girl from the village. The sergeant was laughing happily – he was completely drunk. Then the little excursion took an unexpected turn. 'The couple disappeared over the ridge,' Fausten remembered, 'and a short while later re-emerged in front of the Russian-held village. I watched them through the field telescope. The sergeant remained oblivious to any danger. But the girl spurred the horse forward and the new arrivals were quickly surrounded by Red Army soldiers. The girl was warmly embraced; the hapless sergeant was hauled away with much laughter.

In the north, Russian attempts to reach besieged Leningrad were failing. 'The enemy's planes are now very active,' Soviet Colonel Pavel Lopatin wrote on 19 March. 'They are bombing the villages all around us.' Lopatin was right to be worried:

the Wehrmacht had reorganised its forces. In the forests around
Lyuban, Lieutenant General Vlasov's Second Shock Army was
now being encircled by the Germans.

The balance of power on the Eastern Front was shifting. This
could be seen clearly in the contrasting battles at Lyuban and
Demyansk. In both these places, brave groups of defenders – in the
first, Russian, in the second, German – were holding out against
a numerically superior foe. And initially, their plights were very
similar.

The town of Demyansk, a little over 200 miles north-west of
Moscow, was built on high ground above the marshy delta of
the river Lovat. It was garrisoned by a Wehrmacht Army Corps
of around 90,000 men. Soviet troops subjected these men to two
months of relentless tank and infantry assaults. The beleaguered
Wehrmacht and SS units in Demyansk, supplied by air drop, had
somehow clung to their positions. 'A hail of fire was unleashed on
us,' said German soldier Otto Bense. 'I had to blank everything
out – just concentrate on the task at hand. It was so easy for a man
to lose his life at Demyansk.'

A hundred miles to the north, the Soviet soldiers at Lyuban
were in equally desperate straits. 'The Germans have gone over to
the offensive,' Colonel Lopatin wrote on 23 March. 'The supply
situation is bad – our ration has been reduced to 400 grams of
bread a day.' On 24 March he added: 'A grey, unfriendly morning – the atmosphere is damp and oppressive. It would have been
wonderful to have delivered our beloved city of Leningrad from
the German blockade. But now we ourselves are trapped – and
running out of food.'

Now the fates of the encircled forces diverged. At Lyuban,
Lieutenant General Vlasov appealed to Stalin's high command for
help; none was forthcoming. The Germans at Demyansk were
more fortunate. On 21 March – the first day of spring – a relief
force was despatched under Lieutenant General Walther von
Seydlitz to break the Russian siege.

Fifty-three-year-old Seydlitz approached his task with vigour
and determination. His adjutant, Joachim Sandau, recalled his

distinctive style of command. 'Seydlitz was very approachable,' Sandau said. 'He took the time to talk to people, whether they were officers, sappers or riflemen. Unusually, he always carried a rifle with him, and a general with a rifle over his shoulder has won his men over from the start.' Major General Gustav Höhne, commander of the 8th Infantry Division, added: 'Seydlitz was outstandingly brave. He would put on skis and personally lead reconnaissance missions, and would join those front-line battalions in the most difficult positions. He could grasp the features of a military situation and make decisions quickly. Above all, he had a strong sense of duty and was determined to reach the surrounded German forces at Demyansk. He brought hope to the defenders.'

There was no such hope on the Russian side. The Soviet high command was still striving to win success at Vyazma, its main military priority. At Lyuban, Lieutenant General Vlasov continued to appeal for assistance in vain. 'Nobody seemed aware of our army's position,' he said, 'and nobody was concerned about it.' His Soviet Second Shock Army was caught in the iron grip of the Wehrmacht. 'The snow is melting', Colonel Lopatin wrote on 1 April, 'and we are up to our knees in water. We are trapped in forest and marshland – all routes out are held by the Germans. The enemy attacks constantly and our artillery batteries have no more shells. Food is running very low – in the morning we have a "soup" made out of a few breadcrumbs, in the evening the same.'

To the south, the German relief force moved towards Demyansk. It was fighting its way through 20 miles of enemy-held territory and the Red Army resisted fiercely. 'The Russians defended every village,' Joachim Sandau wrote. 'But our push continued'. 'On 1 April the day-time temperature at last lifted above freezing,' said Major General Höhne. 'Our infantry could now move forward more quickly.'

At Demyansk and Lyuban, increasing German optimism contrasted with growing Russian despondency. 'Our army has been sacrificed, condemned to a certain death in this desolate place,' Lieutenant General Vlasov wrote bleakly.

Easter in both pagan and Christian traditions represents the contrasting themes of death and sacrifice, and of new life. In 1942, Easter Sunday fell on 5 April for both the western and Russian Orthodox faiths. 'We are using the heavily damaged church as a stable for our horses,' staff officer Hans Meier-Welcker wrote. 'But there was an Easter egg hunt in the village – and everyone got a piece.' Occasional gestures of human kindness were still made. On 5 April the church opposite Josef Perau's house in Roslavl reopened, as the town *Kommandant* allowed the local inhabitants to celebrate Easter: 'The response was overwhelming,' Perau wrote, 'the building was completely full.'

On Easter Sunday Heinz Otto Fausten was anticipating a quiet day and a decent evening meal, but events turned out differently. 'In one of the barns we discovered a young Russian, hiding under the straw,' Fausten remembered. 'He was from the neighbouring village, and was trying to escape conscription into the Red Army. But our new sergeant decided that he was a spy and ordered him to be shot. I refused to carry out the order.' Fausten was now the sole survivor of his 240-strong company from the 1st Panzer Division. He had seen thousands of men die: what difference would one more make? And yet, impulsively, Fausten now made a stand. 'I will not shoot this man,' he said to the sergeant, 'nor will anyone else in this unit.' His fellow soldiers gathered around, and there was an ominous silence. Then the sergeant ordered Fausten to report to the commanding officer. The officer listened to Fausten and – remarkably – chose not to punish him. 'We will transfer you,' he said.

When Fausten returned, the sergeant was standing there. He had just shot the young Russian and the corpse lay in the snow. Blood was still seeping from the bullet hole, a close-range shot to the head. 'You're lucky you didn't get a court martial,' the sergeant said. 'You will stand guard over the body, out in the open – for the whole night.' The night-time temperature was still −10 degrees Celsius, but Fausten's comrades brought him hot tea, and he was able to shelter by the side of the barn. 'I spent the whole time wide awake, next to the Russian,' Fausten said. 'I had not known the man – yet I felt a remarkable sense of connection with him. It made no sense. But I held my night-time vigil by his side, nonetheless.'

Near Lyuban, Lieutenant General Vlasov's army was wasting away. 'Many of our men were now incapable of moving through the swampland,' Vlasov recalled. 'The last of the snow has turned to mud,' Soviet Colonel Lopatin wrote on 10 April. 'Rations are down to 200 grams of bread a day. Our soldiers are growing weaker – no supplies are getting through.'

On the same day, German Major General Höhne was pushing closer to Demyansk. He noted: 'Now the snow has begun to melt with a vengeance. The water in the woods is knee-deep. Wide, shallow streams run through field and forest. Roads are covered with a one-metre-thick layer of mud.' Then Höhne added: 'We keep moving towards our trapped comrades – every man knows what is at stake.'

On 12 April Lieutenant General von Seydlitz caught sight of the shattered tower blocks of Ramushevo, rising like a mirage through the haze and smoke. The town, which controlled the crossing point over the river Lovat, was the last major obstacle before Demyansk. A bridgehead on the western side of the river was seized on 15 April, but as the river was swollen by the spring thaw and the Soviet defences there were formidable, this could not serve as a crossing point. Instead, Seydlitz undertook a reconnaissance of the surrounding countryside and then devised a fresh plan of attack.

On 18 April Josef Perau recorded: 'Spring has now arrived – there has been a most dramatic change in the weather. It had been humid and dank, with grey overcast skies. But now the sun has broken through with enormous force and a warm wind is blowing from the south. A comrade called me over to the window. There was a butterfly – a bright, lemon-yellow butterfly.' The following day Perau added: 'We are preparing the wounded for evacuation. On the verandas, our soldiers are sitting, bare-chested, in the sunshine.'

It was unusual for the Wehrmacht to show much sensitivity to nature, but after the horror of the winter retreat German soldiers found the first signs of spring both comforting and deeply moving. They were harbingers of hope. But no such hope existed for their Russian counterparts. Expectations of rapid victory were being cruelly dashed. At Lyuban, Lieutenant General Vlasov's Second Shock Army was running out of its last supplies. 'Rations were reduced to 100 grams of bread a day, and then 50 grams,' Vlasov said. 'Meanwhile, our high command sent out one contradictory order after another.' On 18 April Colonel Lopatin wrote: 'It is a wonderful sunny day and the front line is quiet. But I am growing weak – and it is hard to move very far. Because of the severe food shortage, some of the men are starting to swell up through hunger. I walk over to the edge of the forest. There is no sound. I cannot hear birds or animals – just deathly silence.'

The Wehrmacht's resurgence continued. On 20 April Lieutenant General von Seydlitz captured Ramushevo, launching an unexpected flanking attack through flooded marshlands south of the town and overrunning the Russian defences. German soldiers showed extraordinary determination, wading through waist-deep water from melted snow and then launching an assault on the enemy. The next day Seydlitz established contact with the Wehrmacht troops at Demyansk. A land corridor had been carved out by a force showing new-found confidence and self-belief, and supplies soon began rolling into the beleaguered stronghold. After thirty days of fighting through snow and mud, the German relief effort had succeeded.

11

The Grand Illusion

I N CASUAL CONVERSATION, Hitler once briefly reflected on
the hell of the German retreat. 'Luckily nothing lasts for ever,'
the Führer said, 'and that is a consoling thought. Even in raging
winter, we know that spring will follow. And if, at this moment,
men are being turned into blocks of ice, that won't prevent the
April sun from shining and restoring life to these desolate places.'
Philosophical indeed. It was fortunate for Hitler that the April sun
was shining again on a coherent German front, and that he could
now plan a fresh offensive against the Soviet Union.

By April 1942 the Führer was longing to attack once more:
'The winter battle in Russia has come to an end,' he announced.
'Thanks to their remarkable bravery and selfless sacrifice, our
German soldiers have achieved an extraordinary success. The
enemy has suffered huge losses in men and equipment. Striving to
exploit his *imaginary initial successes* [my italics] he has expended the
main mass of his reserves. As soon as the weather and terrain are
favourable, exploiting their superiority, the German armed forces
must once again seize the initiative and impose their will upon the
enemy.'

Here was the flight into fantasy and illusion. The so-called
'imaginary initial successes' of the Soviet counteroffensive had cost
the Wehrmacht dear. By 31 January 1942 the German forces in the
east had suffered – from the outbreak of the war – 917,985 casualties, and lost more than 41,000 trucks, 207,000 horses and 13,600
artillery pieces. By the end of March 1942 the Germans considered
only 8 of their 162 divisions in the Soviet Union to be 'attack
ready', and their 16 Panzer divisions had only 140 functioning

tanks, fewer than the complement of one full-strength division. Colonel Erhard Raus, commander of the 6th Panzer Division, wrote: 'The German Army would never recover from the enormous losses in men and equipment suffered during the retreat from Moscow. In my own division, we lost more than 80 per cent of our infantry and artillery, the bulk of our motor vehicles and all of our tanks and heavy weapons.'

To return to the offensive, Hitler had to rely on reinforcements from Germany's allies, principally the Romanians, Hungarians and Italians. However, few of these troops had the training or equipment to fight the rapid, mechanised battles that bore the hallmark of the Wehrmacht's earlier successes in the east. The days of blitzkrieg were over.

After months of intense fighting, both sides began information campaigns intended to lower their opponent's morale. On 27 April German staff officer Hans Meier-Welcker noted: 'The Red Army's propaganda section has been busy. Leaflets are dropped by plane over the combat zone, and flutter down towards us. Enemy trucks fitted with loudspeakers are moving backwards and forwards opposite our lines. They produce testimonials from some of our prisoners, saying conditions in the Russian camps are decent and good.' He added: 'We are supposed to be responding tomorrow with our own trucks and speakers.' After the death of more than two million Red Army soldiers in German captivity, it was hard for the Wehrmacht to do so with much conviction.

Even though the front had stabilised, there would be no rest from this war. Army doctor Heinrich Haape recalled the visit of the newly promoted Colonel General Model to the battered remnants of the German 6th Infantry Division. 'Model inspected a small, shrunken group of soldiers, exhausted from the winter fighting,' Haape recalled. 'The general spoke his words of praise, and the men waited expectantly for what was to follow: "Soon you will be sent to France for recuperation." But Model uttered no such promise. "On, comrades, to new deeds" was his final injunction.' Manpower was so short that the soldiers could simply not be allowed leave.

However, on 28 April Heinz Otto Fausten was lucky. His 1st Panzer Division was leaving Sychevka and travelling to a different section of the front, and he vividly recalled the spring thaw: 'The landscape was transformed into a seascape,' Fausten said, 'as the frozen undersoil prevented the melting snow from completely draining away. In the waterlogged fields around Sychevka, dark heaps were emerging – piles of corpses, relics of the winter fighting. Civilians moved around the bodies, scavenging for clothes or personal possessions.'

A military car drew to a halt. A general was inside, and he leant over and asked Fausten: 'Where do I know you from?' Fausten stood to the salute:

'I do not know, Herr General – East Prussia, Sabsk, Kalinin?'
'You have fought in the east from the very beginning?'
'Yes, Herr General, without a break – I am the last of 3 Company!'

The car drove off, but that evening Fausten was summoned to his HQ. The officer looked up at him, and said: 'You have been ordered home on leave, departing on the next military train.' Fausten was stunned by his good fortune.

German troops stationed at Roslavl, behind the front lines, were now fighting increasingly tough battles against Russian partisans. After the mass burning of villages during the German retreat from Moscow, support for the partisan movement had grown; it was now causing the Wehrmacht real problems. On 1 May divisional chaplain Josef Perau wrote: 'Our military cemetery is expanding at a frightening rate. On Monday twenty-two men were buried in a large communal grave. One man – witnessing the burial of his unit commander – thanked me for the words I had spoken. The soldiers gather, a volley of shots is fired and we pay our last respects to the fallen.'

For both sides, the suffering continued. 'A great holiday – a shame about the reception!' Soviet Colonel Lopatin joked grimly the same day. His troops from the 4th Guards Infantry Division, trapped in the forest near Lyuban, were each given 100 grams of vodka and a tiny amount of dried bread. 'I could have eaten a whole loaf,' Lopatin wrote with feeling. 'I have lost so much weight I find it difficult even to move.'

On 5 May the German stronghold at Kholm was relieved, ending a 105-day siege. Major General Theodor Scherer's small garrison of five and a half thousand men was the last Wehrmacht outpost surrounded by the enemy: Army Group Centre had now won itself a breathing space. A week later Hans Meier-Welcker recorded: 'I have put down some thoughts on the events of last autumn and winter. First and foremost, we badly underestimated the capacity of the Russians to continue to resist in the autumn of 1941. One sign of our overconfidence last October was the extraordinary decision to scale down home armaments production. We are still suffering the consequences of that blunder today, as the return to full output takes time and has not yet been fully accomplished.' Meier-Welcker continued:

> Underestimating the enemy, we launched a second, November offensive against Moscow – and completely overreached ourselves. But what was fatal for us was the 'Stand Fast!' order of mid-December. It forced us to cling to every scrap of land – we were only allowed to pull back very slowly, with the Red Army constantly at our heels. The possibility of making a rapid withdrawal – thereby avoiding destructive fighting in terrible winter conditions – was lost.
>
> If we had withdrawn quickly, the weather conditions – and the deep snow – would have worked in our favour, impeding the enemy's pursuit. We would have had to sacrifice some of our heavy equipment, but this happened to us anyway. If we had promptly pulled our lines back, we could have built up a reserve – augmented it with reinforcements from the west – then created specific battle groups, to deal with any Russian break-through attempts. By doing this, we would have avoided placing such extreme demands upon our already exhausted troops.
>
> The lack of any reserves, and the throwing of reinforcements straight into the battle without winter training or acclimatisation, put our armies at a serious disadvantage. From this arose a desperate struggle for survival, and it was only through quite exceptional generalship by some of our commanders and outstanding bravery from their troops that a catastrophe was averted.

Meier-Welcker concluded: 'At this stage, we were assisted by the fact that many of the Russians had very little combat training, that the quality of their junior officers was poor and – as their counter-offensive foundered – that their soldiers' lives were sacrificed in increasingly wasteful frontal attacks. But how much better, if the German Army had been able to face these attacks from an advantageous position.'

Hans Meier-Welcker was an able staff officer. He preferred to discuss strategic options, and pay tribute to the courage of German troops at the end of the retreat. It was harder for him to pay tribute to the courage of Red Army soldiers as the battle for Moscow reached its climax. And while he could be honest about instances of cruelty that he had witnessed – the burning of villages and the mistreatment of Russian prisoners of war – he was unable to engage with the wholesale atrocities committed by German troops and security detachments, although by the spring of 1942 these had claimed millions of lives. But the erosion of his trust in Adolf Hitler, the self-appointed leader of the German Army, was plain to see.

In the spring of 1942 Colonel Hermann Balck, a member of the inspectorate of the German Armoured Forces and a superb Panzer commander, said of the Führer's 'Stand Fast!' order:

Hitler believed that he was a great military leader, and deluded himself after the defeat at Moscow that he had saved the German Army. He claimed that there were no other options other than the halt order he was insisting upon. But this was simply not true. Towards the end of December 1941, the withdrawal of the Second Panzer Army to a pre-arranged fall-back position showed that a rapid retreat would have been possible, and could have been conducted without excessive loss of material. This contradicted the tactical justification for the 'Stand Fast!' order. We were forced to obey the Führer's decree, nonetheless, and paid a terrible price for it – in blood and suffering.

It is not, in fact, entirely clear whether a rapid German withdrawal to a fall-back position – the so-called Königsberg line, running through Rzhev, Gzhatsk and Yukhnov – would have been practicable in the second week of December, in the heavy snow and extreme cold. But many Wehrmacht commanders believed it should have been tried. This was the judgement of military professionals.

After stepping in at a crisis point of the German retreat, and dismissing Field Marshal von Brauchitsch, Hitler had not appointed a professional to succeed him. Instead the Führer himself – entirely lacking in strategic training or understanding – had decided that he could lead the German Army and resolve the situation through sheer willpower.

At a time of adversity, great military leaders have the gift of being able to reach out to their men, to encourage them and lift their spirits. Observers were struck by Napoleon's composure during the retreat from Moscow. 'His presence electrified our downcast hearts and gave us a last burst of energy,' wrote Captain Charles François. 'The sight of our chief walking in our midst, sharing our privations, still elicited our enthusiasm.' A German artillery officer fighting with the *Grande Armée* added: 'He who sees real greatness abandoned by fortune forgets his own suffering and his own cares. As a result we filed past, under his gaze, in silence – partially reconciled to our own harsh fate.'

But Hitler was no Napoleon. Rather than share the privations of his troops, he disregarded them. German staff officer Ulrich Gunzert described the Führer's rigid adherence to his 'Stand Fast!' order: 'We were being overrun,' Gunzert said. 'Yet we were ordered to retake a position lost to the enemy. Our commanding general went to see Hitler and tried to explain to him that to attack in these circumstances would be hopeless. He wanted to withdraw – but the Führer refused him permission.' Then Gunzert added: 'I had to speak to Hitler myself, on the phone. I tried to explain the situation to him. He screamed at me to be quiet, and to do what he said, or I would be hanged. That was our conversation. And then I had to send my men out, without artillery or air support, to advance half a mile across a snowfield at −40 degrees Celsius, armed only with their rifles. The Russians shot them down like rabbits.'

'Hitler's orders no longer corresponded to the reality on the ground,' said Major General Hans von Greiffenberg, Army Group Centre's chief of staff. 'The Führer was unable to grasp the true capabilities of the enemy, and issued wholly unrealistic instructions to our troops, that he expected to be obeyed to the letter.' When Colonel General Guderian had met with Hitler on 20 December 1941 and tried, unsuccessfully, to persuade him to command with less rigidity and allow his generals more freedom of action, his overriding impression was that the Führer was either unable or unwilling to connect with the suffering of his soldiers.

Almost a month later, on 16 January 1942, with the whole of Army Group Centre teetering on the brink of destruction, Hitler had been forced to modify his misjudged halt order. The war diary of the German Third Panzer Army recorded simply: 'A sigh of relief swept the entire front.' It was not only the German Army that had paid a heavy price in blood and suffering. Hitler's assumption of command had accelerated the brutality of the war, and Russian civilians and prisoners of war had died in increasingly large numbers as a result.

Spring had not brought an end to the food problems. In German-occupied Rzhev, Nina Semonova wrote on 20 May: 'I have forgotten what bread even tastes like. To be full, to be able to satisfy my hunger – I can no longer even imagine what that is like.' The Wehrmacht's 6th Infantry Division, stationed close to the town, reported: 'The food situation for the local population is growing more difficult every day. Completely undernourished, many are now dying – the remainder lie about apathetically, and have no energy to do anything.' The 256th Infantry Division noted that civilians from Rzhev, mostly women and children, 'wander around begging, starving and in rags'. The city had a population of 40,000 when the Germans occupied it in October 1941; less than a year later, its population had dropped to only 3,000 inhabitants.

Stalin had been unable to destroy the Wehrmacht outside Moscow, and so repeat Russia's great triumph of 1812 against Napoleon. But the forced retreat of the German armies inspired the Russian defenders. 'We had won an important victory,' Soviet platoon commander Georgi Osadchinsky said, 'and driven the enemy away from our capital. It gave us confidence that we could withstand the German aggressor. Sadly, we proved unable to surround and destroy his main armies. Then, as spring came, our attacks grew increasingly wasteful, and had less and less effect. The war would go on.'

Where that war would now lead, no one really knew. Soviet losses had mounted alarmingly. By the end of April 1942, when the Soviet Thirty-Third Army was finally destroyed, fighting at Rzhev and Vyazma had claimed around 272,000 Russian lives and the battle at Demyansk another 90,000. General Zhukov said: 'If one considers our losses, and the results that were achieved, the latter stages of our counteroffensive were clearly a Pyrrhic victory.'

May 1942 was a grim month indeed for the Red Army. Their forces were defeated along the entire length of the front – in the Crimea, at Kharkov and Lyuban. 'We are winning victories again,' exclaimed German soldier Hans Jürgen Hartmann of Army Group South, 'and this is vital, after the catastrophe of last winter. Now – at last – we can put the terrible suffering of those months behind us.' On 20 May Soviet Colonel Lopatin broke through the German encirclement at Lyuban. He wrote:

> The sky is overcast as we struggle along the railway tracks. Our soldiers are moving slowly, some walking with the help of sticks, others being carried on carts. The enemy's artillery and mortars have opened up – shells are landing all around us, exploding in the marshes, throwing up fountains of mud. My legs are so shaky they no longer seem to obey me. My wet, sodden coat is flapping against my boots. The sounds of combat grow stronger. Dirty, covered in mud, we shelter from the heavy rain under a huge fir tree, trying to regain our breath. Then we move forward again. One comrade says: 'We are entering the valley of death.' There is scarcely an untouched tree, all are torn and distorted by shell fire. Guns are scattered around us, wheels up in the air, abandoned carts, the dead bodies of soldiers and horses, a pockmarked landscape of shell craters.

Lopatin and his comrades escaped the German trap. But most of the Soviet Second Shock Army perished in the marshlands.

Its commander – Lieutenant General Andrei Vlasov, hero of the defence of Moscow – was found by the Germans wandering, lost and disorientated, in the forest. Deeply traumatised by his ordeal, and believing his army had been abandoned by Stalin, he declared to his captors that he was willing to recruit a Russian army and fight against the Bolshevik regime. But Hitler did not respond to his offer.

The die was cast. Unfettered by any restraint on his power, the Führer now led the Wehrmacht in a race war of subjugation. The fighting would become even more ruthless, and destructive almost beyond imagination. Total war was to be unleashed against the Russian people.

Notes

Eyewitness accounts, memoirs and diaries are usually cited on their first appearance in the text.

Chapter 1: In the Shadow of Napoleon

Leopold Höglinger's diary extracts are provided courtesy of his son-in-law, Justin Warman. I owe Wolfram von Richthofen's diary (Bundesarchiv, Freiburg, N671/4) to Richard Hargreaves. The remarks of Stephan Mikoyan, Hans-Erdmann Schönbeck and Heinz Otto Fausten are from interviews with me. For Gotthard Heinrici's diaries see Hürter, *Ein Deutscher General*. Hans von Greiffenberg's observations are from his operational survey, 'The Battle for Moscow 1941–42', in National Archives and Records Administration, Washington DC (henceforth NARA), Foreign Military Studies, MS T-28. Background on Napoleon's Moscow campaign is from Zamoyski, *1812*. The detail on the German 23rd Infantry Division and the shooting of prisoners is in Christian Streit, *Keine Kameraden*. The German soldiers' letters are from Ortwin Buchbender and Reinhold Sterz, *Deutsche Feldpostbriefe*. The comments of Kluge, Manstein and Weichs are from Johannes Hürter, *Hitlers Heerführer*. Material on Wilhelm Schröder is from Imperial War Museum (IWM) private papers, box no. 01/8/1. For Philipp von Boeselager's views on the campaign see *Valkyrie* and Guido Knopp's German TV (ZDF) documentary, 'The Turning Point – Moscow 1941'; for Ulrich de Maizière, *In Der Pflicht*; and for Gerhard Dengler, 'Turning-Point'. The testimonies of Alexander Andrievich, Ivan Nikitin and Vera Yukina are in Walter Kempowski, *Das Echolot*. For the crossing of the Berezina river: Höglinger's diaries and Günther Blumentritt, 'Moscow', in William Richardson and Seymour Freidin, *Fatal Decisions*. Erich Mende's reaction is in his *Das Verdammte Gewissen*. Count von Stauffenberg's visit is from Peter Hoffmann, *Stauffenberg: A Family History*. Hans Meier-Welcker's diary extracts are from *Aufzeichnungen eines Generalstabsoffiziers*. Alois Scheuer's letters are in *Briefe aus Russland;* Karl Fuchs's in *Your Loyal and Loving Son*. Franz Frisch's observation is from *Condemned to Live*. Hitler's indecision is described in Gerhard Engel, *At the Heart of the Reich*. Franz Halder's views on the progress of the war are recorded in Charles Burdick and Hans-Adolf Jacobson, *The Halder War Diary*. Guderian's immediate reaction to the Kiev operation (Dermot Bradley, *Generaloberst Heinz Guderian*) was far more positive than his retrospective account in *Panzer Leader*. The research of Johannes Hürter shows that the majority of Army Group Centre's commanders supported the diversion south, to Kiev. For the planning of Typhoon see Walter de Beaulieu, *Generaloberst Erich Hoepner* and Heinrich Bücheler, *Hoepner*. The *Völkischer Beobachter* piece is from Janusz Piekalkiewicz, *Moscow 1941*.

Chapter 2: Typhoon

For an excellent introduction to Typhoon, issues of logistics and the German order of battle, see Robert Forczyk, *Moscow 1941*. Extracts from Wolfgang Dose's journal, 'Kampfberichte von der Ostfront', have been made available by Gerhard Dose. Hans Jürgen Hartmann's reaction is in *Zwischen Nichts und Niemandsland*. Ernst Tewes's account is from his 'Seelsorger bei den soldaten, 1940–45' in Georg Schwaiger, *Das Erzbistum*. Fedor von Bock's assessment is from his *War Diary*. Heinz Otto Fausten's tank dash to Kalinin is from an interview with me, and his memoir *Wir Haben Uns die Zeit nicht Ausgesucht*. Background material is in Rolf Stoves, *Die 1 Panzer Division*. For comments of Eduard Wagner and Wolfgang Koch, see Wolfgang Paul, *Die Schlacht um Moskau*. Heinrich Haape's first day of combat is recorded in *Moscow Tram Stop*. Background material is from Horst Grossmann, *6 Infanterie-Division*. Shabalin's diary is from Hans Georg Lehmann, 'Das Kriegstagebuch des Sowjetischen Majors der Staatlichen Sicherheit Sabalin (Brjansker Front)', *Wehrforschung* 2 (1974). Andrei Yeremenko's experiences are in his *The Arduous Beginning*. For Wolfgang Fischer, see Russell Stolfi, 'The German 10th Panzer Division's Eastern Front Offensive near Vyazma', *World War Two* (1997). Heinrich Larsen's letter is from Andrew Nagorski, *Greatest Battle*. Ella Zhukova's remarks are from the ZDF documentary 'Turning Point'. Comments of Mikhail Lukhin and Andrei Khrulev are from David Glantz, *Before Stalingrad*. Horst Lange's observations are in his *Tagebücher aus dem Zweiten Weltkrieg.* Stephan Mikoyan's and Zoya Zarubina's accounts are from interviews with me. Werner Lacoste's story, 'Begegnung mit tragischem ausgang', is from the German veterans' magazine *Kameraden* (July/ August 2008). Carl Wagener's views are set out in *Moskau 1941.* The testimonies of Makary Barchuk and Nikolai Nechayev are in Andrei Gorbunov, *'Moscow is Behind Us!'*; Boris Baromykin's account is from an interview with me. On the panic of 16 October, see Rodric Braithwaite, *Moscow 1941* and Bezymensky, *The Battle of Moscow.* For Dmitry Lelyushenko, see Richard Armstrong, *Red Army Tank Commanders.* Georgi Osadchinsky's testimony is from a series of interviews with me; some of his diary extracts are in 'My Infantry Battalion', in the Russian veterans' journal *Forum*, XXXVI– XXXVII (2005). Material on the 78th Infantry Division is from Ludwig Merker's unit history. Josef Deck's account is from *Der Weg der 1000 Toten.* For German combat reports on the growing strength of Russian resistance, see Klaus Reinhardt, *Die Wende vor Moskau.* The letters of Harald Henry are in Hans Bähr, Hermann Meyer and Eberhard Orthbrandt, *Kriegsbriefe Gefallener Studenten.* Gerhard vom Bruch's diary is from Wolfgang Paul, *Brennpunkte*; Robert Rupp's account is in Ingrid Hammer and Suzanne zur Nieden, *Briefe und Tagebücher.*

Chapter 3: At the Gates of Moscow

The comments of Rudolf Schmidt, Adolf Strauss, Georg Thomas and Maximilian von Weichs are all from Johannes Hürter, *Hitlers Heerführer.* The civilian testimonies of Vera Kalugina and Nina Semonova are in Paul Kohl, *Ich Wunder Mich.* Wilhelm Pfeiffer's description of the devastation in Vitebsk is from Gordon Burgess, *Wolfgang Borchert.* Ivan Barykin's account of the 7 November parade is from an interview with me. Ludwig von Heyl's comments on the resumption of the offensive are in his memoir, *Wie Ich Den Krieg Erlebte.* The reaction of Hermann Geyer is found in Earl Ziemke and Magna Bauer, *Moscow to Stalingrad.* Erich Hoepner's letters are from Heinrich Bücheler, *Hoepner.* Anatoly Shvebig's testimony is from Artem Drabkin's 'I Remember' section of www.russianbattlefield.com. Konstantin Rokossovky's account is in his *A Soldier's Duty.* Rodric Braithwaite, *Moscow 1941*, and Chris Bellamy, *Absolute War*, have now printed extracts from Rokossovsky's memoir excised by the Soviet censors: they are extremely critical of Georgi Zhukov's abrasive style of command. Dmitry Vonlyarsky's testimony is from his interview with me; Graf Castell's diary is in Plato, 5

Panzer-Division. The accounts of Hans Braukmann, Peter Biewer and Ernst Jauernick are from Hans Dollinger, *Kain, Wo ist dein Bruder?*; Ivan Panfilov's letter is in Guido Knopp, *Der Verdammte Krieg*. Nikolai Obryn'ba's experiences are from *Red Partisan*. Kurt Grumann's diary is in Elena Rzhevskaya, 'Roads and Days: The Memoir of a Red Army Translator', *Journal of Slavic Studies* 14 (2001). Gerhard Bopp's experiences are from *Kriegstagebuch 1940–43*. Wolfgang Paul's remarkable account is in Hans Schäufler, *Der Weg war Weit*. On 'Lili Marleen': Heinrich Rotard's comments are from Knopp, *Der Verdammte Krieg*; Josef Bailer's are in the ZDF documentary 'Turning Point'.

Chapter 4: The Tipping Point

Gustav Schrodek's account is in Hans Schäufler, *Der Weg war Weit*. For Walther Schaefer-Kehnert, see Laurence Rees, *War of the Century*; Karl-Gottfried Vierkorn's remarks are from an interview with me. The conversation between Walther von Brauchitsch and Fedor von Bock is in Alfred Turney, *Disaster at Moscow*. On Hitler and Tolstoy's estate see Gerhard Engel, *At the Heart of the Reich*. For the defeat of German forces at Lobnya I am indebted to Georgi Osadchinsky and the newly opened T-34 History Museum at Sholokhovo; the first floor of the museum is devoted to the fighting at Lobnya and is a regular meeting place for Russian veterans. The reaction in Kalinin is from Paul Kohl, *Ich Wunder Mich*. Ernst Streng's diary is found in Otto Weidinger, *Das Reich*. Adolf Raegener's comments are reproduced in Wolfgang Paul, *Das Potsdamer Infanterie-Regiment 9*. Alexander Conrady's views are from his *Rückzug vor Moskau*. The 258th Infantry Division letter is in Ortwin Buchbender and Reinhold Sterz, *Deutsche Feldpostbriefe*. Hermann Hoss's testimony is from Hans Schäufler, *So Lebten und So Starben Sie*. Ivan Boldin's comments are in Walter Kerr, *The Russian Army*. Heinrich Link's deeply moving account is from Friedrich Hossbach, *Infanterie im Ostfeldzug*.

Chapter 5: Ten Days in December

I am grateful to veterans Heinz Otto Fausten, Georgi Osadchinsky, Hans-Erdmann Schönbeck and Dmitry Vonlyarsky for discussing the December fighting with me. I have found the observations of Hans von Greiffenberg in his 'Battle for Moscow' (NARA, MS T-28) very useful for the broader military context; Wolfram von Richthofen's diary extracts (Bundesarchiv, N671/4) insightful for the atmosphere at Hitler's headquarters; and Lothar Rendulic's 'The Effects of Extreme Cold on Weapons and Vehicles' and 'Combat in Deep Snow' (NARA, MS D-106) invaluable for the realities of fighting at −35 degrees Celsius. The beginning of the retreat was a shattering experience for German soldiers and an exhilarating one for Red Army troops. For the testimonies of Alexander Cohrs, Wilhelm Hebestreit, Fritz Hübner, Georg Kreuter, Reinhold Pabel and Ivan Savenko, see Walter Kempowski, *Das Echolot*. The utter failure of German intelligence is discussed in David Glantz, *Soviet Military Deception*. The accounts of Peter Biewer, Anton Gründer, Hans Johann Kröhl, Albrecht Linsen, Vladimir Ogryzko and Pavel Ossipov are from Knopp, *Der Verdammte Krieg*. The Cossack cavalry attack on the German 95th Infantry Division is from Willy Reese, *A Stranger to Myself*. The comments of Günther von Kluge on army discipline and Hans von Greiffenberg and Rudolf Schmidt on Russian POWs are from Johannes Hürter, *Hitlers Heerführer*. The remarks of Friedrich von Broich, Hans Reimann and Paul Seyffardt are in Sönke Neitzel, *Tapping Hitler's Generals*. The testimonies of Ekkehard Maurer and Franz Peters are from the ZDF documentary 'Turning Point'. Regimental commander Adolf Raegener confirms Peters's bleak assessment in Wolfgang Paul, *Infanterie-Regiment 9*. The two key Soviet successes were at Klin and Livny. For Klin, see 'The Pocket of Klin – Breakout of a Panzer Division', in US Army Pamphlet *Operations of Encircled Forces – German Experiences in Russia* (1952); for Livny, I am grateful to Robert Westby, on the Axis History Forum, for the key sections of the 134th Division's history and Hermann Metz's report on Conrad von Cochenhausen's death. Background on Cochenhausen is from Richard Hargreaves, *Blitzkrieg Unleashed*.

Chapter 6: Stand Fast!

Material on the 45th Division is from Rudolf Gschöpf, *Mein Weg mit der 45 Infanterie-Division*. Accounts of Wolfgang Buff and Karl Fuchs are in Walter Kempowski, *Das Echolot*; Helmut von Harnack and Werner Pott from Hans Bähr, Hermann Meyer and Eberhard Orthbrandt, *Kriegsbriefe Gefallen, Studenten*. For Albert Neuhaus, and an excellent discussion of the general context, see Richard Evans, *The Third Reich at War*. Extracts from Otto Bente's diary are in Jochen Löser, *Bittere Pflicht*. The comments of Faber du Faur and Rudolf Schmidt are from Johannes Hürter, *Hitlers Heerführer*. Victor Klemperer's perceptive remarks are in his *I Shall Bear Witness*. Alfred Jodl's praise for Hitler's halt order is noted by Klaus Reinhardt, *Die Wende vor Moskau*; for Günther von Kluge's initial support see Wolfram von Richthofen's diary entries for 15–19 December and Günther Blumentritt, 'Moscow', in Richardson and Freidin, *The Fatal Decisions*. But Strauss's immediate criticism of the 'Stand Fast!' decree (cited in Ziemke and Bauer, *Moscow to Stalingrad*) was a far more typical reaction. The complaint of Hellmuth Stieff, *Briefe*, is particularly telling. Werner Pott's description of Hitler's 'scorched-earth' policy is in Bähr, Meyer and Orthbrandt, *Kriegsbriefe Gefallener Studenten*. For Friedrich Bergmann's death, see Wilhelm Meyer-Detring, *137 Infanterie-Division*.

Chapter 7: 'This Is All There Really Is'

Heinz Otto Fausten and Karl Gottfried-Vierkorn have kindly shared with me memories of Christmas 1941 in Russia. Wolfgang Dose's account is from 'Kampfberichte von der Ostfront'; Hans Jürgen Hartmann's in *Zwischen Nichts und Niemandsland*. The Christmas rations counter-attack is from Rolf Hinze, *Hitze, Frost und Pulverdampf*. The extract from the 134th Division's combat diary is in Werner Haupt's unit history. Helmut von Harnack's and Willi Thomas's Christmas experiences are in Hans Bähr, Hermann Meyer and Eberhard Orthbrandt, *Kriegsbriefe Gefallener Studenten*. Wilhelm Schröder's account is from IWM, private papers, 01/8/1. Franz Peters's description is in the ZDF documentary 'Turning Point' and Ludwig Freiherr von Heyl's Christmas preparations are from his memoir *Wie Ich Den Krieg Erlebte*; Gerhard Bopp's from his *Kriegstagebuch*. Erich Mende's recollections are in *Das Verdammte Gewissen*. Willy Reese in *A Stranger to Myself* strikes a very different tone. Alois Scheuer's Christmas letter is from *Briefe aus Russland*; Gustav Wetter's diary entry is in Hans Dollinger, *Kain, Wo Ist Dein Broder?* For Josef Deck, see *Der Weg der 1000 Toten*; for Wilhelm Prüller, *Diary of a German Soldier*. Gotthard Heinrici's letters are in Johannes Hürter, *Ein Deutscher General*. The accounts of Fritz Hübner and Franz Leiprecht are from Walter Kempowski, *Das Echolot*. Gerhard vom Bruch's diary is in Wolfgang Paul, *Brennpunkte*. Heinrich Haape's testimony in *Moscow Tram Stop* has been used alongside Horst Grossmann's *6 Infanterie-Division*. On the Soviet side, I am once again grateful to Georgi Osadchinsky. Pavel Ossipov's account is from Guido Knopp,

Der Verdammte Krieg; Ivan Savenko's is in Walter Kempowski, *Das Echolot.* Chaplain Josef Perau's description of Christmas is from his *Priester im Heere Hitlers*; additional material has kindly been provided by Eugen Perau. The anonymous chaplain's account is in Janusz Piekalkiewicz, *Moscow 1941.* For Russian teenagers stealing German presents, see Paul Chavchavadze, *Marie Avinov: Her Amazing Life.* Hans Schäufler's remarkable account of Christmas at Kromy is in *So Lebten und So Starben Sie.*

Chapter 8: Looking into the Abyss

Nikita Khrushchev's comments are from his *Memoirs: Commissar (1918–1945).* Vladimir Goncharov's diary is in Bernd Martin, *Tagebuch eines Sowjetischen Offiziers.* For Giorgi Zhukov's use of paratroopers see David Glantz, *Soviet Airborne Forces.* Martin Gareis's account of the fighting at Maloyaroslavets is from his *98 Infanterie-Division.* Josef Perau's comments are in his *Priester im Heere Hitlers.* August Schmidt's appraisal of Heinz Guderian is found in his *10 Infanterie-Division*; Joachim Lemelsen's in Johannes Hürter, *Hitlers Heerführer.* Hans–Erdmann Schönbeck's reaction to Guderian's dismissal, and declining morale within the 15th Panzer Regiment, is from an interview with me. Otto Bente's diary is in Jochen Löser, *Bittere Pflicht.* All Army Group Centre reports are from Klaus Reinhardt, *Die Wende vor Moskau.* Klaus Voss's observations on extreme combat fatigue are in *Kameraden* (July/August 2008). Material on Dietrich Karsten and the 189th Infantry Regiment was kindly provided by Lena Karsten. Extracts from Fritz Langanke's 'Operation Sychevka' are reproduced courtesy of Dan Reinbold's *Das Reich* website.

Chapter 9: Enter General Model

Alongside Steven Newton's new biography of Walther Model, *Hitler's Commander,* the insights of Horst Grossmann in *Rzhev: Eckpfeiler der Ostfront* remain valuable. The accounts of Operation Sychevka by Fritz Langanke and Otto Weidinger (in his *Das Reich*) are both very useful. For Model's visit to the 36th Motorised Infantry Division see Franz Kurowski, *Infantry Aces.* Heinz Otto Fausten's account is supplemented by material in Stoves, *Die 1 Panzer.* Luftwaffe commander Wolfram von Richthofen worked closely with Model, and once again I am grateful to Richard Hargreaves for relevant diary entries from the Bundesarchiv, N671/4. For the testimony of Peter Stahl, and an excellent discussion of the use of German air power, see Christopher Bergström and Andrey Mikhailov, *Air War over the Eastern Front*. Additional information on the Rzhev battle is found in Erhard Raus, *Panzer Operations*; Alexander Conrady, *Rückzug* and Hans Meier-Welcker, *Aufzeichnungen eines Generalstabsoffiziers*. For Heinrici and Yukhnov I have used Johannes Hürter, *Ein Deutscher General*, and Hellmuth Stieff, *Briefe*. Nina Semonova's diary is in Paul Kohl, *Ich Wunder Mich*; details on the camp at Rzhev are from Catherine Merridale, *Ivan's War*.

Chapter 10: The First Butterfly of Spring

Heinz Herre's account is from Samuel Newland, *Cossacks in the German Army*. Wilfried Strik-Strikfeldt's comments are in *Against Stalin and Hitler*; Max Kuhnert's encounter is from *A German Cavalryman at War*. Alfred Rosenberg's secret memorandum to Wilhelm Keitel is printed in *Nazi Conspiracy and Aggression*, III (Washington, 1946). The letter from the German 292nd Infantry Division is in Ortwin Buchbender and Reinhold Sterz, *Deutsche Feldpostbriefe*. All material on Hans-Georg Reinhardt's Third Panzer Army is from Franz Kurowski, *Deadlock Before Moscow*. Gotthard Heinrici's account of his meeting with Hitler is in Johannes Hürter, *Ein Deutscher General*. Mikhail Kuznetsov's testimony is from Artem Drabkin's 'I Remember' section of www.russianbattlefield.com. Alexander Rogachev's story is in 'Soldiers of the Great War' on www.english.pobediteli.ru. Pavel Lopatin's diary is set out in Isolda Ivanova, *The Tragedy of Myasnoy Bor*. Mikhail Borisov's comments are from an interview with me; Helmut Mauer's are in *Kameraden* (July/August 2008). The Heinrici material is in Johannes Hürter, *Hitlers Heerführer*. Rudolf Gschöpf's description is from *45 Infanterie-Division*. On the relief effort to Demyansk, see Gustav Höhne, 'In Snow and Mud: 31 Days of Attack under Seydlitz', NARA MS C-034; Joachim Sandau's testimony is from the ZDF documentary 'Turning Point'. Andrei Vlasov's comments are in Joachim Hoffmann, *Die Geschichte der Wlassow-Armee*.

Chapter 11: The Grand Illusion

The Führer's observations on the arrival of spring are from Hugh Trevor-Roper, *Hitler's Table Talk*. On the overall war situation in April 1942, see Evan Mawdsley, *Thunder in the East*. Hermann Balck's comments are from *Ordnung im Chaos*. Nina Semonova's diary is in Paul Kohl, *Ich Wunder Mich*. The suffering of the civilians is from Nick Terry's 'The German Army Group Centre and the Soviet Civilian Population 1942–44' (King's College London, PhD, 2006); an extract is printed on Erik Kooistra's Rzhev website: www.home.hccnet.nl/e.kooistra.

Bibliography

The large number of German sources have been kept in their original form; the relatively small number of Russian ones have been translated. Articles and documentary references are individually cited in the Notes.

Richard Armstrong, *Red Army Tank Commanders* (Atglen, PA, 1994); *Winter Warfare: Red Army Orders and Experiences* (London, 1997)

Hans Bähr, Hermann Meyer and Eberhard Orthbrandt, *Kriegsbriefe Gefallener Studenten 1939–45* (Tübingen, 1952)

Hermann Balck, *Ordnung im Chaos* (Osnabrück, 1981)

Omer Bartov, *Hitler's Army* (Oxford, 1992)

Walter de Beaulieu, *Generaloberst Erich Hoepner* (Neckargemünd, 1969)

Chris Bellamy, *Absolute War: Soviet Russia in the Second World War* (London, 2007)

Christopher Bergström and Andrey Mikhailov, *The Air War over the Eastern Front January – June 1942* (Pacifica, 2001)

Lev Bezymensky, *The Battle for Moscow* (Moscow, 2007)

Gottlob Bidermann, *In Deadly Combat: A German Soldier's Memoir of the Eastern Front* (Lawrence, 2000)

Fedor von Bock, *War Diary, 1939–45* (Atglen, PA, 1996)

Philipp von Boeselager, *Valkyrie: The Plot to Kill Hitler* (London, 2009)

Gerhard Bopp, *Kriegstagebuch 1940–1943* (Hamburg, 2005)

Wolfgang Borchert, *The Man Outside* (New York, 1971)

Dermot Bradley, *Generaloberst Heinz Guderian* (Osnabrück, 1986)

Rodric Braithwaite, *Moscow 1941: A City and its People at War* (London, 2006)

Ortwin Buchbender and Reinhold Sterz, *Das Andere Gesicht des Krieges: Deutsche Feldpostbriefe 1939–1945* (Munich, 1982)

Heinrich Bücheler, *Hoepner: Ein Deutsches Soldatenschicksal des XX Jahrunderts* (Herford, 1980)

Charles Burdick and Hans-Adolf Jacobson, *The Halder War Diary, 1939–42* (London, 1988)

Gordon Burgess, *The Life and Works of Wolfgang Borchert* (Woodbridge, 2003)

Paul Carell, *Hitler's War on Russia* (London, 1966)

Paul Chavchavadze, *Marie Avinov: Her Amazing Life* (London, 1969)

Alan Clark, *Barbarossa* (London, 1965)

Alexander Conrady, *Rückzug vor Moskau* (Neckargemünd, 1974)

James Corum, *Wolfram von Richthofen: Master of the German Air War* (Lawrence, KS, 2008)

Josef Deck, *Der Weg der 1000 Toten* (Karlsruhe, 1978)

Hans Dollinger, *Kain, Wo Ist Dein Bruder?* (Frankfurt, 1987)

Artem Drabkin, *The Red Air Force at War: Barbarossa and the Retreat to Moscow* (Barnsley, 2007)

Artem Drabkin and Oleg Sheremet, *T-34 in Action* (Barnsley, 2006)

Gerhard Engel, *At the Heart of the Reich* (London, 2005)

John Erickson, *The Road to Stalingrad* (London, 1977)

Richard Evans, *The Third Reich at War* (London, 2008)

Heinz Otto Fausten, *Wir Haben Uns die Zeit nicht Ausgesucht* (Pössneck, 2002)

Robert Forczyk, *Moscow 1941* (Oxford, 2006)

Franz Frisch, *Condemned to Live: A Panzer Artilleryman's Five Front War* (Shippensburg, PA, 2000)

Karl Fuchs, Horst Richardson and Dennis Showalter, *Your Loyal and Loving Son: Letters of Tank Gunner Karl Fuchs, 1937–41* (Herndon, 2003)

Bryan Fugate, *Operation Barbarossa* (Stevenage, 1989)

Martin Gareis, *Kampf und Ende der Fränkisch-Sudetendeutschen 98 Infanterie-Division* (Friedberg, 1956)

David Glantz, *Soviet Military Deception in the Second World War* (Abingdon, 1989); *A History of Soviet Airborne Forces* (London, 1994); *Before Stalingrad* (Stroud, 2001)

Andrei Gorbunov, *'Moscow is Behind Us!' – Collection of Memoirs of Participants in the Battle of Borodino, October 1941* (Moscow, 2007)

Horst Grossmann, *Geschichte der Rheinisch-Westfälischen 6 Infanterie-Division* (Bad Nauheim, 1958); *Rzhev: Eckpfeiler der Ostfront* (Friedberg, 1980)

Rudolf Gschöpf, *Mein Weg mit der 45 Infanterie-Division* (Nürnberg, 2002)

Heinz Guderian, *Panzer Leader* (London, 1952)

Helmut Günther, *Hot Motors, Cold Feet* (Altona, 2004)

Heinrich Haape, *Moscow Tram Stop* (London, 1957)

Ingrid Hammer and Suzanne zur Nieden, *'Sehr Selten Habe Ich Geweint': Briefe und Tagebücher aus dem Zweiten Weltkrieg von Menschen aus Berlin* (Zurich, 1992)

Richard Hargreaves, *Blitzkrieg Unleashed: The German Invasion of Poland 1939* (Barnsley, 2008)

Hans Jürgen Hartmann, *Zwischen Nichts und Niemandsland* (Dessau, 2006)

Werner Haupt, *Geschichte der 134 Infanterie-Division* (Bad Kreuznach, 1971)

Ludwig Freiherr von Heyl, *Wie Ich Den Krieg Erlebte* (Heidelberg, 1984)

Rolf Hinze, *Hitze, Frost und Pulverdampf – der Schicksalsweg der 20 Panzer Division* (Pöppinghaus, 1991)

Joachim Hoffmann, *Die Geschichte der Wlassow-Armee* (Freiburg, 1986)

Peter Hoffmann, *Stauffenberg: A Family History 1905–44* (Cambridge, 1995)

Friedrich Hossbach, *Infanterie im Ostfeldzug, 1941–42* (Osterode, 1951)

Johannes Hürter, *Ein Deutscher General an der Ostfront: Die Briefe und Tagebücher des Gotthard Heinrici* (Essen, 2001); *Hitlers Heerführer* (Munich, 2007)

Isolda Ivanova, *The Tragedy of Myasnoy Bor: Collection of Memoirs from Participants in the Lyuban Operation* (St Petersburg, 2001)

Walter Kempowski, *Das Echolot: Barbarossa '41* (Munich, 2002)

Walter Kerr, *The Russian Army* (London, 1944)

Robert Kershaw, *War Without Garlands: Operation Barbarossa 1941–42* (Shepperton, 2000)

Nikita Khrushchev, *Memoirs: Commissar (1918–1945)* (Philadelphia, PA, 2005)

Victor Klemperer, *I Shall Bear Witness* (London, 1998)

Siegfried Knappe, *Soldat* (London, 1993)

Guido Knopp, *Der Verdammte Krieg* (Munich, 1991)

Paul Kohl, *Ich Wunder Mich dass ich noch Lebe: Sowjetische Augenzeugen Berichten* (Güttersloh, 1990)

Max Kuhnert, *'Will We See Tomorrow? – A German Cavalryman at War, 1939–42* (Barnsley, 1993)

Franz Kurowski, *Deadlock Before Moscow* (West Chester, PA, 1992); *Infantry Aces* (Mechanicsburg, PA, 2002)

Horst Lange, *Tagebücher aus dem Zweiten Weltkrieg* (Mainz, 1979)

Louis Lochner, *The Goebbels Diaries 1942–43* (New York, 1948)

Jochen Löser, *Bittere Pflicht: Kampf und Untergang der 76 Berlin-Brandenburgischen Infanterie-Division* (Osnabrück, 1986)

Hans von Luck, *Panzer Commander* (London, 1989)

Ulrich de Maizière, *In Der Pflicht* (Bonn, 1989)

Bernd Martin, *Tagebuch eines Sowjetischen Offiziers vom 1 Januar – 8 Februar 1942* (Freiburg, 1966)

Evan Mawdsley, *Thunder in the East: The Nazi-Soviet War 1941–1945* (London, 2005)

Geoffrey Megargee, *War of Annihilation* (Lanham, 2006)

Hans Meier-Welcker, *Aufzeichnungen eines Generalstabsoffiziers 1939–1942* (Freiburg, 1982)

Erich Mende, *Das Verdammte Gewissen* (Munich, 1986)

Ludwig Merker, *Das Buch der 78 Sturm-Division* (Tübingen, 1955)

Catherine Merridale, *Ivan's War: The Red Army 1939–45* (London, 2005)

Wilhelm Meyer-Detring, *Die 137 Infanterie-Division im Mittelabschnitt der Ostfront* (Petzenkirchen, 1962)

Dado Muriyev, *The Rout of 'Typhoon' 1941–42* (Moscow, 1979)

Andrew Nagorski, *The Greatest Battle: The Fight for Moscow 1941–42* (London, 2007)

Sönke Neitzel, *Tapping Hitler's Generals* (Barnsley, 2007)

Samuel Newland, *Cossacks in the German Army* (London, 2002)

Steven Newton, *Hitler's Commander* (Cambridge, MA, 2006)

Nikolai Obryn'ba, *Red Partisan* (Barnsley, 2006)

Wolfgang Paul, *Die Schlacht um Moskau* (Munich, 1978); *Das Potsdamer Infanterie-Regiment 9* (Osnabrück, 1983); *Brennpunkte: Die Geschichte der 6 Panzerdivision* (Osnabrück, 1984)

Josef Perau, *Priester im Heere Hitlers* (Essen, 1962)

Janusz Piekalkiewicz, *Moscow 1941: The Frozen Offensive* (London, 1981)

Anton Detlev von Plato, *Die Geschichte der 5 Panzer-Division* (Regensburg, 1978)

Wilhelm Prüller, *Diary of a German Soldier* (London, 1963)

Erhard Raus, *Panzer Operations* (Cambridge, MA, 2003)

Laurence Rees, *War of the Century: When Hitler Fought Stalin* (London, 1999)

Willy Reese, *A Stranger to Myself* (New York, 2005)

Klaus Reinhardt, *Die Wende vor Moskau* (Stuttgart, 1972)

William Richardson and Seymour Freidin, *The Fatal Decisions* (London, 1956)

Konstantin Rokossovsky, *A Soldier's Duty* (Moscow, 1970)

Hans Schäufler, *Der Weg war Weit: Panzer zwischen Weichsel und Wolga*

(Neckargemünd, 1973); *So Lebten und So Starben Sie: Das Buch vom Panzerregiment 35* (Bamberg, 1983)

Alois Scheuer, *Briefe aus Russland 1941–1942* (St Ingbert, 2000)

August Schmidt, *Die Geschichte der 10 Infanterie-Division* (Eggolsheim, 2005)

Gustav Schrodek, *Ihr Glaube Galt Dem Vaterland* (Munich, 1976)

Georg Schwaiger, *Das Erzbistum München und Freising in der Zeit der Nationalsozialistichen Herrschaft* (Munich, 1984)

Albert Seaton, *The Battle for Moscow* (New York, 1971)

Hellmuth Stieff, *Briefe* (Berlin, 1994)

Rolf Stoves, *Die 1 Panzer Division: Chronik Einer der Drei Stamm-Divisionen der Deutschen Panzerwaffe* (Bad Neuheim, 1961)

Christian Strcit, *Keine Kameraden: Die Wehrmacht und die Sowjetischen Kriegsgefangenen 1941–44* (Stuttgart, 1978)

Wilfried Strik-Strikfeldt, *Against Stalin and Hitler* (London, 1970)

Hugh Trevor-Roper, *Hitler's Table Talk* (London, 2003)

Alfred Turney, *Disaster at Moscow: Von Bock's Campaigns, 1941–42* (London, 1971)

Carl Wagener, *Moskau 1941* (Bad Nauheim, 1965)

Otto Weidinger, *SS Panzer Division Das Reich, 1941–1943* (Winnipeg, 2002)

Timothy Wray, *Standing Fast: German Defensive Doctrine on the Eastern Front* (Fort Leavenworth, 1986)

Andrei Yeremenko, *The Arduous Beginning* (Moscow, 1966)

Adam Zamoyski, *1812 – Napoleon's Fatal March on Moscow* (London, 2004)

Georgi Zhukov, *Marshal Zhukov's Greatest Battles* (New York, 2002)

Earl Ziemke and Magna Bauer, *Moscow to Stalingrad: Decision in the East* (New York, 1988)

Index

Index